The International Monetary Fund in a Multipolar World:

PULLING TOGETHER

Catherine Gwin, Richard E. Feinberg,
and contributors

Jacques J. Polak
Peter B. Kenen
C. David Finch
Jeffrey D. Sachs
Guillermo Ortiz
Louis M. Goreux
Joan M. Nelson

Series Editors:
Richard E. Feinberg
Valeriana Kallab

 Transaction Books
New Brunswick (USA) and Oxford (UK)

Library of Congress Catalog Number 89-20252
ISBN: 0-88738-313-0 (cloth)
ISBN: 0-88738-819-1 (paper)
Printed in the United States of America

Library of Congress Cataloging-in-Publication Data

Gwin, Catherine.
    Pulling together.

    (Policy perspectives ; no. 13)
    1. International Monetary Fund. 2. International
finance. I. Feinberg, Richard E. II. Title.
III. Series: U.S.-Third World policy perspectives ;
no. 13.
HC3881.5.I58G87   1989   332.1′52   89-202522
ISBN 0-88738-313-0
ISBN O-88738 = 819-1 (pbk.)

TP

The views expressed in this volume are those of the authors and do not necessarily represent those of the Overseas Development Council as an organization or of its individual officers or Board, Council, Program Advisory Committee, and staff members.

The International Monetary Fund in a Multipolar World:

PULLING TOGETHER

Acknowledgments

ODC's IMF Project Directors and Editors:
Richard E. Feinberg
Catherine Gwin

Series Editors:
Richard E. Feinberg
Valeriana Kallab

The Overseas Development Council gratefully acknowledges a special grant from the Alfred P. Sloan Foundation for the preparation of this policy study; support from The Pew Charitable Trusts for the ODC U.S.-Third World Policy Perspectives series, of which this volume is part; and the support of The Ford Foundation, The Rockefeller Foundation, and The William and Flora Hewlett Foundation for the Council's overall program.

On behalf of the Council and the contributing authors, the editors wish to express thanks for valuable comments to John P. Lewis and members of the ODC Program Advisory Committee and to others—notably Charles Dallara, Ellen Johnson Sirleaf, Reiner Masera, and John Williamson—who participated in the workshops at which early versions of the chapters were discussed. Special thanks are also due to the many IMF officials who provided insightful comments at the draft stage. The authors alone are of course responsible for the views expressed in this volume.

The editors also wish to acknowledge and express thanks to Cynthia R. Carlisle and Jill C. Vesty for their administrative contributions to the project; to Melissa Vaughn for editorial assistance; to Danielle M. Currier and Patricia Masters for editorial and production assistance; to Manju Malik for expert statistical assistance; and to Joycelyn V. Critchlow for processing the manuscript.

Contents

IV. THE IMF AND THE DEVELOPING COUNTRIES

Foreword

As industrial and developing countries approach the last decade of this century, the need for effective international institutions remains more important than ever. That need is currently particularly acute in the field of international finance. Yet many observers are now questioning the adequacy of the one major international financial institution created to prevent the economic and financial crises that marked the first half of the twentieth century.

That institution—the International Monetary Fund—is now surrounded by controversy over whether or not it has lost its way. Some analysts believe that the Fund's original role in ensuring a stable international monetary system should be re-emphasized, and that the IMF should once again exercise some influence over international financial relations between the major industrial countries (as it now does over those of many smaller, less powerful countries), and then, over time, be converted into a global central bank.

Others believe that the Fund's major role in the future should be to work with the developing countries, as it has done almost exclusively over the past decade—leaving the major industrial powers to regulate financial matters through common agreement among themselves. The Fund in their view would move closer to the World Bank, and would take on added responsibility in dealing with development issues such as poverty and the environment.

The current controversy over the role of the International Monetary Fund comes at a time when the institution is being asked to take on new challenges in the 1990s. The most immediate challenge is to ease the debt situation, thereby helping restore economic growth in the developing world. Also ahead is the challenge posed by the possible entry of the socialist economies—the Soviet Union and the Eastern European countries—into the international financial system.

This new policy study, co-directed by Richard E. Feinberg, ODC Executive Vice President, and Catherine Gwin, Special Program Advisor at The Rockefeller Foundation, directly addresses the future of the International Monetary Fund. *Pulling Together: The International Monetary Fund in a Multipolar World*—the thirteenth in ODC's U.S.-Third World Policy Perspectives series—is the companion piece to ODC's earlier analysis of the role of the World Bank. That study, *Between Two Worlds: The World Bank's Next Decade,* also directed by Richard E. Feinberg, was published in 1986—a time when the Bank was at a crossroads and about to get new leadership. We are very pleased that this earlier volume helped to shape the debate over the future of the World Bank and that many of its recommendations now have been adopted. We hope that the present policy study of the IMF will have a similar impact.

The analysis in this ODC U.S.-Third World Policy Perspectives volume necessarily ranges wider than the Council's usual "North-South" terrain, addressing some issues generally considered "North-North" in nature. The IMF is extremely important to developing countries, but it can only be understood if examined in the context of the entire spectrum of its responsibilities, including its role vis-à-vis industrial nations. Clearly, developing countries depend on global growth to generate the resources needed for their own development. The IMF's surveillance of the macroeconomic policies of the world's major industrial powers is therefore relevant to the solutions of the Third World's debt crisis—which, in turn, can impact positively on growth in the industrial countries themselves.

The Overseas Development Council gratefully acknowledges a special grant from the Alfred P. Sloan Foundation for the preparation of this policy study; support from The Pew Charitable Trusts for the ODC U.S.-Third World Policy Perspectives series, of which this volume is part; and the support of The Ford Foundation, The Rockefeller Foundation, and The William and Flora Hewlett Foundation for the Council's overall program.

John W. Sewell, *President*
Overseas Development Council

August 1989

I. Overview

Reforming the Fund

Richard E. Feinberg and Catherine Gwin

The International Monetary Fund was designed primarily to ensure stable monetary relations among the major industrial nations. Nonetheless, over the past decade, it has provided most of its advice and all of its credit to *developing* countries. Some argue that the Fund's mission as a result has become indistinguishable from that of the World Bank—and that the two institutions should be merged. That, however, is not the perspective of this study.

The essential purpose of the World Bank is to stimulate development in the Third World. In contrast, the IMF's core function is to foster global macroeconomic conditions conducive to the growth of *all* nations, industrial and less-developed alike. As the world's central monetary authority, the IMF monitors world economic trends and national macroeconomic policies. It provides a forum for discussion of international monetary issues. And it can offer short-term credit to help member countries to manage exchange rates and adjust to payments disequilibria.

Today, important improvements are needed in Fund policies toward both the industrial and developing worlds. Side stepped by the developed countries, entangled in unsuccessful programs in many Latin American and African nations, and lacking effective leadership from its major shareholders, the IMF is in danger of losing its bearings. It needs a course correction and a clear mandate from its member countries to strengthen both its policy surveillance and financing roles.

The Fund should not, however, be expected to solve problems best left to other institutions. For example, it is less well equipped than the World Bank to provide the major help needed by the countries of Sub-Saharan Africa—whose problems are deeply rooted ones of development. Nor can the IMF shoulder responsibility for environmental protection or poverty alleviation, as some would have it. The IMF should make sure that its own programs do not exacerbate these problems, and should help interested governments deal with the adverse social consequences of stabilization programs; but it lacks the instruments for coping with these issues directly. To load such functions onto the Fund would threaten its central monetary activities without ensuring a commensurate impact on poverty or the environment.

In an economically interdependent but politically centrifugal world, a strong central monetary institution is needed to help countries to assess and debate the international implications of their national policies and to arrive at collective responses to complex global economic problems. But only if its member states are willing to delegate it more authority can the IMF fulfill these purposes and help pull together a multipolar world.

The Past as Prologue

The IMF was created after World War II to provide a stable international monetary system free from the disorders of the prewar years. Two decades of beggar-thy-neighbor foreign exchange and trade restrictions and competitive devaluations culminating in global depression and armed conflict supplied the impetus for nations to agree to a highly specific set of rules to govern their monetary practices. As set forth in Article I of the IMF's Articles of Agreement, the institution was, among other things:

- To facilitate the expansion and balanced growth of international trade, and to contribute thereby to the promotion and maintenance of high levels of employment and real income and to the development of the productive resources of all members as primary objectives of economic policy.

- To promote exchange stability, to maintain orderly exchange arrangements among members, and to avoid competitive exchange depreciation.

- To assist in the establishment of a multilateral system of payments in respect of current transactions between members and in the elimination of foreign exchange restrictions which hamper the growth of world trade . . .

To achieve these ambitious objectives, the Articles empowered the IMF to both oversee the agreed code of conduct and provide short-term financing to member countries to enable them to correct temporary payments difficulties "without resorting to measures destructive of national or international prosperity." In other words, a link was established between members' obligations under the rules and their access to IMF financing. Moreover, since 1969, the IMF has had the authority to play a role in the supply of international liquidity through the allocation to member countries of Special Drawing Rights (SDRs)—a form of international currency created by the IMF as a global reserve asset.

In its first two decades, the IMF helped the war-torn countries of Europe stabilize their exchange rates, make balance-of-payments adjustments, return to currency convertibility, and unwind discriminatory trade policies. The IMF could not have fostered these accomplishments successfully had it not been for the leadership exercised by the United States through its provision of Marshall Plan aid and the essential public goods on which the Bretton Woods system thrived: growth and price stability. The relationships between the United States and the other major industrial countries has been described elsewhere as a "bargain" according to which "the United States would maintain domestic economic stability (and) . . . other countries would import this stability from the United States through a fixed exchange rate on the dollar."[1] Through the 1950s and 1960s, the policies of the United States and the momentum of its economy fueled an unprecedented rate of growth in the world economy. And they helped build support for the Bretton Woods system of multilateral economic cooperation. In subsequent decades, however, U.S. leadership waned.

Loss of Leadership

Through the late 1960s and 1970s, the United States witnessed a steady erosion of its relative economic power. After their recovery from the devastation of World War II, both Western Europe and Japan became strong competitors in global markets. Then, in the 1980s, as the United States slipped from being the world's largest creditor nation to being its largest debtor, Western Europe and, especially Japan, took on new significance in international monetary and financial affairs. With this shift in relative economic power, both the systemic assumptions and the political underpinnings that had upheld the IMF in earlier years weakened. American willingness to fund the major multilateral economic institutions declined as did its capacity and readiness to shoulder the major policy responsibility for the management of the international monetary system. Instead, dollar instability, the large U.S. fiscal deficit, and persistent trade imbalance became serious threats to global economic growth and stability.

Japan, which has become the world's second largest economy and has replaced the United States as the world's major creditor nation, could exercise a greater leadership role. In recent years, Japan has boosted its foreign aid levels and offered specific ideas for handling the problems of less-developed-country debt and exchange rate intervention. It has been willing to accept a sharp appreciation of the yen. It has also made adjustments in some domestic economic policies. But Japan's willingness to assume leadership remains in doubt. And the United States has yet to demonstrate that it is prepared to share power with Japan along with sharing responsibility. Thus Japan remains more a potential force than a systemic leader.

Meanwhile, countries of Western Europe have established among themselves a new European Monetary System (EMS) to manage their exchange rates and may eventually move toward a single-currency area. Their present goal is the achievement of a single market by 1992. Whether Europe will in the process turn more or less protectionist in relation to the rest of the world remains to be seen; but it is unlikely to serve as a leader in global economic management until the 1992 agreement is worked out and its effects can begin to be felt.

Breakdown and Redirection

Along with the decline in U.S. leadership, two other radical changes in the global economic system have led to an identity crisis for the IMF: the breakdown of the par value exchange rate system and the explosive growth of international banking. In early 1973, the governments of the major industrial countries began to let their exchange rates float. In 1976 they agreed to a second amendment of the IMF Articles, which in effect legalized floating rates and authorized the IMF to "exercise firm surveillance over the exchange rate policies of members." However, with ready access to international bank credit, most developed countries facing payments difficulties have been able to avoid recourse to IMF credit and the linked obligation to agree to adjustment measures. As discussed at greater length by Jacques Polak in his contribution to this volume, "[T]hese new developments put these [developed] countries beyond the reach of the Fund's conditionality and, at the same time, undercut the main rationale for the allocation of SDRs."

SDRs were created as a means of reducing the world's dependence on the dollar and on gold at a time when countries feared that a shortage of global liquidity would impede growth. But today there is no overall shortage of global liquidity, no consensus about the desirability of reducing dependence on the dollar—and therefore no pressure to give SDRs a greater role. At least for now, therefore, the power to create SDRs has not given the IMF an effective means of control over international liquidity.

In marked contrast to its diminished influence in industrial countries, the IMF has become increasingly involved with the developing economies. The number of these countries belonging to the IMF surged from 49 to 132 between 1960 and 1989. This open admissions policy contributed to the rise in IMF lending to the Third World. But it was primarily the international economic events of the 1970s and 1980s that led to the current concentration of IMF financing in the developing countries.

The IMF had begun to take special account of the payments problems of developing countries in the early 1960s. After much debate, it established the Compensatory Financing Facility (CFF) in 1963 to help countries cope with shortfalls in export earnings due to circumstances beyond their control. The aim, in particular, was to benefit those developing countries heavily dependent on primary commodity exports. As such, the CFF was the first of a number of special facilities created in response to special problems of these countries. In the 1970s and 1980s, the Fund undertook additional initiatives particularly beneficial to developing nations, including measures that expanded access to IMF credit for countries with serious adjustment problems, provided more generous amortization terms for some IMF programs, and offered the low-income countries financing on concessional interest rates rather than on the regular IMF near-market terms.

With these changes came an increase in IMF lending to developing countries. By the close of the 1970s, lending to these countries had risen to $8 billion in response to payments difficulties brought on by the oil price hikes, worldwide recession, and failure to adjust.[2] By 1983, with the onset of the debt crisis, it amounted to $31 billion, peaking at $39 billion in 1985. Developing-country use of IMF credit rose unevenly but inexorably as a percentage of total IMF credit—from an annual average of 58 per cent in the 1950s, to 65 per cent in the 1970s, and to 100 per cent by the mid 1980s (see Figure 1).

These developments are not all bad. Today's global trade and international capital flows far exceed what anyone anticipated in 1944 at Bretton Woods. Although relations among industrial countries are not free of tensions, economic and political relations are far superior to what they were in the 1930s. Furthermore, from the ranks of the developing countries have emerged several highly successful "newly industrializing countries" which are rapidly becoming integrated into the world's production, trade, and financial systems. Yet the new developments have brought new problems as well—evident today in large global imbalances, excessive volatility in the exchange markets, and unsustainable levels of indebtedness.

It is hard to envision solutions to these pressing problems and a firmer management of the global economy over the long term without a

Figure 1. Use of IMF Credit by Developing Countries, 1950-1987

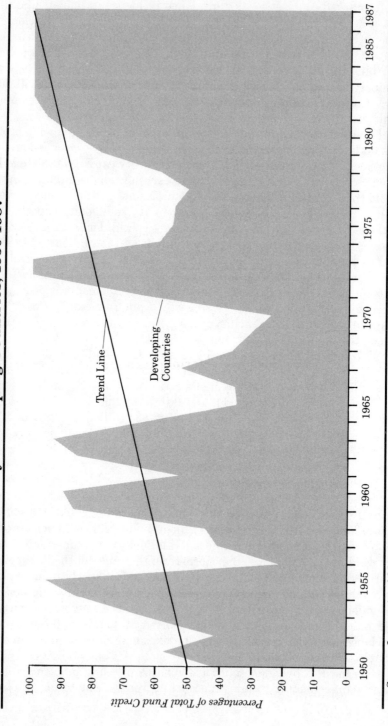

Sources: International Monetary Fund, *International Financial Statistics Yearbook 1988* (Washington, D.C. IMF), pp. 38, 39, 42, 43; and ibid., *Yearbook 1980*, pp. 18, 19, 22, 23.

well-functioning IMF. If the IMF is to be effective, however, member governments will have to reach consensus on the following six tough but vital issues:

1. **Defining a role for the IMF in global monetary management.** In the past, the IMF exerted little meaningful influence over countries whose external balances were in surplus. Now it has little or no influence over deficit developed countries—even though their imbalances have consequences well beyond their national borders. The IMF needs to carve out meaningful modes of interaction with developed countries distinct from its traditional lending authority in order to retain its influence with them and sustain the rationale for its separateness from the World Bank.

2. **Lifting the debt overhang from developing nations.** The contributors to this volume pass rather harsh judgments on the IMF's handling of the Third World debt crisis prior to the recent embrace of the new debt reduction strategy. Now the Brady proposals, while welcome in some respects, threaten to increase IMF risk exposure in uncreditworthy developing countries without significantly alleviating the debt overhang. The Fund's entanglement with struggling developing countries is a challenge to its reputation and a threat to its financial integrity.

3. **Improving economic performance in Sub-Saharan Africa.** The record of IMF-assisted adjustment efforts in Sub-Saharan Africa is discouraging. Many IMF-assisted programs, adopted in response to steep economic decline, have broken down—victims of weak governmental policies and inadequate external funding. Moreover, the Fund has accounted for a net drain of resources out of the poorest countries. It needs to find ways to stay engaged more effectively.

4. **Enhancing cooperation between the IMF and the World Bank.** A troublesome by-product of the Fund's involvement in the twin Third World debt and adjustment crises has been the blurring of the original division of labor between the IMF and the World Bank. Continuing disputes over bureaucratic turf and excessive demands on the time of national officials suggest that recent efforts to apportion responsibilities have not gone far enough.

5. **Helping integrate Eastern Europe and the Soviet Union into the global economy.** Poland and Hungary are members of the IMF, and Soviet President Mikhail Gorbachev has expressed interest in future membership. The Western-controlled agencies can assist in the marketization of Eastern Europe and must decide the prerequisites for the admission to membership of the Soviet Union.

6. **Upgrading the IMF's own capabilities.** To meet these challenges, the IMF needs to change its organizational structure, research

agenda, and style of participation in international public policy debates. Governments should see that the Fund has the financial resources it will need in the 1990s.

These are matters which we now tackle in turn.

Strengthening the IMF's Contribution to Macroeconomic Management in a Multipolar World

In the chapters that follow, Jacques Polak and Peter Kenen make a strong case for a reconstructed role for the IMF in international monetary management. The case rests on the fundamental truth that in today's pluralistic, interdependent, multipolar world, no country is "a macroeconomic island," and no one government can dictate the course of global economic developments.

While the IMF does not have the leverage to compel the major governments to take the effects of their macroeconomic policies on others into account in their economic policymaking, it does have the mandate to analyze these governments' actions, to consult with them on what policy adjustments might be made, and call attention to the consequences of national policies on the global economy.

This surveillance function has never been rigorously pursued, but it is the IMF's core task, and major governments should support specific steps to strengthen it. In addition, governments should acknowledge that the management of exchange rates is an *international* responsibility and should enable the IMF to play a greater role in seeing that this shared responsibility is effectively carried out. Three changes would help to bolster the IMF's macroeconomic management role:

1. **The IMF should have a greater voice as an objective analyst in the process of macroeconomic policy coordination.** Governments cannot cope with the impact of increased production, trade, and financial interdependence—in particular, they cannot maintain reasonably stable prices and rates of growth—unless the key countries coordinate their monetary and fiscal policies. As noted above, when the world economy was dominated by one major power, that country was expected to provide the vital public goods of steady growth and price stability on which an open international system could function. Today, a small group of economic powers dominate the world economy with the predictable result that each wants to be a free rider, not the supplier of public goods. As a consequence, those goods are in short supply.

The major industrial countries have expressed their awareness of the need to coordinate better their macroeconomic policies to achieve desired outcomes for their own national economies. But, as Polak argues, the current process of "mutual surveillance" and coordination is intended to test the compatibility of national policies rather than to manage the global economy. Governments should look beyond the interdependence of their policy actions to the effects of those actions on levels of global economic demand, resource allocations, and growth; and they should let the IMF play a greater role in this expanded process.

There has been some movement in that direction. The Fund's Managing Director now attends meetings of the Group of Seven (G-7) industrialized nations, and Fund staff prepare the main background assessments and economic forecasts that set the quantitative framework for G-7 policy discussions. Nevertheless, there remains too wide a range of issues that the G-7 governments deem "sensitive"—and on which the IMF is excluded from discussion. How well the IMF and G-7 interactions go—whether at the level of ministers or their deputies—still depends too much on personalities and needs to be made more a matter of accepted routine. Moreover, the process of reporting back on the essence of the meeting to the IMF's Executive Board lacks the rigor of specific and meaningful reporting requirements. Rather than being a matter of procedural reform, these improvements in policy coordination depend primarily on the willingness of major governments to let them happen and to accept active participation by the IMF as, in a sense, "the voice" of the global economy.

2. **The IMF should receive a mandate to toughen its surveillance over the national policies of key countries.** Although still nascent, the "mutual" surveillance that has become a part of G-7 efforts at policy coordination is an important development in global economic management essential to the workings of interdependent economies. But mutual surveillance has its limitations and is no substitute for the IMF's role in monitoring the policy actions of individual countries. The principal limitation in multilateral surveillance is the potential for the discussions among governments to delay or diffuse rather than fix responsibility for policy adjustments. Large imbalances reflect large policy mistakes that should be corrected by the countries making them. Bilateral consultations between the IMF and its member countries are intended to encourage such corrections.

No one would claim that IMF discussions with key countries have had a major impact on getting needed actions taken in a timely fashion. That, however, is no reason for the IMF to give over the surveillance of its members countries to a process of mutual surveillance among them. As Polak insists: "Failure to adjust by a major member country remains an issue of prime concern to the Fund, and breakdown of the negotiating process among the Seven should not provide an excuse for such failure." One modest step endorsed by Polak would require developed countries to respond to IMF criticism by reporting back to the IMF on measures taken to deal with the identified problems. "This would at least force the authorities in the country under surveillance to focus, at a high level and in some detail, on observations coming from the international community."

3. **The IMF should play a role in the determination of the exchange rates around which currency stabilization efforts are undertaken. It should also explore various ways in which exchange rate interventions could best be orchestrated—including its own possible participation in associated financing.** The Louvre Accord of 1987 marked a shift to collaborative exchange rate intervention, but the rates agreed to did not prove tenable. Nor, as Polak suggests, will the establishment of tenable rates often be compatible with what the G-7 countries can agree upon. Although the timing and the size of interventions, as well as the distribution of risks, are matters that the key currency countries will have to determine in secrecy, the setting of target rates is a matter of international concern and an appropriate analytical issue for the IMF.

There may also be circumstances under which the IMF could usefully help finance an official, joint intervention. Kenen maintains that the scope for joint intervention now and over the next several years may be limited by the fact that the United States may not have large foreign currency reserves with which to carry out its share of a joint action; and he suggests that the IMF could help ease this constraint. As one approach, the United States might draw down a line of credit from the central banks of major currency countries and then use IMF resources to refinance its overdraft. Unless a new facility were created with different "rules of access" than now apply to normal drawings in the higher credit tranches, the United States would have to negotiate an adjustment program with the IMF subject to standard rules of conditionality when the size of its drawing on the IMF exceeded its first credit tranche. Though governments may not now be prepared to empower the IMF to play this kind of role in exchange rate intervention, they should authorize the Fund staff to analyze the issue.

Ultimately the key to achieving better macroeconomic policy coordination is to build more symmetrical discipline into the IMF system. This was a matter of concern to Keynes in his original design for a world monetary institution but not a matter well built into the functioning of the Fund. In a comment on the Polak and Kenen papers, David Finch, a former senior IMF official, argues that, as a means of exercising mutual discipline over each other, the developed countries should at times forego the practice of providing/accepting unconditional finance from one another and should instead rely on conditional financing provided under the aegis of the IMF. The return to the IMF by the industrial countries would, Finch contends, depoliticize the process of determining policies on monetary financing and hasten macroeconomic adjustments in times of serious disequilibrium. This, however, would still put the principal burden of adjustment on the deficit country.

A different approach to fostering timely adjustment would be to look for automatic or quasi-automatic financial measures such as required issues of foreign currency securities by deficit countries and mandated reserve deposits (possibly with the IMF) by surplus countries as means of inducing countries with excessive imbalances to implement corrective policies. Although neither these nor other means of achieving greater discipline that might involve the Fund are under active consideration by governments, the IMF should be given a mandate to explore this additional subject and develop possible options.

Third World Debt

The IMF's decade-long struggle to cope with the Third World debt crisis can be divided into three stages. Initially, the Fund concentrated on preserving the solvency of the world's major banks by actively orchestrating the partial refinancing of debt service tied to tough austerity programs in debtor nations. Between 1985 and 1988, an overly complacent IMF began quietly to retreat from developing countries, reducing the number of stabilization programs from thirty to twenty, and cutting its own exposure from SDR 35 billion to SDR 26 billion. In a recent turnabout, the Fund has again become heavily engaged, this time tying reform programs to concerted international efforts to increase concessional flows to Africa and to reduce Latin America's debt overhang.

Following Mexico's declaration of bankruptcy in the summer of 1982, Managing Director Jacques de Larosière boldly made use of the Fund's strategic coordination function, as well as its analytical abilities, persuasive powers, and own resources to bring order to a panicky international financial community. In each case, the IMF calculated how much interest the debtor country could afford to pay and asked the banks to refinance the remainder. To encourage commercial bank participation, the IMF and the Federal Reserve Board employed a series of inducements—including official participation in new lending packages, tough IMF-approved austerity measures for the debtors, and telephone calls by Paul Volcker to recalcitrant banks.

No other institution was as well positioned as the Fund to coordinate the actions of all the parties concerned: the financial markets, the key industrial-country governments, and the debtor nations. In this exercise of international leadership the IMF acted consistently with some of its fundamental purposes as it sought to restore confidence to members and to minimize the impact of global imbalances on the multilateral payments systems. At the same time, the political priorities of its main shareholders, as well as the magnitude of adverse global economic shocks, prevented the IMF from upholding other important purposes set forth in its Articles of Agreement: Debtor nations had to sacrifice real incomes, import capacity, and exchange rate stability. In placing its political weight behind the commercial banks, the Fund is partially responsible for the uneven bargains struck between creditors and debtors that ranked debt service to the banks above renewed growth for the developing world. As several contributors to this volume note, the Fund understandably came to be seen as the debt collector for the private banks.

Retreat and Re-Engagement

During stage two, the IMF did not follow through on its initial victories. As the crisis atmosphere eased, it became more difficult to corral banks into participating in new money packages, and many developing countries preferred to escape from IMF tutelage. The IMF itself welcomed a gradual disengagement. Staff projections overestimated developing-country export growth prospects and failed to foresee that dollar devaluation would augment the weight of non-dollar denominated debt.[3] But perhaps more important was the reassertion by key industrial countries and some Fund staff that prolonged involvement with developing nations contradicted the fundamental purposes of the IMF. In this "purist" view, the IMF should keep its powder dry for short-term, emergency lending to major industrial nations whose currencies are key to the international financial system. This view was reinforced by the concern that the exit of the commercial banks from developing-country markets was leaving the Fund with a rising proportion of developing-country risk. Thus, on both analytical and institutional grounds, the IMF contracted its exposure in Latin America and Sub-Saharan Africa.

By the end of the 1980s, the "purist" position had collapsed under the pressure of persistent debt problems and growing demand for renewed collective action. The first cold wind of reality blew out of Africa. Outside experts and the African nations condemned the IMF for extracting resources at a time of deepening balance-of-payments disorder, and several African governments fell behind in their payments to the IMF. In response, member countries agreed to establish new facilities to provide financing at concessional rates and for an extended period to low-income countries. When Michel Camdessus became Managing Director in January, 1987, he persuaded Japan and other industrial nations to provide additional funds to complement these IMF resources.

Camdessus was also an early advocate of debt reduction for hard-pressed Latin American debtors, and he personally gave the green light for Fund staff to fix partial blame for the region's plight on the debt overhang in their April 1989 *World Economic Outlook.*[4] During 1987–88 the IMF served as a forum for the developing countries to explain the adverse impact of the debt overhang and heavy debt service obligations on exchange-rate stability, fiscal deficits, domestic investment, and price stability. One active participant in this debate, which eventually gave birth to the Brady proposals, was Guillermo Ortiz, at that time a member of the IMF Executive Board—and a contributor to this volume.

As a result of the sharp rise in real interest rates in the 1980s and the decline in commercial bank lending, the developing countries have had to pay considerably more in interest and amortization than they have been receiving in new loans from the international financial community. The net transfer of financial resources to the developing world, which amounted to a *positive* $29 billion as recently as 1982, had become a *negative* $34 billion by 1987; the seventeen highly indebted nations suffered a decimating $28 billion swing—from a positive $11 billion to a negative $17 billion.[5] Paradoxically, since 1987, both the IMF and World Bank have themselves become a net drain on developing countries, as interest payments on outstanding loans surpassed net disbursements. For the Fund, during 1987–88, interest charges and amortization surpassed new credits by about $16 billion for the developing world, and by about $5 billion for the heavily indebted nations (Figure 2). While consistent with the revolving nature of the Fund, the timing of these repayments added to the financial woes of many developing countries. However, since their disbursements have generally exceeded amortizations, the exposure of the Bretton Woods agencies has risen both in absolute terms, and especially in relation to the fleeing commercial banks. The combined IMF-World Bank share of the public long-term debt owed by the heavily indebted nations rose from 10 per cent in 1980 to 16 per cent by the end of 1987.[6]

The Orchestration of Net Transfer Reduction

The Brady proposals call upon the IMF and the World Bank to provide about $10 billion each, and Japan an additional $10 billion, over three years to support reductions in the stock of debt and in interest payments. As is customary, these official loans are conditioned upon reforms in debtor nations. Jeffrey Sachs and Guillermo Ortiz concur that the new debt strategy is welcome in several respects. It seeks to reduce the net resource transfer that is draining debtor nations of scarce capital. It seems to be based on a more realistic appreciation of the severity of the debt overhang, and at least in the Mexican case, on the need to make renewed developing-country growth the clear priority. To achieve these objectives, the IMF has reversed tactics and has shifted

Figure 2. IMF Net Resource Transfer to Developing Countries

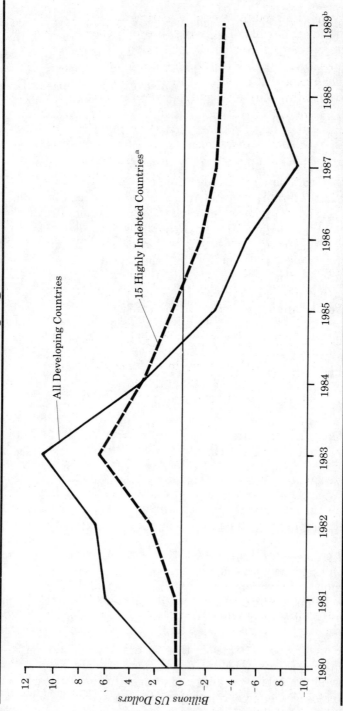

All Developing Countries

15 Highly Indebted Countries[a]

Billions US Dollars

12 10 8 6 4 2 0 -2 -4 -6 8 -10

1980 1981 1982 1983 1984 1985 1986 1987 1988 1989[b]

[a]Argentina, Bolivia, Brazil, Chile, Colombia, Ivory Coast, Ecuador, Mexico, Morocco, Nigeria, Peru, the Philippines, Uruguay, Venezuela, and Yugoslavia.
[b]Figures for 1989 are annualized estimates based on end-June 1989 data for all developing countries and end-May 1989 data for the highly indebted countries.

Sources: International Monetary Fund, *World Economic Outlook* (Washington, D.C., IMF) 1988 and 1989; and International Monetary Fund, *International Financial Statistics* (Washington, D.C., IMF), various issues, 1985–89.

from fortifying the creditor cartel to strengthening the bargaining hand of individual debtors. The new policy of disbursing to countries that undertake reforms even in the absence of agreements with commercial banks, and possibly in the presence of arrears, is intended to foster more balanced deals.

Notwithstanding these advances, several formidable obstacles could derail the new debt strategy. The numbers may not work: As the Mexican debt deal of July 1989 suggests, the current pool of $30 billion in available resources is insufficient to generate significant net debt reduction under the existing set of incentives facing the banks, at least for countries whose debt is not very deeply discounted on secondary markets. The banks may stonewall many debtors: No powerful public coordinator exists to guarantee compliance by a financial community with diverse interests and wide geographic spread. Some debtors may judge that the incentives to play are too weak, while the costs of de facto default have declined—and act accordingly.

The Brady proposals pose an additional, dangerous challenge for the IMF by generating an inherent conflict of interest between the Bretton Woods agencies and the commercial banks. Under the Brady proposals, the Fund and the Bank provide reform-minded debtors new loans as well as credit to be used as collateral to guarantee the discounted debts owed to commercial banks. The danger is that the result will be an increase in IMF exposure in the uncreditworthy developing countries without a significant scaling down of the debt overhang: As of March 30, 1989, developing countries were already $3.4 billion in arrears to the Fund. It is in the institutional interest of the official agencies to minimize the transfer of risk to themselves and to maximize debt reduction by the private banks: This "mini-maxi" solution would optimize the ability of debtors to service official creditors. The banks face the opposite objective function: to maximize the transfer of risk to public institutions and to minimize their own losses. In light of their membership, the IMF and the World Bank must seek a compromise outcome—one that provides enough relief to debtors to enable them to meet their remaining obligations to all creditors so that the risk transferred to the official sector is acceptable.

To make the new debt strategy effective, we recommend that:

1. **The Fund should fill the dangerous power vacuum and provide leadership for a debt strategy based on "guided voluntarism."** As during the "concerted lending" stage of the debt crisis, Fund management should clearly articulate the overall debt strategy and the Fund should be a central forum where strategy is frankly debated and amended as required. Once a nation's financial requirements have been calculated, the Fund should alter its currently rather passive mode and actively engage the commercial banks, working with creditor govern-

ments to orchestrate carrots and sticks to gain compliance. Banks should have the right to choose voluntarily among a menu of options, but not to choose non-participation.

2. **The IMF and the World Bank should have the clear strategic objective of making each country's debt service conform to a payment stream consistent with sustainable growth.**[7] Furthermore, IMF programs must look beyond this year's balances to medium-term sustainability. Although renewed creditworthiness is a long-term aspiration, it is not a realistic near-term objective for most countries.

The IMF's calculations of debtors' financial needs must be as objective as possible, free from political intrusions, and should be firmly endorsed by key industrial-country governments. Otherwise the commercial banks could dismiss IMF projections as biased and negotiations could quickly hit an insurmountable impasse.

Only if the new strategy significantly improves debtors' cash flow outlook will it become sufficiently attractive to induce the participation of the majority of debtors. Right now, there is the danger that many nations, including Argentina, Brazil, and Peru—which account for 70 per cent of the population of South America—will remain on the sidelines.

3. **The IMF should increase its own lending to reform-minded debtors, and net disbursements should become significantly positive.** Such a return to positive net flows is assumed in the IMF's own projections of demand for IMF credit, which are central to the case for a quota increase. Renewed net disbursements would cause the IMF to continue to absorb a rising portion of the external obligations of the heavily indebted nations. Such a transfer can be justified on historical and political grounds. During the period of heavy borrowing, the public sector should have handled a larger proportion of the credit flow than it did. Politically, it is a central function of public sector financial institutions to manage crises through risk absorption. But this risk absorption should be accompanied by a sharing of losses by the private sector, and by a financial reorganization that holds the promise of recovery and eventual repayment of the remaining debt.

4. **Because debt reduction is more complex than new loan packages, IMF staff must become steeped in the regulatory, tax, and accounting regimes that affect banks' behavior and make recommendations to national governments that would reinforce the debt strategy.** This role cannot be left to the Basle-based Bank for International Settlements, which represents the narrower interests of industrial-country central banks. Fund staff must also analyze the various debt reduction instruments not only with regard to their impact on the external balance but also for potential adverse implications for domestic monetary and fiscal targets and inflation.

5. **In negotiating reform programs, the IMF should seek to limit the damage of adjustment on the poor and should be less quick to press for real devaluations aimed at generating abnormal trade surpluses.** Primary responsibility for poverty alleviation must lie with national governments—and between the Bretton Woods agencies, with the World Bank. But Jeffrey Sachs and Joan Nelson agree that the IMF ought to analyze the distributional impact of its recommendations and should propose policies to compensate the poor when stabilization measures are likely to affect them adversely. Noting that in Latin America the wealthy often pay little taxes, Sachs also suggests that progressive tax reforms would help solve the region's chronic fiscal crisis. In addition, Nelson and Sachs maintain that more concern for equity would sometimes improve the political sustainability of IMF programs.[8]

The counterpart of the negative resource transfer has been the large trade surpluses that the developing nations have had to accumulate to generate foreign exchange for debt service. As Sachs argues, the IMF has systematically advocated sharp devaluations in order to spur exports and depress demand for imports. Devaluations have often been warranted to correct badly overvalued exchange rates, but in other instances devaluations have only undermined confidence in government policies and spurred inflation. A successful debt strategy would alleviate pressure on the trade balance and allow the Fund to return to its traditional concern for domestic price stability. In a country with good prospects for fiscal balance, a stable exchange rate can foster confidence in the government's anti-inflationary convictions.

Redefining Relations with the Poorest Nations

Although it gets far less attention, there is another debt crisis that involves the IMF. That is the crisis of the debt-distressed low-income countries, many of which are in Sub-Saharan Africa, and the bulk of whose debt is owed not to commercial banks but to official agencies—both bilateral and multilateral. As of 1987 the total debt of the thirty low-income African countries, with 1987 GNP *per capita* under $425, was $70 billion, an amount equivalent to approximately 500 per cent of their annual exports.

There really is no good solution for this second debt crisis other than to have the official creditors write off their debts or reschedule them on such terms that they cease to be a pressing problem. In the past few years, major donors have agreed to a "menu" of options for easing the burden of African debt, and some have taken steps to write off a portion of concessional loans, but the actions taken to date still leave many poor countries mired in debt that they cannot service and that is seriously eroding their already low standards of living. In addition, their government officials spend too much time in repeated rescheduling negotiations.

The IMF has added its voice to the growing chorus calling for significant debt relief for the low-income countries. But the IMF itself accounted for a net reflow of funds from Sub-Saharan Africa of $1 billion during 1986–87. In the absence of large amounts of new concessional flows from other sources, which would enable the low-income countries to do more than just repay the Fund, this reverse transfer from Africa to the IMF should not be occurring. The IMF ought to "stay in" Africa with positive net flows—at least for the time being.

The Fund also ought to make adjustments in its ways of providing advice and assistance to low-income countries. Of the forty-four countries which had an arrangement with the Fund in the beginning of 1989, twenty-nine were African countries, and another seven were low-income countries outside Africa. In many of these cases, repeated IMF programs have failed to bring progress toward achieving a sustainable payments position.

If the decade of the 1980s could be played over again, the IMF would do better not to become so deeply involved in Sub-Saharan Africa. There is a basic mismatch between the Fund's short-to-medium term financial and analytical timeframe and these countries' fundamentally long-term development problems, the solution of which depends on the gradual build-up of human capital, institutional capabilities, basic infrastructure, and market mechanisms.

The IMF's repayment schedule simply does not meet the major needs of the poorer developing countries, which cannot realistically hope to export their way out of debt and into development in anything but the long term. Even though the IMF has lengthened some repayment schedules to five to ten years, there remains a tendency to expect progress in a much shorter time and to assume that if a country gets its key prices right, the rest (including increased production) will follow. What the past decade has clearly shown, however, is that the supply response in an adjustment effort in the poorer developing countries tends to be weak and slow. Under these circumstances, the IMF cannot, as its standard approach would have it, go into one of these countries and get out quickly—it has to be prepared to stay in a long time.

Moreover, to overcome the supply response problems, it is necessary to deal with the many aspects of development that lie outside the Fund's traditional purview. An IMF mission typically consists of four to five people who visit a country for two to three weeks and talk with officials at the central banks and ministries of finance. But the supply aspects of the poorer developing countries' adjustment problems require detailed attention to a host of sectoral and institutional issues.

The IMF's comparative strength in assisting low-income countries lies in its capacity to develop the data on and work through the implications of a poor country's budgetary, monetary, and external payments problems. However, because of the IMF's focus and its relatively short-term repayment requirements, its help to the poorer countries needs to be set within a broad development policy context. Operationally, this requires a much closer working relationship with the World Bank than the two "sister" institutions as yet have been willing to forge. In most low-income countries, moreover, it means that the World Bank, not the IMF, should take the lead in the structural adjustment dialogue. To perform even a supportive role, however, the IMF must find ways to deal with two subsidiary issues: the cost of IMF credit and the resuscitation of countries in arrears to the Fund itself:

1. **If the IMF is to continue to help the poorer developing countries, it must assure that its financing to them remains on a concessional basis.** Indeed, the case could reasonably be made that all IMF financing to the poorer developing countries—including financing through the Compensatory and Contingency Financing Facility (CCFF)—ought to be at low rates of interest. There are two likely sources of continuing concessional credit. One source might be regular contributions from developed countries. But some fear that dependency on member-country contributions would place the IMF in competition with the International Development Association (IDA)—the World Bank's "soft" loan window—for access to scarce aid resources. A second alternative is to turn to the sale and investment of a portion of the IMF's still-large holdings of 103 million ounces of gold. The sale of IMF gold was used to generate resources for the Trust Fund established in the 1970s, and reflows of Trust Fund loans were subsequently used to finance the Structural Adjustment Facility (SAF). Louis Goreux suggests the possibility of using the earnings from the investment of some portion of the Fund's remaining gold as a continuing source of concessional finance.

2. **The IMF should re-engage with countries in arrears to it who become ready to undertake reforms, and it should help raise new assistance prior to arrears being cleared.** Eleven countries had overdue obligations to the Fund for more than six months as of the end of April, 1989. Existing policy prohibits the Fund from submitting a new program for a country in arrears to its Executive Board before that country has become current. But this estrangement makes it difficult for the IMF to respond quickly to governments that become ready to undertake serious reforms.

For countries whose arrears are not too large in an absolute sense, the IMF can try to mobilize enough outside resources to both clear the arrears and support an adjustment program. For countries whose arrears have become large, however, it might not be possible to mobilize enough resources to do both. In this latter case, the IMF ought to be able to assist a country in formulating and monitoring a recovery program supported by funds other than its own, but with the understanding that the new money would not be used to repay the Fund. In other words, the country's debt to the IMF would remain unpaid for some specified number of years into an adjustment program. The risk for the Fund is that the country might be no better off at the end of that time, and that the arrears would have increased. The way around that danger lies not with the IMF alone, but, in part, with better IMF-World Bank interaction.

IMF–World Bank Relations

Created as "sister institutions" at the time of Bretton Woods, the IMF and the World Bank were previously distinguishable in their financing activities by the kinds of problems they addressed and the terms of financing they provided. Simply put, the IMF was to provide short-term credit for countries with temporary balance-of-payments problems. In contrast, the World Bank was to provide long-term development financing, ordinarily for specific projects, and, after the IDA "window" was opened in 1960, on concessional terms to the poorest nations.

In the 1980s, however, it has been impossible to maintain the old, sharp distinctions between short-term financial distress and long-term development disequilibria that served as the basis for the old division of labor between the IMF and the World Bank in the Third World. Countries now have to cope with finance and development problems simultaneously and over an extended period. In response, both the Bank and the Fund have manufactured increasingly similar lending instruments that focus on similar policy issues. Both extend medium-term balance-of-payments support with conditions targeted at macroeconomic and structural variables.[9] The results have been a confusion of roles, occasionally contradictory advice to countries, compromises struck between the two institutions that leave too little room for input from the recipient country, and excessive time spent by country officials in dealing with overlapping missions.

As each institution has ventured into this new grey area, greater coordination between them has become essential. When the IMF introduced concessional financing for extended programs undertaken by low-income developing countries, the IMF and the World Bank agreed to the joint preparation of "policy framework papers." More broadly, in early 1989 the Bretton Woods "sisters" reached a power-sharing entente that essentially affirmed a 1966 division of labor, restoring "primary responsibility" over macroeconomic issues and exchange rate policies to the

Fund while granting the World Bank primacy over structural or microeconomic matters.

Although the chosen division of labor is the only logical one, it should not be seen as the definitive solution. Precisely because the overlap in activities is the result of the inextricable interrelatedness of policy variables, Bank and Fund staff will continue to cross paths. Therefore, in order to provide borrowing countries with consistent and timely programs and to ensure them a stronger voice in the design of those programs, greater efforts must be made to coordinate IMF and World Bank analyses, program designs, and in-country policy dialogues. To this end, the following four changes would be useful:

1. **The boards of the two Bretton Woods agencies should establish a Joint Standing Committee to discuss policy issues of mutual concern and monitor collaboration efforts.** This JSC could also review medium-term country programs before formal approval by either Executive Board.[10] The Committee should be composed of Executive Directors broadly representative of the various constituencies that make up the membership of the two institutions. The constitutions of the two agencies require, however, that final decisionmaking authority remain with the respective boards.

2. **Countries that regularly have an Executive Director would do well to apppoint a single director to both boards,** as Great Britain, France, and Belgium have successfully done. This would make it more likely that those governments would formulate coherent policies for the Bretton Woods system.

3. **For most countries—low- as well as middle-income ones— prepared to undertake serious adjustment efforts, medium-term country programs should be designed by joint Bank–Fund missions.** The current practices of including representatives from "across the street" in mission teams, and of "parallel missions" that are in-country at the same time, are positive steps but depend too much on personalities to assure coherent programs. (Third World representatives should cease to oppose such collaboration as "cross conditionality," and recognize that Bank and Fund approval processes are already closely linked.)

4. **The World Bank, not the IMF, should take the lead in organizing assistance for low-income countries.** This division of labor would be consistent with the 1989 decision to give the World Bank primacy over structural matters, which are the fundamental problem in the poorest nations, but ought not to prevent the IMF from continuing to assist on macroeconomic problems as needed.[11]

Overall, the objective of these changes should be to foster comprehensive but less time-consuming policy dialogues with economically troubled countries and to fashion consistent policy packages that governments can sustain in efforts to realize stabilization with growth.

The Integration of Socialist Countries into the One-World Economy

The Soviet Union was an active participant in the 1944 Bretton Woods conclave and was offered 13 per cent of the voting shares in the newly created international institutions—but Stalin chose not to join. Consistent with its efforts to participate in multilateral fora and to become more integrated into the global economy, the government of Mikhail Gorbachev has expressed interest in reversing Stalin's isolationist decision and in joining the IMF.

Soviet membership would provide the IMF with a major new mission. Integrating the Soviet Union as well as Eastern Europe into the global economy could become a central purpose of the IMF in the 1990s and beyond.[12] Just as World Bank staff have done in China, Fund staff could provide advice to the Soviet Union on the treacherous transition from bureaucratic centralism to incentive socialism. The IMF possesses expertise in the areas in which the Soviet Union badly needs guidance—e.g., on money and banking, price reform, and exchange and trade relations. If successful in this endeavor, the Fund would have accomplished an important task in its pursuit of a liberal and cooperative world economic order.

Soviet membership would also be consistent with a U.S. foreign policy seeking to move beyond East-West military confrontation to interbloc economic cooperation. The IMF is an obvious instrumentality to serve President Bush's strategic design "to seek the integration of the Soviet Union into the community of nations."[13]

The Soviet Union should only be granted membership after *perestroika* has proceeded further. In the meantime, however, actions can be taken to dilute mutual suspicion among member states and in the Soviet Union about the implications of Soviet entry. We recommend five "confidence-building" measures that could pave the way to membership in the Fund and subsequently the World Bank (the Soviet Union would necessarily enter the Bank as a donor nation but with access to technical advice on structural reform). These measures include: (1) consultations that bring Soviet officials and scholars to the Bretton Woods agencies and that permit IMF and World Bank missions to study the Soviet economy; (2) Soviet provision of data on Soviet loans and concessional assistance to developing nations that is consistent with international classifications; (3) Soviet participation in select World Bank projects through co-financing; (4) Soviet participation in donor consortia in countries where Soviet aid programs are active; (5) cooperation between the Soviet Union and the World Bank in carefully chosen functional areas such as environmental protection. If successful, such cooperative endeavors could help build the trust necessary for a successful working relationship between the Fund and the world's other superpower.

To qualify for membership, the Soviet Union must also meet the Fund's routine data requirements and agree to strive over time to better realize IMF obligations by improving the quality of statistical information and reducing exchange and trade restrictions. Undoubtedly the Fund would seek additional indications that the Soviet Union would not launch a frontal attack on the core values of the organization, nor seek to undermine relations between the Fund and individual members. Even with such assurances, the Fund would still run the risk that Gorbachev could be replaced by hard-liners, but since the Soviet Union would at most be granted 5–6 per cent of the votes on the IMF Executive Board, any disruptive tactics could be contained.[14]

The socialist economies in Eastern Europe are not simply developing countries suffering from an unusually large number of distorting interventions, but have lived with pervasive controls that amount to a qualitatively special case. To effectively advise a reform-minded Soviet Union, the Bretton Woods agencies should become a leading locus for the study of socialist economies in transition.

Strengthening the IMF's Institutional Capacities

To fulfill the ambitious but realistic program outlined above, the IMF will have to strengthen its institutional capacities. Specifically, it should expand its research agenda and become more engaged in public debates. It should alter its bureaucratic structure to allow for more vigorous internal discussion and policy innovation. And it should be provided with more financial resources.

Intellectual Center

In the rapidly changing and complex world of the 1990s, in which power is widely dispersed among many nations and private markets, there is a great need for steady, reliable analysis and advice. On international economic matters, the IMF should perform this function with increased vigor.

As the voice of the global economy, the Fund should be willing to speak out early and forcefully on controversial issues. Member governments should expect the Managing Director to publicly articulate views that may not enjoy unanimous Board approval. De Larosière's willingness to underscore the dangers in the unsustainable U.S. budget deficits and Camdessus' early pursuit of debt reduction are positive examples of such intellectual leadership.

The Fund should continue to publish authoritative statistical series and provide ongoing analyses of official policies and its own recommendations for future action. In addition, the Fund staff should work hard on four of the tough but highly relevant policy issues mentioned earlier: (1) alternative financial mechanisms that could foster greater and more symmetrical discipline in the adjustment of payments imbalances; (2) the net financing needs of debtor nations, individually and collectively, and possible revisions in the banking regulations in creditor nations that could catalyze the required flows; (3) the impact of stabilization measures on the distribution of income and mechanisms for offsetting adverse effects on the poor; (4) the repercussions of a reforming Soviet Union on the international economy and institutions, and the sequencing of reforms during the transition from centralized socialism to a more market economy.

Organizational Reform

If the IMF is to play a demanding and sometimes risky leadership role, changes are needed in its structure and attitudes. The Managing Director should have a strategic planning staff to help him spot emerging issues and to articulate his advice. To foster more innovative and coherent policies, the Fund's vertical structure should be relaxed to allow for more horizontal flow of information between and even within departments. More rapid staff turnover would be desirable to permit the Fund to acquire the necessary know-how as new issues arise. For example, in the 1970s the Fund should have sought more expertise on Africa. Today, it needs more staff or consultants who understand the technical details of financial engineering. Tomorrow it will want economists steeped in socialist reform.

If the Fund is to mold opinion in a more democratic world, it will have to learn to talk not only to central bankers but to a wider public. While recognizing the legitimate requirements of confidentiality, there is considerable room to open access to IMF staff and studies. Some senior members of the research department do circulate, but many researchers and most operational staff maintain a narrow range of contacts outside Fund walls. The Fund could learn from the World Bank's more open posture.

To begin the process of more democratic access to Fund documentation, the U.S. government should agree to the release of the IMF's annual report on the American economy, just as other countries, including China, have released World Bank memoranda on themselves. Sensitive policy discussions between the Fund and member governments require privacy while in progress, but scholars and journalists should be permitted to read papers on general policy matters and the decisions of the Executive Board after a reasonably brief lapse of time. In addition, modernization and simplification of the Fund's arcane language—for example, replacing "purchases" with "credits"—would make the institution more accessible and also more influential.

Fund Resources

At the end of 1989, the Fund expects to be sitting on about $43 billion in usable hard currency and about $35–40 billion in gold at market prices, while having access to contingent lines of credit of an additional $23 billion. From 1985 to end–1989, the Fund expects to have cut its outstanding credit by about SDR 10 billion, thereby increasing its liquidity to abnormally high levels. The Managing Director, U.S. Treasury Secretary Brady, and the finance ministers of many other member countries are already on record in support of a quota increase in 1990. But the size of the increase is yet to be determined. We believe that governments should agree to an increase that would enable the IMF to pursue the several different tasks identified throughout this volume:

- Exercise leverage in reducing the net resource transfer draining heavily indebted countries;
- Stay involved, in cooperation with the World Bank, in the low-income, economically distressed countries;
- Support adjustment in Eastern Europe and build capacity, over time, to assist in the integration of the Soviet Union into the world economy; and
- Continue to stand by as a lender of last resort for countries that encounter intermittent balance-of-payments difficulties.

The IMF's need for a quota increase to implement these tasks rests on the assumption that large macroeconomic imbalances will not smooth out soon; that commercial bank lending to developing countries will not revive significantly over the medium term; and that meaningful IMF involvement in the easing of the debt crisis will require an increase in countries' effective limits on access to Fund resources.

We are not convinced that the size of IMF resources must be maintained in some fixed proportion to total trade and world GNP, since these are no longer good indicators of potential demand for Fund resources. But we are convinced that the amount of resources available to reform-minded developing countries should rise, and that a quota increase ought not be immediately debased by a fully offsetting reduction in access limits. We see the need for governments to reaffirm their support for and adherence to multilateralism in monetary matters. And we believe that the potential influence of the IMF as an intellectual center would be enhanced by the vote of confidence that a quota increase would signal. It is only realistic to note that ideas backed by money tend to be taken more seriously that those that are not.

A 50-per-cent quota increase that raised quotas from the current SDR 90 billion to SDR 135 billion would permit average annual lending of $12 billion during 1990–94, and positive net disbursements of $6 billion, while maintaining IMF liquidity at prudent ratios roughly in line with historic levels. In effect, this increase would enable the IMF to play as dynamic a role in the early 1990s as it did in the early 1980s, at the onset of the debt crisis, though the Fund's specific tasks would be redefined in the ways recommended herein.

Since 1983, the U.S. Congress has considered a quota subscription an appropriation, but not a net budgetary outlay. The U.S. cash payment is immediately offset by the receipt of an enlarged U.S. reserve position in the Fund; that portion of the U.S. quota that must be paid in cash becomes part of the U.S. reserve tranche, which the U.S. can draw on demand. We therefore see no real financial constraint on U.S. support for a moderate 50-per-cent increase next year.[15] However, in the interest of fostering the kind of role we believe that the IMF should now play, the quota increase should be part of a policy package that includes three other elements:

(1) Industrial-country governments should modify the framework of incentives facing the commercial banks to assure their fair participation in reducing the net resource transfer draining debtor nations. The U.S. Congress should require that the administration report on bank cooperation with the Brady proposals, detailing the net resources flows and changes in debt stocks by creditor type for each debtor nation. Otherwise, increased IMF lending could result in an unacceptable transfer of risk to the official agencies without an adequate improvement in the balance-of-payments and growth outlook of the developing countries.

(2) In recognition of its greatly increased economic power and its recent valuable contributions to IMF programs, Japan should be granted the number two ranking in voting shares, behind only the United States. The United States should actively support this realignment, and the affected European nations should gracefully acquiesce.

(3) The U.S. Congress should attach to the quota increase legislation a requirement that the U.S. Treasury work for a more open, accessible, and therefore more accountable Fund.

The IMF can only play the role its member countries allow it to assume. We believe that the times warrant a more transparent, dynamic, and influential central monetary institution. That will require changes in IMF policies and practices as well as a more disciplined approach to monetary matters on the part of all member countries.

Notes

Note: In appreciation for very helpful comments on earlier drafts, the authors would like to express their gratitude to Ralph Bryant, Gerald Helleiner, John Lewis, Barry Newman, Louis Pauly, John Sewell, Robert Solomon, and the other contributors to this volume. The authors alone, however, are responsible for the views expressed herein.

[1] Richard Cooper, "Is there a Need for Reform?" in *The International Monetary System: Forty Years After Bretton Woods* (Boston: Federal Reserve Bank of Boston, 1984), pp. 21–39.

[2] The IMF typically denominates its activities in Special Drawing Rights (SDRs). In this chapter, the SDR-dollar conversion is made at the rate for the year in question. For 1989, as of June 30, one SDR was valued at $1.25.

[3] Fund staff frankly admit this misjudgment in IMF, *World Economic Outlook*, 1989, Box 4, p. 55.

[4] IMF, *World Economic Outlook*, 1989, pp. 52–54.

[5] World Bank, *World Debt Tables, 1988–89*, pp. 30–31.

[6] Ibid, pp. 2, 30.

[7] For an earlier statement of this view, see Richard E. Feinberg and contributors, *Between Two Worlds: The World Bank's Next Decade* (New Brunswick, N.J.: Transaction Books in cooperation with the Overseas Development Council, 1986), p. 9.

[8] The complex interaction between economic reform and political realities, particularly over the long haul, is examined at length in Joan M. Nelson and contributors, *Fragile Coalitions: The Politics of Economic Adjustment* (New Brunswick, N.J.: Transaction Books in cooperation with the Overseas Development Council, 1989).

[9] See Richard E. Feinberg, "The Changing Relationship Between the World Bank and the International Monetary Fund," *International Organization*, Summer 1988, Vol. 42, No. 3, p. 549.

[10] This proposal was first made in Miriam Camps and Catherine Gwin, *Collective Management: The Reform of Global Economic Organizations* (New York: McGraw-Hill, 1981), p. 300.

[11] For an early discussion of this point, see Catherine Gwin, "The Role of the International Financial Institutions," Testimony before the U.S. House of Representatives, Subcommittee on International Development Institutions and Finance, June 17, 1982.

[12] Yugoslavia was a charter member of the IMF. Romania entered in 1972, and Hungary joined in 1982. Poland, which became a member in 1946 and withdrew in 1950, rejoined in 1986, while Czechoslovakia—a charter member expelled in 1954—has recently entered into preliminary membership discussions with the Fund.

[13] Remarks at Texas A&M University, College Station, Texas, May 12, 1989.

[14] A fuller discussion can be found in Richard E. Feinberg, *The Soviet Union and the Bretton Woods Institutions: Risks and Rewards of Membership,* Public Policy Papers of the Institute for East-West Security Studies, 1989.

[15] Assuming a quota increase of 50 per cent, the U.S. share would be about $11.5 billion, about one-quarter of which would have to be immediately paid in SDRs, and the remainder covered by a letter of credit that the Fund would draw on as needed.

II. Summaries of Chapter Recommendations

Summaries of Chapter Recommendations

1. Strengthening the Role of the IMF in the International Monetary System (Jacques J. Polak)

Two developments of the 1970s, the breakdown of the par value system and the development of worldwide banking, have affected the working and the influence of the Fund—in particular in relation to the Western industrial countries. The Fund's influence on their policies has been weakened by the disappearance of par values; the "firm surveillance over exchange-rate policies" mandated by the amended Article IV has not materialized. And ready access to international bank credit has enabled all of these countries to avoid recourse to Fund credit for more than a decade. Yet the Fund, as the ultimate backstop of the system, should arrange its finances so as to be able, if need be, to assist any of its major members. Its next quota review should, accordingly, continue to allow for the potential needs of *all* members.

In the period ahead, the Fund may be particularly helpful to the countries of Eastern Europe, including perhaps the Soviet Union—not only or even primarily by providing finance, but by assisting these countries in their transition to a more market-oriented system.

Through most of its history, the Fund has been a critical source of balance-of-payments finance for the developing countries. In recent years, it has increasingly tailored its credit facilities to the needs of these countries. Under the 1987 ESAF (Enhanced Structural Adjustment Facility), it has for the first time solicited aid funds from its higher-income members to be lent to low-income countries at highly concessional interest rates. If it wants to continue on this road, while avoiding conflict with the established funding procedures of IDA, it should consider investing part of its gold to earn an income from which to subsidize the interest cost of credit to its poorest members.

In spite of the developing-country focus of much of its recent lending activity, it is a mistake to consider the Fund as an aid agency. The
Fund continues to discharge a broad range of responsibilities in the
international monetary system. These responsibilities are most clearly
in evidence in the terms of reference of its Interim Committee, which is
the only international grouping of manageable size (22 members) where
ministers of finance of developed and developing countries seek agreement on major issues in the Fund and the system.

Other organizations or groupings of some (or all) of the Fund's
members also engage in policy advice, finance, or surveillance. Apart
from the World Bank, the two of most direct impact on the Fund are the
European Community (EC) and the Group of Seven (G-7). Until the EC
adopts a regime of fixed exchange rates, the fund's surveillance role
vis-à-vis the EC countries will remain a valuable counterweight to premature exchange rate rigidity.

The agenda of the Group of Seven covers a wide range of policy
areas, including exchange rates, trade, development, debt, energy, and
structural policies, many of which are of primary relevance to the Fund.
The exchange rate regime of managed floating that applies among the
major currencies since September 1985 requires coordination among
the issuing countries with respect to their monetary policies and intervention. The Fund can provide the basic underpinning for these activities by its work on scenarios incorporating alternative exchange rates
among the major currencies. If "peer pressure" by the G-7 can
strengthen the Fund's surveillance over the economies of its major
members, this would expedite adjustment of major external
disequilibria in the system. But there is also a risk that "policy coordination" may unduly politicize, and delay, the working of the adjustment
process. Regular G-7 meetings, supported by Fund staff and management, can prepare the ground for those occasions when common policy
action is needed to prevent the world econony from overheating or sliding into recession.

A large share of the benefits of policy coordination relates to information. It is important to spread these benefits beyond the G-7. The
Fund should also incorporate in its consultation procedures for all members whatever new techniques and indicators may have proven of value
in the context of the G-7.

The increased scope of international bank credit in the last twenty
years has weakened the case for SDR allocations, though they would
still be of benefit to the system and to those countries that lack ready
access to capital markets. But agreement on allocation seems increasingly remote—except, conceivably, as a way to deal with some crisis situation.

2. The Use of IMF Credit (Peter Kenen)

The Fund will face two challenges in the 1990s: It must help to reduce and consolidate the debts of developing countries; and must involve itself in the process of exchange rate management initiated by the Louvre Accord of 1987 and the further reform of exchange-rate arrangements.

Heavily indebted developing countries have been chronic users of Fund credit, and the Fund has been obliged to refinance their obligations. In the process, it has frequently agreed to policy commitments that it would have rejected in ordinary circumstance, impairing its own credibility. The Fund has also begun to finance debt-reduction plans being negotiated by middle-income debtors and their commercial-bank creditors.

The Fund can provide some of the financing needed for debt-reducing operations, but this should not be its main task. The use of Fund credit to buy back or collateralize long-term debt can worsen the debtor's cash-flow problems and reduce the Fund's own flexibility. The Fund should try to avoid a contraction of its claims on the debtor countries, rather than enlarge them, and it should liberalize access to its Compensatory and Contingency Financing Facility (CCFF) to help debtors deal with unforeseen shocks. To achieve this aim, however, the Fund must confront the effects of having relied on borrowed money for earlier extensions of Fund credit. It cannot refinance its members' obligations unless it rolls over its own or draws down its assets to pay them off.

The Fund could roll over its debt without trouble but should reduce it instead and rely less heavily on borrowed resources. Borrowing made sense when OPEC surpluses were very large but makes little sense when surpluses are not sharply concentrated and surplus countries are piling up private-sector claims rather than reserves. Furthermore, reliance on borrowing will reduce support for increases in Fund quotas and thus raise the need for borrowing, which will give the surplus countries too much influence over the Fund's policies. The Fund can afford to pay off its debts. Its holdings of usable currencies and gold are very large and could be drawn down without impairing its liquidity.

The Fund must also modify its policies to keep the supply of Fund from contracting, because drawings by many debt countries already exceed conventional limits. There are two ways to solve this problem: waiving the Fund's rules or liberalizing access by raising Fund quotas.

Waivers have been granted routinely for EFF drawings and certain others. But granting them on an ad hoc basis would come near to violating the Fund's Articles of Agreement, which say that waivers should be granted to members "with a record of *avoiding* large or continuous use of the Fund's general resources." It would therefore be better to raise Fund quotas. Three steps might be taken: (1) a 50-per-cent increase in quotas, partly to provide the Fund with more resources, but mainly to raise drawing rights; (2) an increase in the ceiling for CCFF drawings to 150 per cent of quota, with a cumulative ceiling on all uses of Fund credit at, say, 250 per cent of quota. These numbers are illustrative, not definitive, but would cover most of the middle-income debtors and give them room to draw on the CCFF in case of unexpected shocks. A bigger increase in quotas, by 75 per cent, would be appropriate if the Fund had to make a large contribution to debt-reducing operations.

The Fund must continue to require policy commitments by users of Fund credit. But members should be encouraged to alter their policies *before* applying to the Fund—to seek its endorsement rather than its tutelage. The Fund must continue to monitor implementation but pay less attention to changes in financial and fiscal variables, concentrating instead on changes in trade flows, reserves, and real exchange rates.

The Fund can contribute significantly to the process of exchange rate management: (1) It can play a larger role in policy coordination. (2) It can start to play a role in financing intervention by raising the amount of reserve credit available for this purpose.

A substitution account managed by the Fund could raise usable U.S. reserves and reduce the exchange rate risks borne by other countries. The plan discussed in 1979 focused on the second purpose. A slightly different plan would achieve both purposes. The United States would deposit gold; others would deposit dollars; and all depositors would obtain an SDR-denominated claim that would serve as a reserve asset.

Over the long run, the Fund should be reorganized to use its reserve-creating powers more effectively. Governments hold two Fund-related reserve assets—reserve positions in the General Department and SDR balances in the SDR Department—and they draw Fund credit from the General Department. The Fund's reserve-creating activities should be consolidated in one department and separated clearly from its credit-creating activities. This would help the Fund and its members to make decisions about the size of the Fund and to choose between creating reserves and providing reserve credit.

3. Strengthening IMF Programs in Highly Indebted Countries (Jeffrey D. Sachs)

The broad policy framework of the IMF, with its focus on fiscal prudence as the ultimate source of macroeconomic stability, is an appropriate starting point for IMF programs. Nonetheless, there are many ways in which the IMF can more effectively implement this basic insight in the heavily indebted countries.

The first and most important is to combine the pressure for fiscal adjustment with a realistic dose of debt reduction. A major cause of the shortcomings of IMF programs in the 1980s has been the neglect of the debt reduction alternative. The new Brady Plan is a major cause for hope in this regard, but there are several unsettling features about the early implementation of the new strategy. Most important, the reliance on "voluntary, market-based" debt reduction mechanisms makes little economic or institutional sense. Meaningful debt reduction will only be achieved once the official creditor institutions decide to lead a process of concerted debt reduction. Such concentration is necessary to overcome various manifestations of the "free rider" problems that currently cripples "voluntary" debt reduction operations.

Once debt reduction is achieved, there will be the prospect of more realistic programs. The basic emphasis on fiscal discipline should be continued, but the emphasis on devaluation on recent IMF programs should be toned down. Repeated devaluations can undermine a government's reputation as an inflation fighter and weaken the resolve to maintain budgetary discipline. The Fund typically is overoptimistic in its assessment of the extent to which nominal exchange rate changes can lead to sustained real exchange rate changes.

Another area for reform of IMF practices is in the specification of numerical targets for Fund conditionality. Even in well-designed programs, the Fund lacks the capacity to specify meaningful and *precise* numerical guidelines for money growth and other intermediate targets. The IMF needs to develop more procedures for waiving specific performance tests in circumstances in which the government has effectively undertaken the policy actions demanded, but in which the technical assumptions underlying the IMF's targets were not satisfied. Also, in implementing numerical targets for debt reduction, the IMF must urgently move beyond the "back-of-the-envelope" calculations (e.g., assuming fixed ICORs and a one-sector economy) that now underlie the medium-term balance-of-payments scenarios.

Finally, the IMF must pay far more attention than it has to date to the income distributional consequences of adjustment programs. There is growing evidence, provided by UNICEF and others, that the poor have suffered heavily in the adjustment process of the 1980s. Far more care must be taken to protect the most vulnerable parts of the population, for both moral and pragmatic reasons. In Latin America, in particular, distributional goals could be linked to the adjustment process by a more explicit focus on an increase in progressive taxation.

4. The IMF and the Debt Strategy (Guillermo Ortiz)

The role of the Fund in the debt strategy has taken a major turn since the unveiling of the Brady Plan. One of the most significant changes has been the explicit recognition on the part of the Fund of the consequences of the debt overhang for the restoration of growth and economic stabilization in indebted countries. This is a major—if belated—acknowledgment of the long-standing demands of indebted countries. In practical terms, this change of view has been translated into a more balanced position of the Fund vis-à-vis commercial banks and indebted countries. Some of the most important recent steps have been: the engagement of the Fund's own resources for debt and debt-service reduction operations; a parallel financing agreement with Japan; a modification of the policy on financing assurances; and a tolerance of arrears to commercial banks.

Mexico's recent program incorporates these new features, which form the core of the Fund's new approach to the debt strategy. It is a growth-oriented program that emphasizes reduced resource transfers in a medium-term context through debt alleviation. This is an essential element for the reduction of the level of macroeconomic uncertainty caused by the debt overhang—and a necessary condition for the restoration of economic growth.

Some conclusions of a more general nature can be drawn from Mexico's recent experience:

- In the context of medium-term projections, the Fund should be explicit regarding the amount of debt reduction needed for the restoration of economic growth. This is and will remain a controversial issue, and the Fund's projections will be challenged by commercial banks. Nonetheless, this is an essential point, since the balance-of-payments projections are the basis for negotiations.
- The Fund must take a clear and firm stance with respect to the banks. Just as it was influential in overcoming the resistance of the banks to participation in concerted financing packages in the ear-

lier stages of the debt strategy, it can now use its considerable leverage to facilitate debt reduction operations. In this respect, both policy changes—notably, the modification of the policy on financing assurances—as well as direct Fund action clearly have been supportive of the recently concluded Mexican negotiation.

Regarding the amounts currently available for debt and debt-service reduction, three points are worth mentioning:

- First, these funds seem to be insufficient for allowing a scale of operations that produces a significant impact on indebted countries. This has been a difficult issue in the Mexican negotiations with commercial banks. It will thus be important to augment the catalytic role of the Fund, perhaps along the lines agreed with Japan for the provision of parallel financing for debt reduction.
- A second point has to do with the timing of the delivery of these funds, which constitute the "enhancements" for debt and debt-service reduction operations. These should be "front-loaded" so that countries may benefit immediately from debt alleviation.
- The third point has to do with the unnecessary rigidities introduced in the utilization of the "set-aside" and "interest-support fund" portions of the resources available for debt reduction. These funds should be fungible and utilized indistinctively for any type of debt-reduction operations.

The Fund should also take a firmer stance regarding two issues that have surfaced in recent debt discussions: debt-equity swaps and capital flight. Swaps have been almost unanimously singled out by the economics profession as having inflationary and/or distorting effects. Capital flight will be reversed as confidence is restored. This should not be "factored in ex ante" in balance-of-payments projections.

Finally, it is not clear to what extent the Mexican experience can be replicated by other countries. It should be kept in mind that Mexico has had a long—and largely sustained—record of adjustment and has undertaken deep structural reforms. Not all indebted countries are in the same position, or can count on the same degree of political support from some of the major industrialized countries. Despite the long-standing opposition to the creation of a debt facility along the lines proposed by several authors (see chapter by Jeffrey Sachs in this volume), such a facility may have to be established to deal in a systematic manner with other more difficult cases. It is difficult to envisage a general application of the Mexican experience.

5. The Fund and the Low-Income Countries (Louis M. Goreux)

Fund programs were originally conceived to assist countries experiencing temporary balance-of-payments difficulties. But no industrial country had a program with the Fund during the last twelve years, while African countries presently account for 60 per cent of Fund programs. Most countries now assisted by the Fund are low-income countries with structural problems that can be solved only in the long term.

The Fund has acquired a unique expertise in assessing the implications of fiscal and monetary policies on the external payments situation of countries. It can very effectively assist countries in designing the macroeconomic policies that are necessary for growth, but implementing these policies is not sufficient to induce the supply response. Having become more involved with low-income countries, the Fund had to rely more heavily on the Bank for the supply side of the economy. But the supply and the demand sides have to be fully integrated in the design of realistic growth-oriented programs and, for this purpose, the staffs of the Fund and the Bank have to cooperate more closely than they have done in the past.

Use of Fund credit was intended to be temporary, but this has not been the case for most low-income countries, which need program assistance year after year to solve their structural problems. Since its normal terms of financing did not fit the repayment capabilities of low-income countries, the Fund in 1986 and 1987 established two new facilities, the Structural Adjustment Facility (SAF) and the Enhanced Structural Adjustment Facility (ESAF), with resources that had to be repaid over longer periods (5–10 years) and that carried lower interest charges (0.5 per cent a year). These resources will soon be fully committed, and the Fund will have to replenish them if it is to provide further financial assistance to low-income countries. The Fund could do that by using its regular quota resources and subsidizing their use through a special account. The income required for this account could be the interest earned by selling part of the Fund's gold and investing the proceeds of the sales. In this manner, the Fund would be able to simplify the present structure of its facilities.

The leverage of Fund programs does not result only from the money lent by the Fund, but also from the doors opened to countries implementing Fund programs—particularly with respect to the refinancing of the external debt. Through successive Paris Club reschedulings, the claims of official creditors have become unrealistically large; from 1980 to 1987, claims of bilateral creditors on low-income African countries have almost tripled in relation to the export earnings of debtor countries. The Toronto debt reduction plan aims in the right direction, but it will have to be followed by other steps.

Because the debt of low-income countries is not a serious problem for the banks, it has not been covered by the Brady Plan. But the debt service paid to the banks presents serious problems for a number of low-income countries. To facilitate the negotiation of debt reduction schemes with the banks, the Fund should modify its position regarding the treatment of arrears.

Since 1980, balance-of-payments assistance by the Fund has been supplemented with adjustment lending by the Bank. With this new instrument, the Bank has been able to support structural adjustment in much the same way as the Fund did. This development has been valuable, but it has also raised problems. When the Bank was dealing essentially with investment projects and the Fund with short-term balance-of-payments problems, the boundaries between the respective functions of the two institutions were straightforward. When both the Fund and the Bank moved into structural adjustment lending on concessional terms, the boundaries became blurred.

The author concludes that:

- The Fund should remain involved with low-income countries because it has acquired a unique macroeconomic expertise;
- The Fund should extend credit to low-income countries on concessional terms, preferably by establishing a subsidy account;
- The IMF and the World Bank should be complementary and not competing;
- Each institution should concentrate on its area of special expertise, but no firm boundaries can be drawn between the respective responsibilities of the two institutions; and
- The most fruitful approach would be to reinforce the cooperation between the two staffs. For example, joint Fund/Bank missions with a single head might negotiate the Policy Framework Paper (PFP) with the national authorities, and the Fund and the Bank might treat the PFP as their major policy document.

III. The IMF and the World Economy

Chapter 1 —————————————————————————————————

Strengthening the Role of the IMF in the International Monetary System

Jacques J. Polak

The Purposes of the Fund

The dominant concern underlying the concept of the International Monetary Fund, as agreed at Bretton Woods in 1944, was to provide the postwar world with an effective international monetary system. In the interwar period, monetary conditions, both national and international, had gone from crisis to crisis. The broad vision of the role of the Fund is set out in Article I of the Articles of Agreement, called Purposes (reproduced in the Overview chapter).

One of the most interesting features of the Fund contained in the Purposes is the close link between the Fund's policy prescriptions and its credit facilities. Because it was realized that many of the currency disorders of the preceding decades had originated as responses to foreign exchange shortfalls, the institution that was to administer the agreed rules was at the same time equipped with large financial resources. These could be lent out to its member countries to facilitate their continued observance of the rules—even when they found themselves in a difficult payments position. Thus the Fund's credit mechanism was designed to back up the observance by members of the Fund's code of behavior and to discourage them from "resorting to measures destructive of national or international prosperity" (Article I-v).

Although the Fund's regulatory powers related to external policies only, adherence to the par value system made an important contribution to domestic stability in many countries as well. As Cooper has

pointed out, this followed from the "bargain between the United States
... and the rest of the world. The bargain was that the United States
would maintain domestic economic stability [and] . . . other countries
would import this stability from the United States through a fixed
exchange rate on the dollar."[1] By the second half of the 1960s, the
United States had begun to renege on its part of the bargain by relaxing
its financial policies, but most of the other members of the Fund continued to perceive the discipline of the par value system to be an important
factor for their own pursuit of stable domestic policies.[2]

The balance between the Fund's regulatory and financial activities
has shifted over the years. In its first decade, when the Fund extended
only a limited amount of credit (in part because the Marshall Plan
amply provided for the credit needs of Europe), there was strong emphasis on ensuring that members observed their legal obligations under the
Articles—with respect both to par values and to such other matters as
the prices at which governments could deal in gold or the avoidance of
multiple rates. Deviations from these rules—such as France's devaluation without the Fund's concurrence (1947), or Canada's decision to
allow its currency to float upward under the market pressures set off by
the Korean War (1950)—produced veritable crises in the organization.
By the end of the 1950s, the Fund became a much more active financial
organization, and its extreme preoccupation with the policing of legal
provisions began to wane. The practical merits of floating rates were
recognized for some countries experiencing high inflation and such
rates were no longer considered a bar to the use of the Fund's credit; the
recourse to a temporary float by Germany in 1969 was (implicitly) welcomed by the Managing Director.[3]

With the adoption of the first amendment to the Articles of Agreement in 1969, the Fund's purposes were in fact extended to include a
certain responsibility for the adequacy of international liquidity. The
Fund was authorized to allocate special drawing rights (SDRs) "to meet
the [long-term global] need, as and when it arises, for a supplement to
existing reserve assets."[4] The Fund was instructed to work toward this
new purpose "in such a manner as will promote the attainment of its
[other] purposes and will avoid economic stagnation and deflation as
well as excess demand and inflation in the world."[5] The primary purpose of the amendment giving the Fund these new responsibilities was
to counter the concern felt in the late 1950s and 1960s that the steady
growth of world output and trade might grind to a halt due to an insuffi-
ciency in monetary gold and U.S. dollars for a matching growth in countries' reserves. At the same time, and reflecting a shift in attitude from
that of twenty-five years earlier, the Fund was reminded to conduct its
policies with due recognition of the risks of inflation—a term for which
one would look in vain in the original Purposes.

The first quarter-century after World War II represented a period of extraordinary success for the world economy. There is no way to determine to what extent this success was attributable to good policies in the major industrial countries, to the design of the international monetary system, or to other factors. But whatever its precise contribution, the Fund, as the institution that stood for the major policy approach of that period, could not but gain in stature as the world economy followed the course set out in the second of the Fund's Purposes.

Changes in the System and their Effect on the Fund

From the late 1960s on, however, a number of fundamental changes in the world economy began to undermine the major premises on which the Fund's central position in the system had been built. Two of these deserve particular attention:

1. *The liberalization of capital movements well beyond what had been foreseen at the time of Bretton Woods subjected the par value system to pressures for which it was ill prepared.* At the same time, the position of the United States as the financial anchor of the system began to erode as fiscal deficits and monetary expansion in that country exposed the rest of the world to the risks of an excessive supply of dollars and uncertainty concerning the solidity of the gold value of the dollar.

2. *Following the quadrupling of the price of oil in early 1974, the petroleum-exporting countries began to run huge current account surpluses.* These surpluses, which accumulated in the banks of the industrial countries at a time when their domestic economies were sliding into recession, put pressure on these banks to make a quantum jump in their foreign lending. The immediate effect for the Fund was to remove one of the pillars underlying its role: that countries in payments difficulties would find themselves forced to seek credit from the Fund and thus agree to adjustment measures demanded by the Fund as part of its conditionality. In the 1960s, very few countries had been able to obtain sovereign credit from international banks; this had been one of the arguments for the creation of an international system to provide countries with reserves, in the form of SDRs, that they otherwise would have to earn through current account surpluses. By the late 1970s, most countries had access to sovereign credit from the world's commercial banks, with no questions asked. These new developments put these countries beyond the reach of the Fund's conditionality and, at the same time, undercut the main rationale for the allocation of SDRs (see discussion below, in section on "The Future of the SDR").

These changes in the system affected the Fund's relations with developing countries much less than those with developed nations. The great majority of developing countries continue to have exchange arrangements under which they peg their currency either on the currency of a reserve center (mostly the U.S. dollar and the French franc) or on a basket of currencies. For countries that do not adequately control inflation, the peg frequently leads to a degree of overvaluation, and hence to balance-of-payments problems. At least since the debt crisis, few developing countries have had ready access to bank finance. The Fund thus remains a major source of balance-of-payments finance for these countries, and their consultations with the Fund, while containing a good deal of technical assistance, also remain the instrument through which the Fund tries to steer these countries through the adjustment process.

At the same time, industrial countries—even those about whose policies the Fund was highly critical in its consultations—have had no difficulty financing themselves in the Euro-markets. The last time the Fund concluded a stand-by arrangement with an industrial country was in 1976 (with the United Kingdom and Italy). Moreover, members of the Common Market have had access to balance-of-payments credit from this source on less demanding conditions than the Fund would typically impose. Pushed into third place, behind the market and for many of its European members behind the Economic Community (EC), the Fund has ceased to be actively considered a source of finance for the Western industrial countries. It is quite likely that this change will be lasting. But the rapid shifts that have frequently occurred in world capital markets should caution against drawing excessively firm conclusions from the experience of one or two decades. More particularly, an institution that functions as the ultimate backstop of the international monetary system should not arrange its finances in such a manner as to make it unable to provide assistance to any of its members, should this prove necessary. For the Fund this means that its Ninth Review of Quotas, which is now under way, should make ample allowance for meeting the potential needs of its industrial as well as developing-country members. Through its policies on access as percentage of quota, the Fund can ensure that the resulting increase in its liquidity will not be used excessively to finance the non-industrial members, leaving enough funds available should they be needed by industrial countries.

Other shifting tides have to be taken into account when looking toward the future. While the Fund's influence in the industrial countries of the West has declined, its role in relation to the industrial nations of Eastern Europe, including perhaps the Soviet Union, is clearly on the rise. That role can extend well beyond the provision of balance-of-payments finance. In the difficult transition of these countries to more market-oriented systems for their economies, the Fund can be of great help in providing practical, non-ideological assistance based on its worldwide experience.

Recall also the most recent involvement of the Fund in a stabilization exercise for an industrial country, namely the United States. On November 1, 1978, President Jimmy Carter, declaring that the continuing decline in the exchange value of the dollar was unwarranted by the fundamental economic situation, initiated a series of domestic and international measures to strengthen the dollar and to counter inflationary pressures. The domestic measures included a one-point increase in the discount rate and the establishment of supplementary reserve requirements on large time deposits. These measures were accompanied by financing arrangements that included a drawing on the Fund for $3 billion (which led the Fund to activate the General Arrangements to Borrow) and the use of $2 billion in SDRs.[6] True, the rather modest policy arrangements were not the result of discussions with the Fund, and the money did not represent credit from the Fund, but U.S. use of reserve assets that were at its free disposal. The policy measures were, however, clearly packaged with money from the Fund (as well as from bilateral creditors) to associate the Fund with the U.S. stabilization effort.

The recent concentration of the Fund's credit activities on the developing countries has undermined the original linkage between policy prescription and Fund credit mentioned in the opening section of this chapter. The belief among industrial countries that recourse to the Fund is not likely to be necessary even if inadequate policies lead to payments difficulties inevitably weakens the weight of the Fund's advice. And once the Fund is seen primarily as a credit institution for the developing countries, the temptation grows to extend credit to these countries, even when there are serious doubts about the temporary character of the credit.

As demand for Fund credit became concentrated in the developing countries, the Fund also moved to adjust the supply of such credit to meet the particular needs of these countries, thus introducing increasingly explicit distinctions among its membership—distinctions that it previously had tried to avoid. When the Compensatory Financing Facility (CFF) was introduced in 1963, it was formulated in terms that entitled all members to use it—although there was an unwritten understanding that the industrial countries would not do so. The Oil Facility (1974–76) was designed for use by all oil-importing members; ten developed countries, including Italy and the U.K., drew on it. But the Extended Fund Facility (EFF), created in 1974 (in part as a consolation prize for the failure of the reform exercise to produce "the link" between SDR allocations and development aid), was clearly aimed at financing structural adjustment in developing countries; the profits on the sale of part of the Fund's gold, and on potential future gold sales, were specifically directed to developing countries. To finance the Enhanced Structural Adjustment Facility (ESAF, established in 1987), the Fund has turned to soliciting aid funds from its higher-income members to be lent to low-income developing countries at concessional interest rates.[7]

Against this increasingly dichotomous background, it is not surprising that in recent years the Fund often has been mistaken for an aid agency: developed countries provide the resources, which are then passed on to those developing countries that are prepared to accept the accompanying constraints of Fund conditionality. In this view, the distinction between the Fund and the World Bank is also becoming increasingly vague; both institutions have shifted their policies to the point where they now provide similar types of credit on similar terms to the same groups of countries.[8]

As long as the Fund applied its conditionality to developed and developing countries alike, being a lender of last resort to both, it could point to the evenhandedness of its policies. Now that its credit policies apply in practice to one group of members only, it has become even more difficult than before to convince critical observers, in the North as well as the South, that the Fund is not engaged in imposing Northern principles of economics on Southern countries. Second, the high concentration of Fund credit in certain developing countries whose creditworthiness has been open to question since the onset of the debt crisis is undermining what has been called "the monetary character of the Fund": the concept of the Fund as the repository of central banks' liquid reserves that are used on a revolving basis in short- or at most medium-term credits to sovereign borrowers. The Fund's outstanding arrears (some SDR 2.8 billion as of April 30, 1989) are not yet of a magnitude to invalidate the reserve-like character of creditor-countries' reserve positions in the Fund[9] (standing at about SDR 27 billion at the same time), and the Fund is making strenuous efforts to reduce these arrears. But the hesitation shown by some creditor countries[10] with respect to the further extension of credit against the background of the debt crisis reveals an incipient concern about the quality of claims on the Fund.

The membership of the Fund and the Bank will have to sort out the allocation between the two institutions of their lending activities for the benefit of various groups of members. In particular, a decision will have to be made—no later than when the Fund's ESAF funds run out sometime in 1991—about whether the Fund should continue with its current policy of conducting the bulk of its lending to low-income countries at near-zero interest rates. (Earlier concessional loans to these countries, under the Trust Fund and SAF, represented special operations financed from resources that the Fund had acquired as a result of the sale of part of its gold.) Given the unremitting poverty in many of its low-income member countries, especially those in Africa, the Fund may well take the view that its balance-of-payments credits to these countries should, at least for another decade, be made at very low interest rates. This would imply that the Fund would have a special window for these countries—in much the same way as the Bank operates its International Development Assistance (IDA) window for the same countries.

Should the Fund come to that conclusion, it could usefully simplify its structure of facilities. In the Bank, IDA credits differ from Bank credits only in their financial terms (interest rate, grace period, repayment period). In the Fund, by contrast, various forms of access (under stand-by arrangements, the EFF, SAF, and ESAF) differ not only in financial terms, but also in nuances of conditionality that seem to have only a historic explanation.

A decision by the Fund to consolidate its ESAF experiment by means of an IDA-type window would bring into focus a new aspect of Fund–Bank relations. Until recently, these two institutions relied on clearly distinct sources of finance. The Bank borrows in capital markets, and funds for IDA are collected in triennial rounds of pledging from the aid budgets of high-income countries. Prior to ESAF, the Fund received its resources from the foreign exchange reserves of its members (including some low-income members) that were in a sufficiently strong position to hold part of their reserves in the form of claims on the Fund. On these resources the Fund pays (roughly) a market interest rate, which means that, to break even, it must also charge its borrowers an interest rate close to the market rate.

If an important part of the Fund's credit operations is to continue lending at a near-zero interest rate, the Fund will have to reconsider its financial structure. It could approach its richer members for grants to finance interest subsidies, as it did in the 1970s; that experience proved difficult and raised important issues of equity among the contributors. Alternatively, could the Fund organize periodic contribution rounds parallel to those for IDA? It seems unlikely that the Fund, depending on the same source of finance for similar credits to the same group of countries, would long be able to justify an independent existence—at least as far as its relations with these members were concerned. Even if aid finance for part of the Fund's activities could be arranged, one might question the advisability of eroding the "monetary character" of the Fund in this way.

These considerations suggest that the Fund should seriously consider another source of finance: the investment of part of its gold. A concrete suggestion to that effect is discussed in the Overview.

The Continued Role of the Fund in the International Monetary System

The current preoccupation of the Fund with credit extension to developing countries, in particular in the context of the debt crisis, should not
be allowed to obscure the range of responsibilities that the Fund continues to discharge. The broadest job description for the Fund is its responsibility for the functioning of the international monetary system. The
widespread dissatisfaction with the system that existed a few years
ago—and that, for example, induced President Ronald Reagan in his
1986 State of the Union address to direct Treasury Secretary James
Baker to determine the advisability of convening a world conference "to
discuss the role and relationship of currencies"—has abated somewhat
as the value of the dollar has come down to a more reasonable level. At
this stage, many observers would probably agree with IMF Managing
Director Michel Camdessus that the crucial need is not for "major negotiations to recast the present arrangements."[11] But it would be difficult
to feel comfortable with the notion that broadening and deepening the
current G-7 process of policy coordination is all that is needed to reform
the system. If that *were* so, the business of reform could be left to the
G-7 to sort out. When in the mid–1960s the issue of international liquidity threatened to be monopolized by a small group of industrialized
countries, then Managing Director Pierre-Paul Schweitzer claimed in a
much-noted statement that "international liquidity is the business of
the Fund."[12] Surely the same comment applies to the reform of the
international monetary system. (The relations of the Fund and the
Group of Seven are discussed in greater detail later in this chapter.)

The general responsibility of the Fund for the system and for its
reform contemplated at that time was made explicit in the work of the
IMF "Committee [of Twenty] on Reform of the International Monetary
System" (1972–74). In its aftermath, the IMF established in 1974 an
Interim Committee on the International Monetary System[13] representing, directly or indirectly, the entire membership of the Fund; its tasks
included "supervising the management and adaptation of the international monetary system" and "dealing with sudden disturbances that
might threaten the system."[14] That Committee dealt expeditiously with
the unfinished business of reform of the Committee of Twenty, reaching
a consensus on some of the main outstanding issues in January 1976 in
Jamaica. Originally scheduled to meet three or four times a year, the
Interim Committee soon found two meetings a year sufficient—one in
the spring and one just before the Annual Bank/Fund Meetings.

The Committee constitutes the most visible evidence of the Fund's
concern with the international monetary system. Its discussion of the

world economic situation, based on the staff's *World Economic Outlook (WEO)* papers, often serves to marshall the common view of finance ministers against other voices in their governments—for example, urging adherence to anti-inflationary policies in the early 1980s despite their immediate recessionary effects. In informal sessions, where attendance is limited, the members of the Committee have found it possible to engage in give-and-take discussions that could establish the necessary consensus for the Fund to move forward on pressing issues. Matters such as the size of quota increases, the allocation of SDRs (1978), or access limits to Fund credit are typically resolved in meetings of the Interim Committee, with formal decisions taken subsequently by the Board of Governors or the Executive Board. On some occasions, the Committee has given impetus to initiatives that had not been referred to it by the Executive Directors, such as its endorsement of more liberal export credit policies in April 1985, and of the relending of Trust Fund money to low-income countries in October of that year.

In absolute terms, there is no reason for great enthusiasm about the achievements of the Interim Committee in recent years. But that Committee is the only international grouping of manageable size where finance ministers from developed and developing countries meet, at regular intervals, and where they manage to dispose of the business at hand.[15] Compared to the drawn-out meetings of the U.N. Economic and Social Council (UNESCO), or of the U.N. Conference on Trade and Development (UNCTAD), the Interim Committee is a model of efficiency and cooperation. If and when the time is ripe, it could provide a forum with experience and legitimacy to deal with the reform of the system; or it could serve to approve emergency action if that were needed because of threatening "sudden disturbances."

The Process of Consultation with Members

One essential characteristic of the value of the Fund to its membership is its intimate knowledge of, and in many instances its close association with, the policies of its members. The process of consultation, through which the Fund's expertise in this field has been built up over the years, is analyzed in this section.

The original Articles of the Fund required the Fund to consult annually, starting in 1952, with each member that "still" retained exchange restrictions under the postwar transitional arrangements of Article XIV—to establish whether the country could get rid of restrictions and make its currency convertible.

From the start, the Fund took the attitude that the "need" for restrictions was closely related to a country's policies. In accordance with this approach, the staff consultation reports not only described the country's restrictive practices but also analyzed a broad range of its policies. Over time, the staff's appraisal of these policies, based on in-depth discussions with the country's senior policymakers, has come to be regarded as by far the best source available to other governments (better, for example, than their own embassy reports) on the economies of the countries concerned.

Countries consulted also soon came to appreciate the value of the consultations to themselves. Countries have few opportunities to lay open their policies for analysis by experts with wide experience in other countries, who are well informed and have no domestic political axes to grind. Over the years, as the consultations ranged more and more broadly over countries' economies, their original purpose—to guide countries away from payments restrictions—became a matter of declining concern. Monetary and fiscal policy, wage policy, stagflation, development—and later structural policies, trade policy, aid policy, and commodity policy—all found a place in the staff's discussions and their reports. At the same time, in many countries, the annual consultations also contain an important element of technical assistance: building up statistics, advice on techniques of monetary policy, and so on.

The second amendment to the Fund's Articles, which went into effect in 1978, placed an obligation on each member to consult with the Fund about its exchange rate policies, but more generally the Fund was to oversee the compliance of each member with its obligations under Section 1 of Article IV. These obligations refer to a handful of general policy rules that the country must follow, or try to follow, including "orderly economic growth," "reasonable price stability," avoidance of overvaluation of its currency, and "exchange policies compatible with the[se] undertakings" (whatever that means).

Under the new legal regime as under the old, the consultation discussions that the Fund mission conducts in a member country continue to represent an important international input into national policymaking. This is most obvious when the country has, or would like to have, a financial arrangement with the Fund. In that setting, the consultations often merge with policy discussions on conditionality for the use of the Fund's resources. But in a substantial number of countries where the question of financial assistance from the Fund is not a consideration, the authorities may make active use of the mission's recommendations to influence domestic policy formation. In the last ten years or so, Belgium and Italy, for example, have frequently drawn on the Fund mission's recommendations in the domestic governmental and parliamentary policymaking process. In other industrial countries, the policy influence of the consultations may have been less direct but nevertheless important. The mission's views are typically conveyed as explicitly as possible to the highest government levels concerned with financial policy—usually the Minister of Finance or his deputy.

In the last two decades, surveillance based on consultations with individual countries has increasingly been complemented by description and analysis of the working of the world economy as a whole. By the late 1960s, concern began to arise about the smooth operation of the world economic system, in particular the stability of the exchange rate system. Against this background, the Fund started to prepare papers on the world economic outlook that would permit the Board to focus on the economic situation and policies of the main industrial countries together, rather than individually as in the consultation process.[16] The depth of these *World Economic Outlook* papers, published since 1978, has greatly increased over the years, and this has enabled the staff to trace the effects of a wide variety of policy changes on major groups of countries. Of greatest interest, perhaps, was the possibility of demonstrating by means of "scenarios" the effects that would follow over time from alternative assumptions about exchange rates among the major currencies—thus gradually breaking down the taboo that had inhibited discussion of this subject before.

Even though Article IV consultations are valuable for the countries involved, for all other countries, and for the Fund's knowledge of the manifold interrelations of the world economy, they and the *WEO* discussions have proven to be of limited effectiveness in influencing the national policies of the major industrial countries. Surveillance over floating exchange rates under the new Article IV gives the Fund far less grip on a country's policies than when these policies had to be compatible with the maintenance of an agreed par value. Moreover, the injunction in Article IV, Section 1(iii) against "manipulating exchange rates" is interpreted by some as casting doubt on the legitimacy of substantial intervention to support a pegged or managed rate[17] and also as putting a freely floating rate virtually beyond the range of Fund surveillance.

This weakness of Fund surveillance has been noted both by the deputies of the Group of Ten (G-10) and by the Group of Twenty-four (G-24) in their respective 1985 reports on the international monetary system. As the G-10 deputies so tactfully put it: "These countries appear to have been able on occasion to sustain policy courses not fully compatible with the goals of international adjustment and financial stability."[18] There are no easy remedies for these shortcomings. For the most part, the recommendations offered by the G-10 and the G-24 for improving the effectiveness of surveillance of the main industrial countries seem to hold out little promise. "Supplemental consultations," introduced in 1979[19] as a mandatory procedure when a member's exchange rate policies "may have important effects on other members," have been held only twice—on both occasions with smaller countries.

They would not be helpful in the Fund's coming to grips with the issues underlying exchange rates of the major countries. If five discussions a year (Article IV consultations, two *WEO* papers, and two sessions of the Interim Committee) do not produce results, a few more rounds of the same will not help. Widening the agenda of consultations by the inclusion of subjects on which other agencies have responsibilities and a comparative advantage,[20] such as detailed trade policies for foreign aid, diverts attention from the central issue: adjustment. There seems merit, on the other hand, in the G-10 suggestion that in important cases countries should report back to the Fund on "the measures introduced or considered to deal with the problems identified by the IMF and to respond to specific policy suggestions."[21] This would at least force the authorities in the country under surveillance to focus, at a high level and in some detail, on the observations coming from the international community.

The Fund and Other Groupings of Members

Throughout most of its history, the Fund has had to take into account the fact that other international organizations as well as less formal groupings to which some (or all, in the case of the World Bank) of its members belonged were also engaged in activities similar to those of the Fund in the areas of policy advice, finance, or surveillance. With some of these, such as the regional economic commissions of the United Nations, the Fund's relations have most of the time been perfunctory. With others, such as Working Party No. 3 of the Organisation for Economic Co-operation and Development (OECD), whose purpose is "the promotion of better international payments equilibrium," the Fund has had rather close collaboration based on a basic similarity of views. With other bodies, in particular those that take a strong view on exchange rate policies, there is the potential both for fruitful collaboration and for policy conflict. Two of these groups, the European Community and the Group of Seven (G-7), will be discussed here in some detail. Issues of competence have also surfaced with urgency between the Fund and the World Bank as their respective spheres of activity began to overlap; these issues are addressed elsewhere in this volume.

Most members of the European Community adhere to an exchange rate regime consisting of a set of mutual pegs that is explicitly recognized in Article IV, Section 2(b) of the Fund's Articles. The central values of these pegs have been adjusted on a number of occasions in response to what would have been called fundamental disequilibria under the par value system. But there is no guarantee that the views held in the European Monetary System (EMS) on exchange rates for the currencies of its members will at all times coincide with the outcome of the Fund's surveillance under Article IV. In the late 1970s, when the EMS was new and strongly attached to its mandate for exchange rate stability and the Fund was keen on discharging its new surveillance responsibilities, a few instances arose of rather sharply conflicting positions. Subsequently, though the Fund and the European Community may not always have agreed on exchange rates for the currencies of common members, the Fund has not strongly pressed any divergent views, in part because it recognized that moderate overvaluation of the currency of an EC country has a useful role to play in the downward convergence of the EC's inflation performance and, in any event, does get corrected by realignment before too long. The further integration of the EC will only further shift the weight of exchange rate surveillance from Washington to Brussels. This process will be completed if and when the EC adopts a common central bank, together with fixed exchange rates. But until that stage is reached, the Fund's surveillance role in the EC countries will remain a valuable counterweight to any tendency toward premature exchange rate rigidity.

At present, the opportunities both for close collaboration and for potential conflict seem most pronounced in the Fund's relationship with the G-7 (the United States, Canada, France, Germany, Italy, Japan, the United Kingdom). These countries, or the five largest of them, have a long history of meeting on economic and financial matters of common concern, going back at least to the early 1970s.[22] The arrangement was formalized at the 1982 Versailles Summit of the G-7, where these countries declared their readiness "to strengthen our cooperation with the IMF in its work of surveillance." However, the period from 1981 to 1985, when the United States pursued a policy of "benign neglect" with respect to the exchange rate, was hardly propitious either for the surveillance activities of the Fund or for active policy coordination by the major countries.

The formal reversal of the U.S. policy of disinterest in the exchange rate for the dollar came at the September 1985 Plaza Meeting, which, although convened "in the context of their [the G-5's] agreement to conduct mutual surveillance," did not include the Managing Director of the Fund, who had attended previous G-5 meetings.[23]

The rediscovery by the major countries of their common interest in exchange rates for their currencies set the stage for a much-needed revival of active discussion among these countries of their financial and economic policies. Such discussions had been a well-established feature of the international scene during the 1950s, the 1960s, and most of the 1970s. But the format of current discussions is less closely associated with the two most relevant international institutions, the Fund and the OECD, than was the case in the earlier period. If the Fund is to remain the central monetary institution in the world, and if the G-7 is to make its maximum contribution to the welfare of the world economy, both the Fund and its major members will have to face up to certain issues that their coexistence presents. Some may shrink away from a discussion of these issues in view of the fact that the G-7 countries together exercise about half the voting strength in the Fund.[24] But broad issues concerning the future policy direction of the institution are not determined by an up or down vote, but by a process of gradual persuasion toward a consensus; and groupings of members such as the G-7 are not monolithic blocs. In this connection it is instructive to recall how on earlier occasions an apparent consensus on a particular course of action of a slightly larger group, the G-10, did not lead to the adoption of those actions.[25]

Among the issues of direct relevance to the Fund that the G-7 address, three deserve particular attention: (1) exchange rate management; (2) balance-of-payments adjustment; and (3) the avoidance of worldwide deflation and inflation.[26]

In singling out these three subjects, one must bear in mind that the agenda of the G-7 extends well beyond them and involves "cooperation . . . on all important economic issues such as trade, development and debt, energy and structural policy . . ."[27] And in discussing the three subjects separately, one must acknowledge their interrelationship, particularly that between (1) and (2). In situations of severe payments imbalance, cooperation on exchange rate management, which involves financing, cannot be achieved without a degree of understanding among participants on how the underlying problem is to be corrected by adjustment policies.

Exchange Rate Management

When the United States shifted its exchange rate policy from free-floating to a managed float in September 1985, it needed to reestablish close operational contact with the other main financial centers. Under a system of managed exchange rates, coordination of monetary policy is essential: The positions of the main participants on their respective monetary policies will have to produce interest rate differentials in keeping with their understandings on exchange rates. Intervention in exchange markets, which on occasion has been massive, requires frequent understandings on a number of critical issues: when and where to intervene, by how much, by whom, and at whose risk. It has become clear from the description given by Funabashi that these were matters of active negotiation among the Seven.[28]

Although exchange rate management for the major currencies has implications for all countries in the system, it must be conducted by a

small group of countries; five or seven is a plausible number. The particular version of exchange rate management applied so far has also
required a high degree of secrecy. The Fund has no role to play in these
operational activities and no reason to attend their preparation. But the
Fund does of course have a major interest in, and a contribution to make
to, the exchange rates around which stabilization is being sought. If
exchange rate management by the G-7 is to be successful in the long
run, it will have to be based on the best professional, non-political esti-
mate of a set of tenable rates. This may not always be compatible with
what ministers can agree on. Although the Louvre Accord of February
1987 deserves recognition as a major achievement in the area of monetary cooperation, the actual rates agreed on that occasion soon proved
untenable.[29] At the 1988 Annual Meeting, the Fund staff's professional
view (as expressed in the *World Economic Outlook*) that with current
policies and exchange rates the U.S. current account deficit in 1989
would show no further decline proved hard to reconcile with the G-7
communiqué asserting that adjustment was making adequate progress.[30]

Balance-of-Payments Adjustment

The achievement of the Fund's Purposes (including "the expansion and
balanced growth of international trade") requires that countries pursue
policies aimed at internal and external balance. International agencies
such as the Fund and the OECD have focused their attention primarily
on the avoidance of external imbalance—a surplus or deficit on current
account in excess of what the country can finance over the medium
term. When imbalances arose, their elimination normally has been
approached in a decentralized manner; any country experiencing a
large imbalance (in terms of its trade or reserves) has been expected to
bring that imbalance down.

There are a number of good reasons for this decentralized approach.
First, almost all countries' policies are overwhelmingly more important
for their own economic health than in terms of their impact on the
world economy. This is reflected in the fact that in the Fund's annual
consultations with all countries except the United States, Japan, and
Germany—with rare exceptions such as the Far Eastern newly industrializing countries (NICs)—the focus is entirely on the benefits or
otherwise that countries derive from their own policies. In its consultations with the U.K., France, Italy, and Canada one would look in vain for
the Fund urging a particular set of macroeconomic policies as being
desirable from a world point of view.[31]

Second, the decentralized approach provides a practical (even if not
theoretically perfect) answer to the question of which countries should

take action, and how much: Each country with a substantial unsustainable external disequilibrium should take enough action to reduce its disequilibrium to manageable proportions.

Third, the approach is likely to place the adjustment burden largely on the country where the disequilibrium originates. That country will have a large surplus or deficit, while the resulting deficits or surpluses in all other countries will tend to be much smaller in proportion to their trade flows. (It should be noted that this approach provides only qualified support for the proposition that adjustment should be symmetrical. *Yes,* in the sense that countries responsible for surpluses should be under as much of an obligation to adjust as countries responsible for deficits; likewise, industrial deficit countries with ready access to foreign capital should be as willing to adjust as developing deficit countries without such access. But *no,* in the sense that any country responsible for an imbalance should be able to count on the rest of the world assuming half of the responsibility for its elimination.)

The international effort to have individual countries take the necessary adjustment measures called for by the decentralized process just described cannot boast a striking record of success. Countries large and small have only too often tried to avoid or delay the needed adjustment action. The Fund's surveillance task is never done. But these observed shortfalls in country performance do not invalidate the approach; nor do they provide support for the view that a multilateral effort would be more successful. In recent years, the United States has advocated the search for a multilateral solution to the current disequilibrium in world payments, consisting of a reduction of the fiscal deficit in the United States accompanied by fiscal expansion in the countries with large surpluses.[32] But fiscal expansion abroad would prevent a decline in world interest rates and would bring about some of the U.S. adjustment by crowding out investment rather than reducing consumption.[33] Considerations such as these would point toward easing up on monetary, rather than fiscal, policy abroad should U.S. fiscal correction lead to reduced growth.[34]

Thus, though policy coordination is essential to exchange rate management and may at times help control the level of world demand, there is reason for healthy skepticism about the contribution it can make to the adjustment process. Under favorable circumstances, it may quickly lead to a constructive set of adjustment measures satisfactory to all parties. Alternatively, and more probably, the outcome will be a power struggle to determine which country accepts what share of the collective adjustment burden—an essentially political process complete with appeals to national and international public opinion. Since the outcome is inherently indeterminate, the coordination approach to adjustment puts a premium on "patience"—on the ability of one partner to wait for the other to move[35]—and it carries a built-in delay factor.[36] If negotiations slow down rather than expedite adjustment, this is costly in any event; but the delay factor may turn out to be extremely costly if on some occasion the game of "chicken" is carried on a little too long.

Thus, even with an active G-7, it remains the Fund's task to exercise surveillance over *all* of its members. If peer pressure among major members can assist that process, so much the better.[37] But the Fund cannot contract out surveillance over its major members in the form of mutual surveillance among them. A major member country's failure to adjust remains an issue of prime concern to the Fund, and breakdown of the negotiating process among the Seven does not provide an excuse for such failure.

The Avoidance of Worldwide Inflation and Deflation

Adjustment action by individual countries does not ensure a satisfactory level of world activity. Nor can this result be expected from the regulation of international liquidity, on which (as discussed briefly above) the Fund can exercise one-way influence at best: It can raise liquidity by making SDR allocations, but it cannot prevent, or offset, excessive liquidity creation brought about by large-scale dollar support operations.

The main industrial countries do have at their disposal an important policy instrument for influencing the level of world demand: the world interest rate. After some false starts in the course of 1987, the G-7 appears to have made some progress toward a form of cooperation in monetary policy that targets both absolute and differential interest rates. The difficulty, as far as monetary policy is concerned, may not be so much one of technique as of judging the direction in which the wind is blowing—as was evident, for example, from the quick transition from bearish to increasingly bullish forecasts for the growth in industrial countries in the course of 1988. The problem can perhaps be mitigated by reliance on an indicator of world commodity prices, as announced by the G-7 at their Toronto meeting (June 1988), but it cannot be avoided. As the Fund's *Annual Report 1988* notes with respect to such an index, its "reliability as an early warning signal [of] shifts in global inflationary tendencies . . . has not been thoroughly tested."[38]

The use of fiscal policies in the main countries to regulate world demand is severely restricted by the constraints that most of the major countries have adopted in the flexible use of such policies for domestic demand management.[39] But even without the assurance of instant success, regular half-yearly meetings of the G-7 to appraise the world situation with Fund staff assistance[40] are an important safeguard to the system because they prepare the ground for the rare occasions—most likely due to "unexpected disturbances"—where common action is clearly needed, and would then also prove possible, one would hope. Should such a situation arise, policy action would certainly need to be extended beyond the G-7. A regular or special meeting of the Interim Committee would provide the appropriate setting for addressing such a contingency.

In the view of many academic observers, a large share of the benefits of policy coordination may ultimately derive from the fact that coordination makes national policymakers better informed about the policies and policy intentions of their colleagues in other countries and about the workings (including the decisionmaking processes) of other economies. The G-7 process can contribute to this dissemination of information. It is a matter of concern, however, that these benefits of information are limited to a small group of countries. Smallness of the group is essential to its coherence and the efficiency of its decisionmaking, but the *costs* of smallness should not be ignored. It means the inability of other countries to present their interests, their intellectual contributions, and the relevant characteristics of their economies. It also means that the countries not represented fail to acquire important information for their own decisionmaking. Enlargement of the group is obviously not the answer. The presence of the Managing Director and, at the G-7 deputies level, Fund staff can help marginally. At a minimum, the Managing Director and the staff (who now regularly attend G-7 coordination meetings at the ministerial and deputy levels, respectively) should seek confidential procedures for debriefing the Fund's Board after attending G-7 meetings, as was instituted for G-10 meetings in the 1960s. But a major part of the remedy lies in the fullest exploitation of the established facilities of the Fund. If indicators and five-year projections for the G-7 countries prove their merit, they should become part of the Fund's consultation procedure for the G-7 countries and others as well. While there is reason to keep the contents of the negotiations among the G-7 secret, it should be the Fund staff's task to gather, for the benefit of the membership as a whole, all relevant information on the G-7 countries through the Fund's regular consultations and its special contacts in connection with the *WEO*.

The final contribution will have to be made by the G-7 themselves. They should heed the lesson—which the United States has had to learn and relearn over the last forty years—that great powers can often most effectively achieve policy changes in other countries by acting through the established channels of international organizations. The Fund's role as guardian of the financial system benefits its major members as well as its nearly 150 other members. For the long run, legitimacy in the process of decisionmaking in international organizations is essential.[41] Hence the G-7 should avoid presenting themselves as the Fund's self-

appointed directorate and refrain from publicly taking views on the policies of other members of the Fund (such as the exchange rates for "certain newly industrialized economies" discussed in its April 13, 1988
communiqué).[42] The G-7 can be more effective supporting Fund views
than preempting them.

The Seven would do well to strengthen the Fund's surveillance over
their economies; only thus can the Fund enhance its surveillance over
other members. The Seven should also rely on the Fund's established
fora, especially the Interim Committee and the Executive Board, to
achieve consensus on all issues that transcend the group. The April
1989 process of international consensus-building on the Brady proposal
for the debt crisis constituted a good example of preparation of a subject
by the G-7 followed by deliberation and wider consensus-building in the
Interim Committee.

The Future of the SDR

The changes that have taken place in the international monetary system over the last twenty years have removed the need for SDR allocations to avert a global shortage of reserves. But the "global need" that
the Articles require for allocation is not so narrow a concept as to bar
allocations in this new setting, as confirmed by the 1978 decision to
allocate. There remain, moreover, a number of supplementary reasons
that support the resumption of allocations, but they are less compelling
than they were when reserve creation by the Fund was first introduced.[43]

First, while industrial and some developing countries can acquire
reserves by borrowing at market interest rates, this is not the case for
middle-income countries with recent debt problems or for many low-
income countries. For them, raising reserves means either borrowing at
high-risk premiums over market rates or forgoing imports, that is, keeping down the growth rate. SDR allocations would help these countries.
There is no reason to see any drawback for the rest of the membership
in an allocation as long as its magnitude does not undermine the Fund's
conditionality—as long as it is small compared to countries' access to
Fund credit.[44]

Second, reserves obtained from SDR allocations, unlike reserves
obtained from bank loans, do not run the risk of melting away at the
very time when they are most needed, namely, when banks are unwilling to roll over loans that fall due. From this angle, allocations that lead
to a corresponding reduction in the borrowing of reserves would
improve the quality of reserves even if they did not raise the quantity.

Third, there is widespread agreement that, whatever the need for the SDR at present, this international component of the system needs to be preserved for potential future use, requiring allocations to prevent SDRs from becoming an insignificant proportion of total reserves.

None of these arguments have so far been seen as compelling by the main industrial countries, most of which, with the exception of France and Italy, oppose SDR allocations. As the last allocation decision (taken in 1978) fades further into history, the resumption of regular allocations becomes increasingly unlikely. In recent years the power to create SDRs tends to be referred to in the context of some highly unusual situation, such as a crisis in the world financial system,[45] or a specific operation of major financial interest (the proposal of French President François Mitterrand to allocate SDRs for a guarantee fund to service international debt would fall in that category).

Under the Fund's Articles, SDRs can be brought into circulation by allocation only. The Fund has, however, on a number of occasions studied the possibility of issuing SDRs in exchange for reserve currencies through the introduction of a substitution account.[46] The latest consideration of such an account—envisaging initial substitution of perhaps $50 billion by SDRs—was occasioned by the U.S. stabilization measures of 1978. For about a year and a half, this effort made considerable progress, propelled by the confluence of (a) a desire to improve the reserve assets system and enlarge the role of the SDR, (b) the willingness of the United States to lighten the reserve currency role of the dollar, and (c) the interest of large official holders of dollars in the diversification of currency risks without engaging in conversion operations. But the project came to nought at the April 1980 meeting of the Interim Committee. One reason for this was the strengthening of the U.S. dollar, which cooled the interest of potential depositors. But the project was also handicapped by the assumption that, while the liabilities of the substitution account would be expressed in SDRs, paying the SDR interest rate, its claims on the United States would be expressed in dollars and would earn the prevailing interest rate on U.S. Treasury bills. This construction—which seemed unavoidable at the time—presented major problems for the maintenance of financial balance in the account. Attempts to solve these by partial guarantees by the United States or the commitment of some of the Fund's gold proved unavailing.

If interest in a substitution account were to arise anew—which would seem likely only in the context of a renewed concern about the value of the dollar—a simpler approach should recommend itself. The balance of the account could be automatically preserved if its assets as well as its liabilities were expressed in SDRs and earned the SDR interest rate. This would not mean that the entire exchange risk of dollars deposited in the account would be transferred to the United States. Since the dollar has a 40 per cent weight in the SDR currency basket, creditors would maintain 40 per cent of the dollar risk while the United States would assume 60 per cent of that risk. This is the same distribution of risk that applies when the United States buys yen for intervention against SDRs as envisaged under the Reagan–Takeshita joint statement of January 13, 1988. These and other recent instances of SDR use by industrial countries[47] provide evidence of the system's continuing need for an international asset that is not a national currency—a function for which gold no longer qualifies.

Concluding Observations

The task of the Fund remains to be concerned with the international monetary system. To perform that task, it keeps in close contact, through its consultations and otherwise, with all of its members. It is equipped to provide balance-of-payments credit to any member in need of such credit that is willing to pursue a set of policies likely to turn around its position over a short- or medium-term horizon. The large international flows of credit from the commercial banks since the 1970s have put one group of Fund members—roughly the industrial countries—in a position where they no longer rely on credit from the Fund. These credit flows led to the overindebtedness of another group of Fund members, which makes them highly dependent on credit from the Fund (and from the World Bank) to shake off the debt overhang and resume growth. For the period ahead, the Fund will need to assist the latter members with policy advice and credit while remaining involved in the difficult task of urging the reduction in the continuing imbalances among the former.

Notes

[1] Richard N. Cooper, "Is There a Need for Reform?" in Federal Reserve Bank of Boston, *The International Monetary System: Forty Years After Bretton Woods* (Boston: Federal Reserve Bank of Boston, 1984), p. 23.

[2] See Report of Executive Directors, *The Role of Exchange Rates in the Adjustment of International Payments* (Washington, D.C.: International Monetary Fund, 1970).

[3] International Monetary Fund, *Summary Proceedings of the 24th Annual Meeting of the Board of Governors,* September 29–October 1, 1969 (Washington, D.C., 1969), p. 10.

[4] Article XV, Section 1. The explanatory parenthetical clause is from the comparable provision in Article XVII, Section 1(a).

[5] Article XVIII, Section 1(a). This Article, unlike the more general Article XV, refers not only to the allocation, but also to the cancellation of SDRs. The potential power (it has never been used) to reduce the total stock of world liquidity is, however, obviously limited, since it can only apply to SDRs that were previously allocated. There is also a question as to whether it would ever be possible to find an 85 per cent majority for a decision under which all members would have to give up some of their reserves.

[6] These transactions left the United States with only SDR 2 billion in SDRs and reserve position in the Fund combined at the end of 1978, compared to SDR 6.2 billion a year earlier. At the end of 1988, the United States held a total of SDR 14 billion ($19 billion) in these two accounts combined.

[7] ESAF contributions include loans to the Fund at concessional interest rates, loans at market interest rates, and grants to enable the Fund to charge a nominal interest rate on money lent to it at market rates. The Fund announced in December 1987 that it expected ESAF to have resources of SDR 6 billion; about 90 per cent of that target appears to have been met.

[8] See Louis Goreux's chapter in this volume on the parallel provision of credit to the low-income countries by the two institutions (ESAF from the Fund and IDA from the Bank, integrated by means of joint policy papers); and Guillermo Ortiz's chapter on the similar relationship vis-à-vis the middle-income countries (Extended Fund Facility from the Fund and policy-based lending from the the Bank).

[9] A member country's "reserve position in the Fund" constitutes the sum of the assets the member has contributed to the Fund, on which it can draw unconditionally in case of need. This position is the sum of (i) amounts in gold, SDRs, or convertible currencies paid as quota subscription, (ii) net use by the Fund of the member's currency, and (iii) its creditor position under various borrowing arrangements. (For minor qualifications to this definition, see "Introduction" in any monthly issue of *International Financial Statistics*).

[10] "Creditor countries" refers to countries holding creditor positions, which are defined as the sum of items (ii) and (iii) in the preceding note.

[11] Michel Camdessus, Remarks before the American Enterprise Institute at conference on "Monetary Policy in an Era of Change." IMF Press Release, November 17, 1988 (Washington, D.C.: International Monetary Fund, 1988).

[12] J. Keith Horsefield, *The International Monetary Fund, 1945–1965* (Washington, D.C.: IMF, 1969), p. 471.

[13] The Committee was designated as "interim" pending the establishment, under the Articles as they were to be amended, of a new decisionmaking body, the "Council." Although provisions covering the Council are contained in the amended Articles, there has never been sufficiently strong support for such a body to bring about its creation by the required 85 per cent majority of the Board of Governors. The composition of the Interim Committee is the same as that of the Executive Board, with appointed members for the largest countries and the remaining members (for a total of twenty-two members) elected by groups of countries.

[14] International Monetary Fund, *Annual Report 1974*, p. 111.

[15] The Development Committee, with a similar composition as the Interim Committee in terms of constituencies, consists partly of ministers of finance and partly of development ministers and has been notably less influential than the Interim Committee.

[16] Margaret G. de Vries, *The International Monetary Fund, 1972–1978* (Washington, D.C.: International Monetary Fund, 1985), p. 786.

[17] Under Section 3004 of the Omnibus Trade Act, the U.S. Secretary of the Treasury must "consider whether countries manipulate the rate of exchange between their currency and the U.S. dollar for purposes of preventing effective balance-of-payments adjustments or gaining unfair competitive advantage in international trade." In October 1988 the Secretary considered Taiwan and Korea guilty of manipulation. (U.S. Treasury, Report to the Congress on International Economic and Exchange Rate Policy, October 15, 1988, pp. 17 and 19). The consultations of the Fund with Korea did not lead to a finding that Korea engaged in exchange rate manipulation (Taiwan is not a member of the Fund).

[18] Group of Ten, "The Functioning of the International Monetary System," A Report to the Ministers and Governors by the Group of Deputies, (n.p.) 1985, paragraph 36.

[19] International Monetary Fund, *Annual Report 1979*, p. 136.

[20] As the Managing Director said when he addressed the Ministerial Mid-Term Review of the Uruguay Round in Montreal on December 6, 1988: "It would be a mistake to have all of us trying to address all sides of these interrelated problems, irrespective of our individual mandates and fields of expertise."

[21] Group of Ten, "The Functioning of the International Monetary System," op. cit., paragraph 45.

[22] Joseph Gold, "The Group of Five in International Monetary Arrangements," in Cheng, Bin, and E.D. Brown, eds., *Contemporary Problems of International Law: Essays in Honour of George Schwartzenberger on his Eightieth Birthday* (London: Stevens & Sons, 1988).

[23] Saccomani has drawn attention to the fact that since Versailles the emphasis among the major countries shifted from collaboration in surveillance by the Fund to "self-surveillance" or mutual surveillance conducted by the group. The Plaza Communiqué

reflects this shift. Fabrizio Saccomani, "On Multilateral Surveillance," in Paolo Guerrieri and Pier Carlo Padoan, eds., *The Political Economy of International Cooperation* (London: Croom Helm, 1988), pp. 72–73.

[24] They control about 47 per cent of the votes in the Board of Governors and slightly over 50 per cent in the Executive Board, where the Canadian and Italian directors exercise the votes of all countries that have elected them, and where the voting power of South Africa (and a few new members) is not exercised.

[25] One could cite the 1961 G-10 proposal for a borrowing arrangement outside the Fund, the 1964–65 G-10 understanding that reserve creation by the Fund should benefit only the limited group, and one G-10 choice for a new Managing Director that did not materialize. Of interest, too, is the fact that the G-5 agreement on West Berlin as the place for the 1970 Annual Meeting did not carry the day against strong opposition from some smaller countries: That meeting was held in Copenhagen.

[26] The distinction between (b) and (c) parallels that between "relative" and "absolute" coordination made by the Group of Thirty and Currie, et al.—a rather infelicitous choice of modifiers. See Group of Thirty, *International Macroeconomic Policy Coordination* (New York and London: 1988); and David Currie, Gerald Holtham, and Andrew H. Hallett, "The Theory and Practice of International Economic Policy Coordination: Does Coordination Pay?" in Ralph C. Bryant, et al., eds., *Empirical Macroeconomics for Interdependent Economies* (Washington, D.C.: The Brookings Institution, 1988).

[27] Hans Tietmeyer, "Comment," in Wilfried Guth (Moderator), *Economic Policy Coordination*, Proceedings of an international seminar held in Hamburg in May 1988, International Monetary Fund-HWAA Institute für Wirtschaftsforschung-Hamburg (Washington, D.C.: International Monetary Fund, 1988), p. 136.

[28] Yoichi Funabashi, *Managing the Dollar: From the Plaza to the Louvre* (Washington, D.C.: Institute for International Economics, 1988).

[29] C. Fred Bergsten, *America in the World Economy: A Strategy for the 1990s* (Washington, D.C.: Institute for International Economics, 1988), p. 119.

[30] *World Economic Outlook*, 1988, p. 15; and Reuters, September 25, 1988.

[31] Similarly, in the par value era, the Fund dealt with proposals for par value changes on an individual basis, with the notable exception of the realignment of 1971 that involved the U.S. dollar.

[32] U.S. Secretary James Baker III, in International Monetary Fund, *Summary Proceedings of the 42nd Annual Meeting of the Board of Governors*, September 29-October 1, 1987 (Washington, D.C.: International Monetary Fund, 1987), p. 107; and Bergsten, *America in the World Economy*, op. cit., p. 102.

[33] W. Max Corden, "Trade Policy and Macroeconomic Balance in the World Economy," *IMF Working Paper* 88/101 (Washington, D.C.: International Monetary Fund, 1988).

[34] William H. Branson, "International Adjustment and the Dollar: Policy Illusions and Economic Constraints," in Guth, *Economic Policy Coordination*, op. cit., p. 72.

[35] Giorgio Basevi, "International Monetary Cooperation under Tariff Threats," presented at a Symposium on International Trade and Global Development, November 1988, Erasmus University, Rotterdam. Forthcoming.

[36] Guth, *Economic Policy Coordination*, op. cit., p. 212.

[37] Crockett's notion that "surveillance by the Fund can be seen as complementing and extending the G-7 process" puts cart and horse in the wrong sequence. Andrew Crockett, "The Role of International Institutions in Surveillance and Policy Coordination," in Bryant, et al., eds., *Empirical Macroeconomics for Interdependent Economies*, op. cit.

[38] International Monetary Fund, *Annual Report 1988*, p. 43.

[39] Jacques J. Polak, "Economic Policy Objectives and Policymaking in the Major Industrial Countries," in Guth, *Economic Policy Coordination*, op. cit.

[40] Crockett, "The Role of International Economic Institutions," op. cit.

[41] Emile Van Lennep, "The Political Aspects of International Economic Cooperation and Coordination," Speech given at the John F. Kennedy School of Government, Harvard University, October 5, 1988 (photocopy). Two efforts to find legitimacy for a special G-5 role in the Fund deserve to be mentioned. Joseph Gold sees a connnection between the G-5 and the provision in the Fund's Articles under which the countries with the five largest quotas appoint an Executive Director (Gold, "The Group of Five in International Monetary Arrangements," op. cit.). Robert Roosa suggested in 1982 that the Fund have "a special relationship with the [five] reserve currency countries because all of its own liabilities are stated in SDRs, which in a very meaningful sense are related to the prospects for the countries whose currencies determine the value of the SDR" (Robert V. Roosa, "The Multiple Reserve Currency System," in Group of Thirty, *Reserve Currencies in Transition*, New York, 1982, p. 14). More recently, Roosa referred to the G-5 as "the five countries whose currencies had been chosen at the beginning of 1981 by the 150 members of the IMF to form the SDR and thus to represent the central core of currency values for the world mon-

etary system" and hence (presumably because *noblesse oblige*) as the countries that "move forward toward a harmonized convergence of economic performance" (Robert V. Roosa, "Restoring Stability Within a System of Floating Exchange Rates," in David B. H. Denoon, ed., *Changing Capital Markets and the Global Economy,* Papers from the 8th Monetary and Trade Conference, Global Interdependence Center, Philadelphia, 1987, pp. 73–74). The communiqué of the Versailles Summit (1982) that formally established the G-5 adopted Roosa's phrase for the G-5 in announcing its readiness to develop surveillance "on a multilateral basis taking into account particularly the currencies constituting the SDR."

[42] *IMF Survey,* April 18, 1988, p. 116.

[43] Jacques J. Polak, "The Impasse Concerning the Role of the SDR," in Weitze Eizenga, et al., eds., *The Quest for National and Global Economic Stability* (Dordrecht: Kluwer Academic Publishers, 1988), pp. 175–89.

[44] If the Fund decides to allocate SDRs, allocations are made to all members in proportion to their quotas. Members can take themselves out of an allocation by voting against it, but if more than 15 per cent of the membership votes against an allocation, it is rejected. Countries not needing allocated SDRs can repay debt with them or borrow less.

[45] Group of Ten, "The Functioning of the International Monetary System," op. cit., paragraph 72.

[46] R.R. Rhomberg, *Constructing the SDR: Evolution of Ideas and Techniques* (forthcoming, IMF).

[47] The Bundesbank bought yen for intervention from the Bank of Japan against SDRs in 1987. Funabashi, *Managing the Dollar,* op. cit., p. 191.

Chapter 2

The Use of IMF Credit

Peter B. Kenen

The International Monetary Fund changed greatly in form and function during the 1970s and 1980s. Designed originally to meet the needs of industrial countries and to maintain orderly relations among their currencies, the Fund has become increasingly concerned with the needs and problems of developing countries—the only users of Fund credit in the 1980s.

A number of events combined to bring about these changes. The shift to floating exchange rates in 1973 was decisively important; it weakened the major countries' obligations to the Fund and reduced their need to use its resources. The oil shocks of the 1970s, the rapid growth in lending by commercial banks, and the debt crisis of the 1980s changed the Fund in other ways. It had been designed to function as a credit union: Each member would contribute to the Fund's resources, and each could then draw on them to meet its balance-of-payments needs.[1] Faced with huge demands for balance-of-payments credit in the wake of the two oil shocks, and even larger demands at the start of the debt crisis, the Fund began to function as a financial intermediary, borrowing resources from one group of countries to meet the needs of others.

The changes in the Fund's role as a financial institution were accompanied by changes in its policies and practices. These had been designed to safeguard members' rights by protecting the liquidity of the Fund itself, but they began to take on broader purposes. The improvement of national policies became a goal in itself, and the Fund encouraged its members to use Fund credit as soon as they ran into balance-of-payments problems, to expose them to the Fund's advice and policy conditions. For this same reason, however, the Fund was increasingly criticized for being paternalistic. In the 1980s, moreover, the Fund was widely seen as a debt collector for creditor governments and banks because it would not disburse Fund credit to any member that was not up to date in its interest payments. Finally, the Fund began to be part of the debt problem rather than part of the solution as it started to draw net resources away from the debtor countries instead of making more money available to them.

The Fund will need to change further in the 1990s to keep pace with the evolution of the monetary system and to help its members deal with new problems. Changes will be needed in all aspects of its work, including the surveillance of national policies and the provision of financing. This chapter concentrates on the Fund's financial activities, while its policy role is examined in other chapters. It focuses primarily on two requirements. First, the Fund must help reduce and consolidate the debts of developing countries, including the $33 billion owed to the Fund itself, and it must modify its policies to make that task easier. Second, the Fund must involve itself in the process of exchange rate management initiated by the Louvre Accord of 1987 and the further reform of exchange rate arrangements that must take place eventually.

The Breakdown of the Bretton Woods Bargain

The Bretton Woods Agreement of 1944 was a neatly balanced bargain. On the one hand, participating governments acknowledged that exchange rates are shared variables, not to be chosen or altered unilaterally; that decisions about exchange rates would not be taken without the consent of the Fund. On the other hand, governments were promised that they could use Fund resources to deal with balance-of-payments problems; they would not have to sacrifice important domestic objectives to maintain exchange rate stability.

The bargain was balanced in another way. When one country purchased a second country's currency from the pool held by the Fund, the second country's drawing rights would rise automatically. The second country could thus expect to purchase the first country's currency when it began to run a balance-of-payments deficit. The Fund's resources would revolve automatically if balance-of-payments deficits rotated regularly. As that might not happen, however, the Bretton Woods bargain contained two provisions to protect its members' rights by protecting the liquidity of the Fund. The first was the Scarce Currency Clause, which allowed the Fund to declare that a particular currency was scarce, ration its own holdings of that currency, and authorize its members to control commercial uses of that currency. This clause has never been invoked. The second provision authorized the Fund to adopt rules and policies designed to guarantee that members would repay their drawings on the Fund rather than become permanent debtors.

At first, the Fund relied on a complicated formula that held that part of any increase in a member's own reserves must be used to pay back drawings. It also relied on assurances by the Fund's staff that a member wanting to use Fund credit was taking steps to solve its balance-of-payments problem. The formula proved to be cumbersome, however, and the Fund soon moved instead to fixed-term use of its resources and more elaborate forms of conditionality.[2] Ordinary credit-tranche drawings had to be repaid in three to five years, and a member wanting to use Fund credit beyond the first credit tranche had to submit a "letter of intent" describing the policies it would follow to solve its balance-of-payments problem and proposing precise "performance criteria" by which the Fund might monitor its progress.[3] If it failed to meet those self-imposed objectives—by letting its money supply grow too fast, for example, or by reducing its budget deficit too slowly—and could not offer satisfactory reasons for its failure, the Fund would not allow it to draw down the rest of the stand-by credit established in response to its initial application.

The Bretton Woods bargain seemed to be working fairly well at the start of the 1970s, and there was reason to hope that the Fund would exceed its founders' expectations. In 1969, the First Amendment to the Fund's Articles of Agreement addressed an important issue neglected by the original bargain—the management of international liquidity. The Fund was given the power to create its own reserve asset, the Special Drawing Right (SDR), to supplement supplies of other assets, and 9.3 billion of SDRs were created within the next three years.

But much was wrong with the monetary system in 1970. The Fund did not have the power to propose exchange rate changes, and the exchange rate system had become too rigid:

> From the vantage point of today it takes an effort to realize the extent to which parity changes were resisted. . . . Maintenance of a constant parity was treated as tantamount to maintenance of stable social arrangements, and the contemplation of parity changes as the equivalent of 'thinking the unthinkable.'[4]

It is worth recalling, however, that the initial breakdown of fixed parities in August 1971 was engineered by the United States to achieve a realignment of pegged exchange rates—not to replace them with floating rates—and that the Fund played a role in the process. The Fund helped to produce the Smithsonian Agreement, which defined the new set of exchange rates. That agreement, moreover, led to the creation of the Committee of Twenty, charged with proposing long-run reforms of the monetary system, and its *Outline of Reform* favored an exchange rate regime "based on stable but adjustable par values."[5]

Fund credit was not used heavily, but it was used widely. In 1968–72, the five years preceding the first oil shock, eleven industrial countries drew on the Fund, including the United States and five other Group of Seven (G-7) countries (Japan was the exception); their drawings totaled SDR 7.8 billion. But only two of those countries (France and the United Kingdom) made credit-tranche drawings, and all drawings had been repaid by the end of 1972. Drawings by developing countries were more numerous but still fairly small, and their use of Fund credit was even more modest; thirty-three developing countries used Fund credit in that five-year period, but when their drawings peaked in 1968, they came to only 23 per cent of the total quotas of developing countries.[6] At the end of 1988, in contrast, the use of Fund credit by developing countries amounted to 73 per cent of their total quotas, and thirty-five developing countries were using amounts larger than their quotas.

The effects of the shift to floating exchange rates—the weakening of obligations to the Fund and reduced reliance on Fund credit by the industrial countries—did not show up immediately. The float was considered temporary, and the balance-of-payments effects of the first oil shock led to large drawings by developed as well as developing countries. Drawings by the U.K. and Italy totaled SDR 7.5 billion, amounting to 39 per cent of total drawings in 1974–77, and the use of Fund credit by developed countries exceeded 32 per cent of their total quotas at the end of 1977.

But the size of the imbalances caused by the first oil shock and differences in national responses to it appeared to rule out an early return to pegged exchange rates, and the Fund's Articles of Agreement were amended in 1978 to make law conform to fact and legitimize floating exchange rates. The Fund was to "exercise firm surveillance over the exchange rate policies of members" and to formulate guidelines for that purpose (Article IV, Section 3), but each government was free to peg or float its own exchange rate. The basic obligation of the Bretton Woods bargain was transformed by the migration of a single word: the commitment to a system of stable exchange rates became instead a commitment to "a stable system of exchange rates" (Article IV, Section 1). Thereafter, none of the G-10 countries used Fund credit.[7] In 1979, moreover, when the European Community (EC) countries established the European Monetary System (EMS), they set up their own credit facilities, allowing them to stabilize the exchange rates among their currencies without drawing on the Fund; the credit lines are open-ended in the short run and backed by the longer-term credit facilities of the European Monetary Cooperation Fund (EMCF).[8]

The Fund as a Financial Intermediary

The large drawings that took place after the first oil shock represented a turning point in the Fund's own history. At that point the Fund began to function as a financial intermediary, rather than a credit union, by using money borrowed from some members to make loans to others.

The Fund had borrowed before. In 1962, the Group of Ten (G-10) countries entered into a standing agreement with the Fund, the General Arrangements to Borrow (GAB), promising to lend their currencies to the Fund "when supplementary resources are needed to forestall or cope with an impairment of the international monetary system," but only when one of the participating countries was about to make a drawing. In effect, the G-10 countries took on obligations to each other by undertaking to assure that the Fund would have the particular currencies needed to facilitate their own drawings.[9]

In the 1970s, however, the Fund began borrowing to supplement ordinary drawings rather than to facilitate an ordinary drawing by relieving an impending shortage of a particular currency. In 1974 and 1975, it borrowed SDR 6.9 billion from sixteen industrial and oil-producing countries to set up two oil facilities.[10] In 1977, the Interim Committee found "grounds for believing that the Fund's role as a *financial intermediary* could contribute significantly to promotion of international adjustment" and endorsed the creation of supplementary arrangements for members that "will face payments imbalances that are large in relation to their economies."[11] Accordingly, the Fund established the Supplementary Financing Facility (SFF) in 1979, under which it would borrow an additional SDR 7.8 billion from fourteen countries.

The SFF was supposed to be temporary and was due to expire in 1982, but its resources were fully committed in 1981, and the need for large drawings was expected to continue. Therefore, the Fund embarked on a third exercise in intermediation to finance what it called the policy of Enlarged Access to Resources (EAR). The policy and borrowings associated with it were meant to bridge the gap between the expiration of the SFF and an increase in Fund quotas (which was not due to take place until 1984, but was completed in 1983 because of the outbreak of the debt crisis). The EAR remains in place, however, although it is a

ghost of its former self, and total lending under the EAR amounted to
SDR 13.1 billion by the end of 1988 (of which SDR 8.6 billion was still
outstanding). Saudi Arabia was the largest lender of resources for the
EAR (and the Fund owes it about SDR 6 billion for its contributions to
the SFF and the EAR). The Fund's position as financial intermediary is
summarized in Table 1.

Table 1. Scheduled Repayments of Borrowings from and by the Fund (millions SDRs, fiscal years ending April 30)

Payable by End of Fiscal Year	Owed to the Fund	Owed by the Fund
1989	3,741	3,690
1990	2,849	2,907
1991	2,176	1,159
1992	1,396	590
1993	902	350
1994	607	300
1995	319	75
Total	11,990	9,070

Source: International Monetary Fund, *Annual Report 1988*, pp. 180–81. (Detail may
not add up to total because of rounding.)

At the start of the 1970s, the rules governing access to Fund credit
were quite simple. Drawings on the first credit tranche were not subject
to formal conditionality; a member merely had to demonstrate that it
was making reasonable efforts to deal with its problems. Drawings on
the higher credit tranches were reviewed more rigorously and usually
conditioned on performance criteria. Drawings on the Compensatory
Financing Facility (CFF), established in 1963, were meant to offset fluc-
tuations in a member's exports arising from causes beyond its control.
Therefore their size depended on the size of the export shortfall. But
cumulative drawings on the CFF could not exceed a member's quota,
and when they reached 50 per cent of quota, the Fund had to be satisfied
that the member was cooperating with the Fund "to find, where
required, appropriate solutions for its balance of payments difficulties."[12] But CFF drawings were not subject to any other form of conditionality at that time, although they were subject to the same fixed-
term repayment rule as ordinary credit-tranche drawings.

Access to the Extended Fund Facility (EFF), created in 1974, was governed by somewhat different conditions. The EFF was designed to help countries adopting "comprehensive" adjustment programs, including policies to correct "structural imbalances in production, trade, and prices," as well as macroeconomic policies. As structural adjustments take time to implement and even longer to affect economic behavior, EFF drawings may take three years, amount to 140 per cent of quota, and be amortized over a six-year period starting four years after each year's drawing. By its very nature, however, the EFF is highly conditional; compliance is monitored by performance criteria, and programs are reviewed annually, before the next year's drawings can be made.

Access to the two oil facilities was subject to certain limitations relating to the increase in the member's oil-import bill, quota, and reserves, but not to the usual forms of conditionality. Drawings on the SFF, however, were tied mechanically to credit-tranche drawings, and similar rules were used for the EAR. Under both arrangements, the size of each drawing was decided first, in light of the member's needs, but its character was governed by so-called mixing rules. A member drawing on the first credit tranche would draw an additional 12.5 per cent of quota from the Fund's borrowed resources; and when it went on to the higher credit tranches, it would draw an additional 30 per cent with each tranche. In consequence, a member's drawing could be as large as 202.5 per cent of quota, with 100 per cent coming from the credit tranches and 102.5 per cent coming from the Fund's borrowed resources. Under the EAR, moreover, a member might be authorized to draw more than this amount, within certain annual and cumulative limits, and would thus use more borrowed money. In brief, the SFF and EAR made much more credit available, just when it was needed, but on stricter terms than those that governed access to the oil facilities. Amounts of Fund credit outstanding from these and other facilities are shown in Table 2.

Soon after putting these facilities in place, however, the Fund began to tighten access to them and to other forms of Fund credit. The tightening started in 1983, when the Fund reduced the ceiling on cumulative use of the CFF from 100 per cent to 83 per cent of quota, preventing the automatic increase in access that would have been produced by the general quota increase of that year, and it made the terms of access to the upper 33 per cent virtually the same as those that apply to the higher credit tranches. And similar rules were adopted in 1988, when the CFF was replaced by the Compensatory and Contingency Financing Facility (CCFF). The CCFF is more liberal than the CFF because it covers additional contingencies, such as an increase in debt service payments resulting from higher world interest rates. But this additional insurance is available only to those members that have other

Table 2. Fund Credit Outstanding from
Principal Facilities
(billions of SDRs, January 31, 1989)

Facility	Amount
Ordinary Resources:	
Credit-tranche drawings	5,810
Compensatory Financing Facility (CFF)	3,833
Extended Fund Facility (EFF)	5,208
Borrowed and Other Resources:	
Supplementary Financing Facility (SFF)	1,334
Enlarged Access to Resources (EAR)	8,363
Structural Adjustment Facilities (SAF and ESAF)	1,005
Total	25,552

Source: International Monetary Fund, *International Financial Statistics,* March 1989. (Detail may not add up to total because of rounding).

highly conditional credit arrangements with the Fund.[13] During and after 1984, moreover, the Fund cut the annual and cumulative limits on drawings under the EAR. The annual use of Fund credit cannot exceed 110 per cent of quota, and cumulative use cannot exceed 440 per cent. These ceilings cover all credit-tranche and EFF drawings, as well as drawings on borrowed resources.

The Fund continues to create new facilities, however, as it seeks to deal with new problems. The Structural Adjustment Facility (SAF) was established in 1986 to provide long-term concessional credit to low-income countries; it was part of the Fund's response to the 1985 Baker Initiative, which sought to combine adjustment with growth in heavily indebted countries. The Enhanced Structural Adjustment Facility (ESAF) was established in 1988 and dedicated formally to the same objective, but it had a more immediate purpose: to refinance low-income countries' obligations to the Fund.

Thus the Fund acted speedily and flexibly to meet new problems in the 1970s and 1980s, but its own flexibility and credibility were damaged in the process—especially by the Fund's involvement in the debt crisis. To contribute effectively to the solution of that problem and to play a central role in the further evolution of the international monetary system, the Fund must modify some of its policies and consolidate its own financial operations.

The Fund and the Debt Crisis

The shift from low to high conditionality that occurred when the SFF replaced the oil facilities was followed by a tightening of conditionality itself. Some trace this policy change to the advent of the Reagan administration; others trace it to the judgment made earlier by many governments that there had been too much financing and too little adjustment after the first oil shock, and that a tougher stance was needed to deal with the second shock.[14] Nevertheless, there was little difference between the amounts of Fund credit used by developing countries following those shocks. Net drawings totaled SDR 6.6 billion in 1979–81, compared with SDR 5.8 billion in 1974–76. And the stock of Fund credit rose hugely with the start of the debt crisis, as a large number of countries resorted heavily to Fund credit (see Table 3).[15]

Table 3. Numbers of Countries Using Fund Credit in Amounts Larger than their Quotas, 1982–88

Level of Use	1982	1985	1988
From 100 to 200 per cent of quota	14	20	22
From 200 to 300 per cent of quota	14	22	11
Larger than 300 per cent of quota	10	7	2
Total	38	49	35

Source: International Monetary Fund, *International Financial Statistics,* February 1989; data for end of each calendar year.

The Fund's involvement in the debt crisis is discussed extensively elsewhere in this book and need not be examined comprehensively here. Three comments will suffice:

1. Although the terms of access to Fund credit had hardened before the crisis and conditionality was being tightened, the Fund should not be blamed for the painful measures that debtor countries had to take. They had to reduce their current account deficits when bank lending ceased, and expenditure-reducing measures were the fastest way to do so.

2. The Fund *can* be faulted for putting its seal of approval on unrealistic policy packages. But ultimate responsibility for this error resides with the governments of the creditor countries. They wanted the Fund to deliver those packages quickly, so that commercial banks could be persuaded to provide new money and reschedule the debtors' obligations.[16]

3. The Fund was chronically optimistic about the prospects for growth and inflation in the debtor countries, and the evolution of debt burdens, which is perhaps to say that it put too much trust in the technical and political feasibility of the policy packages it endorsed.[17]

The Changing Debt Strategy

At the start of the debt crisis, debtor and creditor governments were virtually unanimous in adopting the "liquidity" view of the problem and in their concern to prevent a crisis of confidence in the banking system—a concern quite different from solicitude for the banks themselves.[18] The debtors were deemed to face a short-term problem reflecting the unusual combination of worldwide recession and high interest rates brought on by the shift in the policy stance of the major industrial countries. On this view, it was eminently sensible for the debtors to take on more debt temporarily to service their existing debts and preserve their creditworthiness.

When the problem proved to be more obdurate, the case for short-term borrowing weakened, and there was less justification for using Fund credit. The Baker Initiative of 1985 recognized this tacitly when stressing the need for long-term, growth-oriented lending by the multilateral development banks rather than balance-of-payments lending by the Fund. By 1988, moreover, it was becoming clear that the most heavily indebted countries could not be expected to grow out of their debt problems, even with the help of long-term lending, and the official community began considering ways to reduce the stock of debt.

At the Toronto summit, the major industrial countries agreed to grant debt relief to the low-income debtors, but pointedly excluded the middle-income debtors. At the 1988 IMF-World Bank Annual Meeting in Berlin, however, the Interim Committee went further, agreeing that the "menu" of methods for dealing with debt problems should be broadened to include "voluntary market-based techniques which increase financial flows and which reduce the stock of debt without transferring risk from private lenders to official creditors."[19] In March 1989, moreover, U.S. Secretary of the Treasury Nicholas Brady called for a three-year waiver of the clauses in existing loan agreements that stand in the way of debt reduction "to accelerate sharply the pace of debt reduction and pass the benefits directly to the debtor nations" and suggested that the Fund and World Bank could contribute to the process.

A portion of their policy based loans could be used to finance specific debt reduction plans. These funds could support collateralized debt for bond exchanges involving a significant discount on outstanding debt. They could also be used to replenish reserves following a cash buyback. Moreover, both institutions could offer new, additional financial support to collateralize a portion of interest payments for debt or debt service reduction transactions.[20]

The Executive Board of the Fund responded in May 1989 by adopting guidelines for the Fund's support of debt and debt service reductions. Such support, it said, will be linked to medium-term adjustment programs and to programs involving appropriate flows of new money, and it will be governed by these rules:

(1) In appropriate cases, part of a member's access under an extended or a stand-by arrangement could be set aside to support operations involving principal reduction, such as debt buybacks or exchanges. The exact size of the set aside would be determined on a case-by-case basis, but would involve a figure of about 25 per cent of the arrangement, determined on the basis of existing access policy. . . .

(2) In appropriate cases, the Fund would be prepared to approve requests for additional resources of up to 40 per cent of a member's quota, where such support would be decisive in facilitating further cost-effective operations. . . . The additional resources from the Fund are to be used for interest support in connection with debt reduction or debt-service reduction operations. . . .

(3) Recognizing the need for cautious adaptation of its policy . . ., the Fund may, on a case-by-case basis, approve an arrangement outright before the conclusion of an appropriate package is agreed between the member and commercial bank creditors. . . .[21]

The Board went on to warn that an accumulation of arrears to banks may sometimes be tolerated, but repeated its refusal to tolerate arrears to official creditors. Immediately after adopting these guidelines, the Fund approved drawings by Costa Rica, the Philippines, and Mexico, each involving a set-aside for debt reduction.

There is an impeccable case for debt reduction. In certain special circumstances, partial debt forgiveness can benefit a debtor and its creditors by raising the debtor's ability to service its remaining debt.[22] In a much larger class of cases, reductions in debt or debt service payments can benefit both parties if they are accompanied by measures that raise the quality of the remaining debt. A debt buyback does this by replacing the remaining debt with other assets, but the debtor may not gain if the assets it uses or borrows to buy back debt could be devoted to other productive purposes.[23] Other methods for reducing debt or debt service payments do this by reducing the riskiness of the remaining debt. This can be accomplished by posting other assets as collateral to guarantee the principal or interest payments or by obtaining a third-party guarantee.

Yet there are risks and problems here. The amounts of financing available from the Fund and the World Bank may be too small to support large amounts of debt reduction, and large amounts are needed to generate significant improvements in the debtor countries' policies and prospects. (The figure commonly quoted—a 20-per-cent cut in annual debt service payments resulting from reductions in interest rates or principal—would be far too small even if combined with new lending by the banks, and debtors have asked for much larger cuts.) The opportunity cost of debt reduction may be very high if debtors must borrow what they need to buy back debt or post collateral for interest payments. And the speed with which Fund credit must be repaid, even on EFF or ESAF terms, calls into question the wisdom of using it for debt-reducing purposes. A debtor's cash flow problem may get worse if it must use medium-term credit to buy back or collateralize long-term debt.

The Case for a Quota Increase

The Fund can continue to provide some of the money required for debt reduction, along with the World Bank and other multilateral institutions. But the Fund must not encourage the belief that it can be the principal provider and must not base the case for an increase in its own resources on that unrealistic premise. The amounts of money required for meaningful debt relief are larger than those that the Fund can be expected to supply without concentrating its efforts and resources far too narrowly on the particular countries involved, and the terms on which Fund credit is normally provided are inappropriate for the purpose. If the scale and character of debt reduction come to be conditioned on the quantity of credit available from the Fund and World Bank, there will be too little debt relief and an excessive concentration of the corresponding risks on those two institutions.

It will be hard enough for the Fund to prevent the debtors' cash flow problems from getting worse in the next few years, as its claims on those countries fall due. It must find ways to roll over those claims, and it must liberalize access to the CCFF to help the debtors deal with unforeseen contingencies.[24] To keep its own claims from contracting, however, the Fund must confront the consequences of having relied on borrowed money to finance the SFF and EAR, and it may have to modify the conduct of conditionality.

A small but growing number of countries, including Peru and Sudan, have failed to repay their obligations to the Fund, and it has declared formally that they are ineligible for more Fund credit. But this stance is symbolic, and the Fund is rightly reluctant to take the next step: expelling a member completely. Indeed, it has engaged whenever possible in its own oblique form of debt rescheduling: A member that cannot repay its old drawings submits a new letter of intent, containing a fresh set of performance criteria, draws once again on the Fund, and uses the proceeds, in whole or in part, to meet its old obligations. In consequence, some twenty countries have been continuous users of Fund credit for more than a dozen years. This sort of refinancing has not been available to Peru and the other countries that have fallen far behind in their payments to the Fund; they have been unwilling or unable to produce acceptable letters of intent. In other cases, however, the Fund has accepted letters of intent that it might have rejected in ordinary circumstances. In effect, it has been forced to choose between two unpalatable practices: declaring that some of its members cannot continue to draw on the Fund or papering over the problem by accepting letters of intent that are not very credible and thus tarnishing the Fund's own seal of approval.[25]

The nature of the problem facing the Fund and its link with the Fund's own borrowing are illustrated by the position of Mexico, the largest user of Fund credit (and the second largest user relative to quota). Its obligations to the Fund are shown in Table 4.[26] The credit-tranche drawings are recent and not yet due to be repaid; the EFF drawings were made some time ago, and Mexico is starting to repay them. But that distinction is less important than another. Much of Mexico's debt to the Fund is matched by the Fund's own debt to Saudi Arabia, the Fund's main creditor. The Fund cannot roll over its claims on Mexico unless it can roll over its own debts or use its own resources to pay them off.

It would not be impossible for the Fund to refinance its debt. Saudi Arabia may not want to renew its lending, given its own situation, but Japan and other surplus countries might be willing to replace it. (The Fund already has a medium-term credit arrangement with Japan.) Over the long run, however, the Fund should rely less heavily on borrowing, apart from temporary borrowing under the GAB to meet a shortfall of liquidity or the need for particular currencies. Borrowing made sense when OPEC surpluses were very large, and the world might be better off today if the Fund had played a larger role in recycling them. Borrowing makes less sense, however, when current account surpluses are less sharply concentrated or when, as now, surplus countries pile up private sector claims rather than reserves at the disposal of their governments. Finally, reliance on borrowing may gradually reduce the Fund's ability to mobilize support for increases in quotas, and that in turn would increase its reliance on borrowing, as well as its vulnerability to the views and circumstances of the surplus countries. The influence of individual governments on the Fund's decisions was meant to depend on vot-

Table 4. Fund Credit Outstanding to Mexico, December 1988

Type	Millions of SDRs	Percentage of quota
Ordinary Resources:		
Credit-tranche drawings	674	57.8
Extended facility	998	85.6
Borrowed Resources (EAR):		
Credit-tranche drawings	1,017	87.2
Extended facility	881	75.5
Total	3,570	306.1

Source: International Monetary Fund, *International Financial Statistics,* February 1989.

ing power, which depends on quotas, and the distribution of quotas is renegotiated periodically. The distribution of influence over the Fund's decisions should not change haphazardly because of a change in the distribution of surpluses and deficits or the state of the Fund's own liquidity.

It is therefore more sensible for the Fund to pay off its debts with some of its own assets. It has, in fact, been doing this (which is why Table 1 shows that the Fund is owed more than it owes), and it can go on doing so. The Fund's total debts amounted to about SDR 9 billion at the end of the most recent fiscal year. Its holdings of usable currencies amounted to about SDR 41 billion.[27] The Fund must be ready to meet its members' needs, but it has additional sources of liquidity: Its drawing rights under the GAB amount to SDR 18.5 billion, and it holds 103 million ounces of gold, worth more than SDR 3.6 billion at the Fund's accounting price but close to SDR 31 billion at the current market price. (It could not sell that gold in the open market without depressing the market price, but it could borrow against it at market-related prices.)

If the Fund ceased to rely on borrowed resources, however, it would have to recast its policies regarding the use of its own resources. Credit-tranche drawings do not normally exceed 100 per cent of quota, and drawings under the Extended Fund Facility (EFF) do not normally exceed 140 per cent of quota. Yet Mexico's total drawings already are greater than 300 per cent of quota, and those of several other middle-income debtor countries exceed 200 per cent of quota.

The Fund can deal with this difficulty by waiving its own rules on a case-by-case basis or by liberalizing access with an increase in Fund quotas. The second method is far better than the first.

When the Fund set up the EFF and SFF, it agreed in principle to waive the quota-based ceiling on the use of its resources, and it did this again for drawings under the EAR. Hence waivers were granted routinely to individual members that were qualified to use those facilities. For the Fund to do so on an ad hoc basis, however, to refinance its claims on large, chronic users of Fund credit, would come close to violating its Articles of Agreement. The Articles state that the Fund may grant such waivers at its discretion but "on terms which safeguard its interests" and "especially in the case of members with a record of *avoiding* large or continuous use of the Fund's general resources."[28]

It would thus be more prudent to rationalize the situation by raising quotas, which would safeguard the Fund's liquidity as well as its integrity. Three steps might be taken:

(1) A 50-per-cent increase in quotas, partly to provide the Fund with the additional resources it will need eventually, but mainly to raise drawing rights.

(2) An increase in the ceiling for EFF drawings from 140 to, say, 180 per cent of quota.

(3) An increase in the ceiling for all CCFF drawings to 150 per cent of quota, with a cumulative ceiling on the use of Fund credit at, say, 250 per cent of quota.

If these proposals were adopted, Mexico's quota would rise from SDR 1,166 million to SDR 1,749 million, and the upper limit for an EFF drawing would rise to SDR 3,148 million. Mexico could refinance most of its debt to the Fund; it would have to pay back only SDR 400 million (about $520 million) net. And it could still enter into contingency arrangements amounting to 70 per cent of its quota (250 per cent *less* 180 per cent) or SDR 1,224 billion.

The numbers in this example are meant to be illustrative, not definitive. In fact, they would not cover Mexico completely, although they would cover most of the other middle-income debtors.[29] Countries with obligations smaller than 150 per cent of their present quotas would be covered by the credit-tranche ceiling; those with obligations smaller than 270 per cent of quota would be covered by the new EFF ceiling (if they qualify for EFF drawings in all other relevant respects).[30] And all of them would still have room to enter into CCFF arrangements to protect them from unforeseen shocks.

A quota increase of less than 50 per cent on average would make no sense at all. Too much time and trouble would have to be invested. A somewhat bigger increase, averaging 75 per cent, will probably be needed if the Fund is to make a large financial contribution to the debt reduction process—and that is the widespread expectation, even though it is not entirely appropriate.

Making Conditionality Less Intrusive

Some heavily indebted countries pose problems more complicated than those of Mexico. The Fund and Mexico have been able to agree on a new stand-by arrangement and a new policy package to go with it. It would be far harder for the Fund to reach similar agreements with many other debtor countries. Their political situations would prevent them from making the appropriate policy commitments, while their economic prospects could prevent the Fund from endorsing the very best sets of policies that their political situations would permit them to produce. To keep the supply of Fund credit from shrinking, conditionality must be made more palatable without damaging the Fund's own credibility.

The Fund is frequently described as the scapegoat for decisions that governments must take but do not have enough political support to take by themselves. Furthermore, governments are not monolithic, and officials concerned with balance-of-payments and debt problems do not always win their bureaucratic battles because they do not have powerful political constituencies. The Fund can strengthen their bargaining positions. These arguments make sense when the Fund can provide financing for a country that confronts a short-term problem and can protect its creditworthiness by dealing boldly with it. They make less sense under present circumstances because they are myopic. A government that hides behind the Fund will be accused of failing to defend its independence from foreign interference and will find it increasingly hard to return to the Fund to refinance its obligations. It would be helpful, however, for the Fund to devise less intrusive forms of conditionality—to make "going to the Fund" less traumatic and "staying with the Fund" less embarrassing.

The Fund must continue to ask for policy commitments, including, where appropriate, commitments aimed at long-term structural adjustment as well as those concerning monetary and fiscal policies. Whenever possible, moreover, governments should be encouraged to change their policies *before* they apply for Fund credit. They should be seen as seeking the Fund's endorsement, not its tutelage.[31] The Fund should offer its advice during the annual consultation that it holds with each member, not in the negotiations that precede a drawing.

The Fund must continue to monitor implementation, but it should not pay so much attention to the short-term evolution of financial or fiscal variables such as the growth rate of domestic credit or the level of public sector borrowing. It should focus instead on the evolution of the external situation by monitoring trade flows, reserves, and the path of the real exchange rate. If these are behaving badly compared to projections made in the member's letter of intent, the Fund should ask for an explanation. In some cases, external circumstances will be to blame, and the member may need help from the CCFF. In other cases, domestic policies will be to blame, and the member should be asked to intensify its efforts by adhering more faithfully to its policy commitments or revising them. Under multiyear EFF programs, of course, a member's situation and policies should be reviewed at the end of each year, and it should be asked to modify commitments made for the coming year if it has not made satisfactory progress.

The Fund has begun to move in this direction. The transformation of the CFF into the CCFF will force the Fund to make balance-of-payments projections and monitor subsequent developments closely, because it may have to decide whether a member has been adversely affected by external circumstances. Furthermore, the Fund appears to be putting less emphasis on short-term movements in domestic indicators. But it should go further. Domestic trends are very important for the sustainability of a country's external position. An increase in the budget deficit is likely to worsen the current account balance, and inflation is bound to affect competitiveness. A country with a high inflation rate, however, should be expected to adjust its nominal exchange rate frequently, not necessarily to reduce its inflation rate quickly.

In brief, the Fund should administer conditionality in keeping with its own obligations and purposes. It should try not to complicate the problems of the heavily indebted countries while striving to make sure that those countries' problems do not complicate its own, and it should not allow creditor governments and commercial banks to use the institution for their own purposes.

The Fund and the Developed Countries

Industrial countries have not used the Fund's resources for many years, but they may need them in the future. Exchange rate arrangements are changing, and reserve arrangements will have to change with them.

At the start of the 1980s, the governments of the major industrial countries were mildly schizophrenic about the exchange rate regime. On the one hand, they appeared to believe that it was desirable and possible to peg exchange rates within Europe and to defend them by official intervention. On the other hand, they favored freely floating rates for the key currencies and doubted the wisdom or feasibility of large-scale intervention.[32]

A few years later, however, they were trying to manage exchange rates intensively. In the Plaza Communiqué of September 1985, governments chided foreign exchange markets for failing to take account of changes in national policies and other "fundamentals" affecting exchange rates. They called on markets to bring down the dollar and warned that they would intervene when and if that would be helpful. In the Louvre Accord of February 1987, they went much further. In 1985, they had agreed on the "wrongness" of current exchange rates, which was not very difficult in light of the large U.S. trade deficit and the protectionist pressures it was producing. In 1987, they agreed on the "rightness" of current rates—that the dollar had fallen far enough—and intervened heavily to stabilize them. In fact, foreign official purchases of dollars financed most of the U.S. current account deficit in 1987. In early 1988, moreover, skillfully executed intervention helped to halt the depreciation of the dollar triggered three months earlier by the stock market crash.

The Louvre Accord marked a major change in the international monetary system, and it has been widely criticized. Some critics say that it is wrong in principle and bound to fail in practice—that governments should not try to second-guess markets and will not be willing to coordinate their policies, most notably their monetary policies, closely enough to stabilize exchange rates effectively.[33] Other critics believe that present arrangements are not tight or transparent enough. They want governments to commit themselves explicitly to exchange rate targets, although they disagree about the most appropriate methods of choosing and defending them. Some of them favor wide, soft bands, which would be defended by coordinating interest rate policies; others favor narrower and harder bands, which would have to be defended by intervention as well as by interest rate coordination.[34]

This is not the appropriate place to argue the case for exchange rate management. It is fitting, however, to ask what role the Fund should play in a highly managed system, and the answer has two parts. The first relates to its role in policy coordination, which is necessary for successful exchange rate management; this issue was examined by Jacques J. Polak in Chapter 1. The second relates to the financing of official intervention, which is the issue addressed in the balance of this chapter.

Economists continue to debate the role of official intervention in exchange rate management.[35] But one lesson taught by recent experience has importance for the future of the Fund. Intervention is most effective when conducted jointly:

> When governments give the appearance of being united and of holding their views firmly, while market participants are divided and uncertain, official pronouncements about exchange rates can have large effects, especially when backed by intervention or the threat of intervention, and intervention can be effective even when markets are skeptical about the governments' pronouncements.[36]

But the ability of the United States to intervene jointly with other countries is rather limited, because it does not have large foreign currency reserves. It has ample access to short-term reserve credit but not to longer-term financing. There are many ways to rectify this situation, and some of them involve the Fund.

The Fund might be asked to manage a substitution account that would make the monetary system more symmetrical by raising the readily usable reserves of the United States and reducing the exchange rate risks borne by other governments.Under arrangements proposed in 1979, when the subject was last discussed in the Fund, governments and central banks holding dollar balances would have deposited some of them with the Fund in exchange for SDR-denominated claims. They could not have used those claims for intervention, because foreign exchange markets do not deal in SDRs, but they could have sold them to other governments in exchange for those governments' currencies. It was agreed in principle that the costs and benefits of the arrangement would be shared by the United States and the depositors, and Washington interpreted this understanding to mean that the depositors would bear some of any losses.[37] But other countries did not buy this interpretation, and discussions of the subject ended in 1980, when the United States shifted its own position, proposing that all losses be borne by the Fund, which would set aside some of its gold for the purpose. In fact, the whole proposal became less attractive when the dollar began to appreciate.

The 1979 proposal would have reduced the exchange rate risks borne by the holders of dollar reserves but would not have raised U.S. reserves. A variant of the proposal would do both, however, and would reduce the risk of loss. The United States would deposit gold. Other governments would deposit dollars. Both would obtain an SDR-denominated claim to be used as a reserve asset.[38]

The creation of a substitution account would serve an additional purpose: making the SDR a more important reserve asset. A change in the functioning of the Fund itself would serve that same purpose and prepare the Fund for a larger role in a more highly managed monetary system. Under present arrangements, governments hold two reserve assets with the Fund, their reserve positions in the General Department and their SDR balances in the SDR Department, and they obtain Fund credit from the General Department. To complicate matters, allocations of SDRs are made on the recommendation of the Managing Director, using explicit criteria set out in the Fund's Articles of Agreement (Article XVIII, Section 1), while reserve positions are reviewed automatically whenever Fund quotas are reviewed, but without reference to explicit criteria (Article III, Section 2).

These arrangements are cumbersome and blur the functional distinction between the two departments of the Fund. One department is involved in providing Fund credit, but both departments are involved in creating reserve assets. Furthermore, these arrangements blur the nature of each member's rights and obligations: Its rights are defined with respect to its SDR holdings, reserve position, and access to Fund credit. Its obligations are defined with respect to the acceptance of SDRs and by the size of its quota (currency subscription). Finally, basic decisions about the creation of Fund-related reserve assets are not adequately integrated. Governments are not required to look at the size of the Fund as a whole in relation to global reserve needs and supplies from other sources.

The Fund's structure should be altered eventually to consolidate its reserve-creating activities and simplify its members' obligations to provide financing through the Fund.[39] Decisions affecting the size of the Fund should be taken on the basis of consistent criteria relating to the need for balance-of-payments financing, global supplies of reserves and reserve credit, and the appropriate division of Fund-related financing between reserve creation and extensions of Fund credit. These aims can be advanced by shifting the boundary between the two departments of the Fund. These basic organizational issues should be addressed in conjunction with the Tenth General Review of Quotas, due to take place in the mid-1990s.

Conclusion

In the late 1970s, some observers wondered whether the Fund had a future. Its members' obligations had been weakened by the shift to floating exchange rates, and the rapid growth of international bank lending was seen as likely to reduce the importance of the Fund as a source of reserve credit. The debt crisis gave the Fund new responsibilities, and it has a role to play in solving the problem. Nevertheless, the international community must rely less heavily on the use of Fund resources to deal with debt and on the use of the Fund as tutor to the debtor countries. At the same time, the industrial countries must come to rely more heavily on the Fund's resources and advice as they move toward a more managed monetary system.

Notes

[1] On the Fund as a credit union, see Peter B. Kenen, *Financing, Adjustment, and the International Monetary Fund,* Studies in International Economics (Washington, D.C.: The Brookings Institution, 1986), pp. 2–6.

[2] For contrasting views on the origins and purposes of conditionality, see Sidney Dell, *On Being Grandmotherly: The Evolution of IMF Conditionality,* Essays in International Finance, 144 (Princeton, N.J.: International Finance Section, Princeton University, 1981), and C. David Finch, *The International Monetary Fund: The Record and the Prospect,* Essays in International Finance, 175 (Princeton, N.J.: International Finance Section, Princeton University, 1989); see also John Williamson, ed., *IMF Conditionality* (Washington, D.C.: Institute for International Economics, 1983), Chapters 1–3, 7.

[3] Most readers will be familiar with Fund terminology, but repetition may be helpful. Every member's quota serves four purposes: (1) It determines the member's voting power; (2) It determines the member's contribution to the Fund. One quarter of each member's quota was payable in gold under the original Articles of Agreement and is currently payable in Special Drawing Rights (SDRs); the rest is payable in the member's own currency; (3) It determines the member's share in any allocation of new SDRs; (4) It determines the member's access to Fund credit. Access is defined by five tranches—each equal to one quarter of the member's quota. One is the reserve tranche, which the member is entitled to treat as an ordinary reserve asset; it can be drawn down and reconstituted at the member's discretion. The other four are credit tranches, which cannot be used without the Fund's approval. Drawings on the first credit tranche are approved rather routinely; drawings on the higher credit tranches are subject to close scrutiny and, as indicated in the text, various sorts of conditionality. All credit-tranche drawings must be repaid in full.

[4] Michael Artis and Sylvia Ostry, *International Economic Policy Coordination,* Chatham House Papers, No. 30 (London: Royal Institute of International Affairs and Routledge & Kegan Paul, 1986), p. 33.

[5] On the engineering of the 1971 crisis and subsequent events, see Robert Solomon, *The International Monetary System, 1945–1981,* expanded edition (New York: Harper and Row, 1982), Chapters xi-xiv.

[6] The credit-tranche drawings listed above include drawings on the Compensatory Financing Facility (CFF) as well as ordinary credit-tranche drawings. There were no other Fund facilities at that time, apart from the small Buffer Stock Facility. (Unless otherwise indicated, all figures in this chapter relating to the Fund come from its *Annual Reports* or from *International Financial Statistics.*)

[7] The United States drew on the Fund in November 1978, when it also borrowed from other G-10 countries to mobilize reserves for halting a depreciation of the dollar. But this was a reserve-tranche drawing that did not involve the use of Fund credit.

[8] For details, see Francesco Giavazzi and Alberto Giovannini, *Limiting Exchange Rate Flexibility: The European Monetary System* (Cambridge, Mass: MIT Press, 1989), Chapter 2. Initially, the EC countries planned to convert the EMCF into a European Monetary Fund, but that has not happened. The existence of these credit facilities does not rule out recourse to the IMF, which could indeed be necessary if the EMS countries wanted to combat a depreciation of their currencies against outside currencies such as the dollar and yen, but the size of their reserves makes this unlikely. The United States is more likely to need Fund credit, because its foreign currency reserves are small.

[9] The GAB was put in place to furnish the currencies the Fund would need to finance a drawing by the United States, because U.S. drawing rights were very large compared to the Fund's holdings of the other countries' currencies. The GAB was revised in 1983 to allow the Fund to use it when the participants' currencies are needed for drawings by nonparticipants. This change, however, came much later in the process by which the Fund became a financial intermediary.

[10] A total of fifty-five countries borrowed from the oil facilities, including the two largest users of Fund credit, the U.K. and Italy; these borrowings were repaid in full by 1983 (so references to problems arising from the use of borrowed resources relate entirely to subsequent borrowings).

[11] Press Communiqué, April 29, 1977, in International Monetary Fund, *Annual Report 1977,* p. 115. Emphasis added.

[12] International Monetary Fund, *Annual Report 1980,* p. 137.

[13] Complicated ceilings and sub-ceilings apply to the various forms of contingency financing; some are tied to the member's quota and some to the size of the other credit arrangement.

[14] For the first interpretation, see John Williamson, "The Lending Policies of the International Monetary Fund," in Williamson, ed., op. cit., pp. 640–48; for the second, see Jacques J. Polak, "The Role of the Fund," in *The International Monetary System: Forty Years After Bretton Woods* (Boston: Federal Reserve Bank of Boston, 1984), p. 251.

[15] As Fund quotas rose by an average of 50 per cent during this period, the figures in Table 3 understate the increase in reliance on the Fund.

[16] See Joseph Kraft, *The Mexican Rescue* (New York: Group of Thirty, 1984).

[17] On the bias in the Fund's forecasts for growth and inflation, see Peter B. Kenen and Stephen B. Schwartz, "An Assessment of Macroeconomic Forecasts in the International Monetary Fund's World Economic Outlook," *Working Paper G–86–04* (Princeton, N.J.: International Finance Section, Princeton University, 1986), pp. 30–33. When forecasting the overall debt service ratio for all non-oil developing countries, the Fund was low for four years running (1983–1986) and high in 1987 (when Brazil's moratorium on debt service payments reduced the actual ratio).

[18] See Kraft, op. cit., who suggests that Mexican officials were even more worried about this aspect of the problem than some of their U.S. counterparts. (Otherwise, they might have taken a tougher stance in their early dealings with banks and creditor governments.)

[19] Press Communiqué, September 26, 1988, in *IMF Survey,* October 17, 1988, p. 325.

[20] U.S. Treasury Press Release, March 10, 1989.

[21] IMF Press Release 89/17, in *IMF Survey,* May 29, 1989, pp. 172–73.

[22] See, for example, Paul R. Krugman, "Market-Based Debt-Reduction Schemes," *Working Paper 2587* (Cambridge, Mass.: National Bureau of Economic Research, 1988).

[23] Jeremy Bulow and Kenneth Rogoff, "The Buyback Boondoggle," *Brookings Papers on Economic Activity,* 1988:2 (Washington, D.C.: The Brookings Institution).

[24] The low-income debtors present special problems, discussed in Louis Goreux's chapter in this volume, and the solution proposed below will not work for them. The Fund's claims on those countries must be replaced by concessional (ESAF) credits. But the problem facing the Fund in respect of the middle-income countries will arise eventually in respect of the low-income countries. They can use ESAF credits to repay their ordinary drawings on the Fund, in fact if not in form, but ESAF credits have to be repaid by 2002 (ten years after the final deadline for disbursement), and Goreux rightly asks what will happen then. Will ESAF be replenished by new loans (or the conversion of old loans into grants), allowing it to refinance its clients' debts, or will those countries have to draw on other Fund facilities to repay debts to ESAF?

[25] David Finch proposes one way out of this dilemma. Heavily indebted countries that are able to give "credible assurances that future debt servicing would be paid in full" should negotiate reductions in their debts to commercial banks and have access to a new, highly conditional Fund facility structured to provide them with additional credit. Countries that cannot offer such assurances should have access to another new facility with low conditionality, in order to refinance some of their obligations to the Fund, but they should repay the rest gradually. (C. David Finch, "An IMF Debt Plan," *The International Economy,* March/April 1989.) I have two difficulties with this approach. (1) Access to new Fund credit should not be made to depend on a country's ability to reach agreement with its commercial bank creditors. The ultimate success of a debt-reducing agreement may indeed depend on *prior* assurance that the debtor will have access to additional Fund credit. The Fund cannot be the main provider of the cash required to implement a debt reduction plan, but unused access to Fund credit may be an important assurance that the country will be able to meet its obligations to the banks. (2) There is something odd about an arrangement that imposes high conditionality on countries that are able to manage their affairs competently but low conditionality on countries that cannot do so—even though the arrangement offers additional Fund credit to the former and takes away some of it from the latter.

[26] These figures pertain to the situation before the 1989 agreement. Drawings under that agreement would add to Mexico's obligations, but repayments of old drawings would offset them partially. Use of the figures for Mexico should not be taken to imply that Mexico has failed to fulfill its obligations to the Fund. On the contrary, it has met its financial obligations fully and tried hard to carry out its policy commitments.

[27] International Monetary Fund, *Annual Report 1988,* p. 74.

[28] IMF Articles of Agreement Article V, Section 4.

[29] They might even be made to cover Mexico. Under present rules, a member may make an EFF drawing on top of an ordinary credit-tranche drawing if the two together do not exceed 165 per cent of quota. Mexico would be covered completely if this limit were raised to 200 per cent when the EFF limit was raised to 180 per cent. It should perhaps be emphasized that these revisions are meant mainly to facilitate the refinancing of mem-

bers' obligations, not to encourage larger drawings; in language used frequently in Fund decisions, the numbers are ceilings, not targets.

[30] This group includes Argentina, Brazil, Chile, Morocco, and the Philippines.

[31] The Managing Director of the Fund has stressed this point in recent statements; see, for example, *IMF Survey,* April 3, 1989, p. 99.

[32] It is not impossible to reconcile these two views. It can be argued, for example, that the EC is an "optimum currency area" within which exchange rates should be fixed, and that the whole world is not. Alternatively, it can be argued that the EMS is a Deutschemark zone, with one key currency, in which pegging is sensible and feasible. It can also be argued that capital controls have facilitated exchange rate management within the EMS. These issues are examined in Giavazzi and Giovanni, op. cit., Chapters 4–7, and in Peter B. Kenen, *Managing Exchange Rates* (New York: Council on Foreign Relations Press for the Royal Institute of International Affairs, 1988), Chapter 4.

[33] See, for example, Martin Feldstein, "The Case Against Trying to Stabilize the Dollar," *American Economic Review,* May 1989, pp. 36–40.

[34] For proposals of the first type, see John Williamson and Marcus H. Miller, *Targets and Indicators: A Blueprint for the International Coordination of Economic Policies* (Washington, D.C.: Institute for International Economics, 1987); their advocates appear to believe that foreign exchange markets are fairly well behaved, and that the main task is to influence monetary policies. For proposals of the second type, see Kenen, *Managing Exchange Rates,* op. cit., Chapters 3–4; their advocates tend to be critical of foreign exchange markets and believe that the main task is to influence the markets' expectations. The issues and evidence are reviewed skillfully in Paul R. Krugman, *Exchange-Rate Instability* (Cambridge, Mass.: MIT Press, 1988).

[35] Recent evidence and views are surveyed in Richard Marston, "Exchange Rate Coordination," in Martin Feldstein, ed., *International Economic Cooperation* (Chicago, Ill.: University of Chicago Press, 1988).

[36] Kenen, *Managing Exchange Rates,* op. cit., p. 26.

[37] Losses would occur if the dollar had depreciated in terms of the SDR over the lifetime of the account and the effects of the depreciation had not been offset by the net interest income of the account.

[38] A numerical illustration is given in Kenen, *Managing Exchange Rates,* op. cit., pp. 70–72; Jacques J. Polak's chapter in this volume suggests a different way of dealing with the problem of losses, but it would not increase U.S. reserves.

[39] For one such plan, see Kenen, *Financing, Adjustment, and the IMF,* op. cit., pp. 65–69.

Comment by C. David Finch:
Conditional Finance for Industrial Countries

In the preceding two chapters, Jacques Polak and Peter Kenen have addressed many aspects of the IMF role with industrial countries, but they have treated conditional financing lightly. In my view, they undervalue the past importance of conditional finance and, more importantly, avoid the most important current issue of international finance: the arrangements needed to assist the return of the U.S. balance of payments to viability.

While it is true that the enormous growth of the international banking system has drastically changed the role of conditional official finance, neither this development nor the continuing flexibility of exchange rates has eliminated the need for such finance. Monetary authority financing for balance-of-payments problems has remained important and will grow with the continuing attempts to produce more order in exchange rates among the major countries. At present, conditions attached to such financing for industrial countries are virtually nonexistent. But time will force a change if the weaknesses of the U.S. current account persist. Although any immediate needs are likely to be met through bilateral and major power understandings, there are many advantages for all sides in moving toward using the IMF. Such an evolution would reinvigorate international collaboration and have profoundly beneficial effects for the international monetary system.

In 1944, no question would have been raised about the need for official balance-of-payments financing as an essential element in plans to produce a better-functioning system. In 1989, with the key exchange rates flexible, the need is not so universally accepted. Yet in practice, official financing is still sought and used to limit disturbances to international monetary and trading conditions. In essence, the willingness to allow an exchange rate to depreciate only transforms a weakness from showing as a loss of exchange reserves to a weakness shown by accelerating price increases. And the desire for financial resources to limit these price increases creates a search for official finance very similar to that to replace exchange reserve losses. Thus in 1976 the United

Kingdom, despite newly introduced exchange rate flexibility, had virtually the same need for official financing that it had under fixed exchange rates in the late 1960s.

The growth of private financing, particularly by the commercial banks, has had perhaps an even stronger impact on the attitude toward official financing. Quite clearly, the original Bretton Woods concept of an IMF providing large financial resources for a wide range of industrial countries on a cyclically compensating pattern has proved to be totally mistaken. In 1989, no one doubts that the normal financing requirements of industrial countries will be met by the private capital markets. But that does not mean official financing has no remaining role. In domestic markets, commercial banks provide for the normal needs of the economy, but this financing is underpinned by a clear central bank commitment to act as lender of last resort when any major bank suffers a loss of confidence. So in the international sphere, the growth of private lending carries with it the danger of disruption when confidence is lost and in consequence creates a similar need for a lender of last resort. For developing countries, this was dramatically shown when Mexico had its crisis in 1982.[1] For industrial countries the need presently is less apparent, but in 1976, loss of confidence was the cause of problems for the United Kingdom that were met with official support through the IMF. The success of this conditional operation is one factor behind the present illusion that creditors of industrial countries are free from the dangers of losses shown in Latin America.

The recent balance-of-payments problems of the United States have demonstrated that an ebbing of confidence creates financing problems for even the largest country. In 1987, the loss of confidence was met by official financing, totaling probably over $120 billion, provided through purchases of U.S. dollars by other central banks. This financing, centering around the Group of Seven Louvre Accord of February 1987, was not conditional and not provided through the IMF. But it was official, it did have a joint objective to limit exchange rate disorder, and it was so effective in achieving that objective that a reassured private sector resumed capital flows sufficient to finance the U.S. savings gap and to cause the U.S. dollar to appreciate. Unfortunately, because there was no conditionality, continuing U.S. action to reduce that gap was not assured, and the underlying payments weakness persists.

This was not due to U.S. resistance. To the contrary, Secretary Baker was the originator of the joint approach, using it in September 1985 to achieve the Plaza Agreement to facilitate the orderly depreciation of the U.S. dollar needed to reduce trade tensions. And the U.S. Congress had shown its concern about the savings gap independently when it enacted the Gramm-Rudman-Hollings limits. No, the absence of conditionality stems from the attitude of the governments with payments surpluses that, despite the desire of their financial officials to see an improvement in U.S. savings, were so anxious to limit U.S. dollar depreciation that they freely supplied the official support. This readiness to make almost unlimited finance available owed much to the strength of political presssures inevitable under G-7 procedures.

Fundamentally, by determining policies on monetary financing in a political forum, it allows other issues to intrude. In particular, governments with payments surpluses find themselves held responsible for the U.S. dollar exchange rate. Without any separation available, their politicians are vulnerable to requests from lobbies of their exporters to the United States that a depreciation of the U.S. dollar be prevented. This attitude is understandable but shortsighted. Politically, depreciation is an essential element in reducing political pressure in the United States for restraints on those exports. And the economic reality is that, in the long term, the scope for exports to the United States is dependent on an early return to better payments balance. The longer the overall U.S. current account deficit persists, the greater the debt service payments that directly reduce future exports to the United States.

The setting may also encourage some mercantilist political sentiment that welcomes the declining economic power of the United States implicit in the current rapid build-up of foreign debt. It takes a deep understanding of the issues to recognize that too easy an acceptance of the present imbalances leads to serious danger for all participants in the world economy. As noted above, the United States is all too likely to react to its growing weakness by abandoning its commitment to open trade. This would be devastating to the current GATT round of trade negotiations, the success of which is crucial in this period of waning U.S. hegemony. Moreover, no one should underestimate the damage to all countries from weakness in the key reserve currency—a weakness that becomes the more dangerous the slower the reactions.

The technical experts of the financial authorities for all the G-7 countries are of course acutely aware of the concerns widely expressed by economists about the sustainability of the present U.S. imbalance and already have tried to ensure that the G-7 collaboration encourages a U.S. response. They certainly favor continuing reduction of the U.S. current account deficit through faster reduction of the U.S. fiscal deficit. But the present unconditional financing mechanism has made the efforts of the technical experts virtually fruitless. It is all too likely that when the next round of U.S. dollar weakness returns, they will remain ineffective.

It now seems likely to be triggered by rising pressure on resources, causing interest rates to rise in the surplus countries, particularly Japan and Germany. Ultimately the downward pressure on the U.S. dollar will become strong enough to raise the issue of official financing.

Withholding that financing until the U.S. public is made aware of the extent of their dependence on foreign savings could be a key element in strengthening U.S. public support for effective action to reduce the U.S. fiscal deficit. An unchecked drop in the dollar would quickly lead to a rise in U.S. prices and especially in interest rates.

Will this opportunity be used? At present, it seems rather unlikely. Withholding of exchange support would have to last long enough for the needed U.S. action to achieve adequate political momentum. The major surplus countries are most unlikely to be ready to face the political risks involved. They will fear being held directly responsible for a "hard landing" involving significant increases in unemployment from cumulating private market reactions.

Moreover, without a multilateral source of financing, effective attempts to introduce conditions would have a strongly bilateral flavor. Financing seems certain to be heavily concentrated on Japan. The reaction in the United States and Japan to this dependence—particularly if financing is delayed sufficiently to facilitate U.S. fiscal action—would undoubtedly increase the role of those suspicious that non-economic political motives have been important. Even if the eventual financing has little conditionality, concerns on both sides may well grow, particularly as a recurrence of the U.S. gap may well be expected. Any G-7 facade that can be provided will help but cannot substitute adequately for an identifiable financial intermediary with a clear non-political role.

What are the advantages of an IMF framework? It separates the payments deficit from other issues and focuses political attention on the measures necessary to reverse dependence on foreign official support. The experience of the United Kingdom in 1976 once again is instructive.[2] Although the role of the IMF was dependent on backing by the United States and Germany, local press attention focused on the adequacy of the U.K.'s fiscal measures to assure payments recovery—not on what outside governments were doing. And because the private market had the same economic concerns, private capital quickly showed its confidence that the process would generate the right policies by giving support well before the agreement was completed.

How would a beginning be made toward an IMF role in meeting the inevitable U.S. official financial needs? The first step would have to be discussion among the G-3 financial authorities. The attitude of U.S. officials would be crucial. They would need to be convinced that the arrangements would be adequate in size to meet their financing needs as well as effectively supportive of their struggle to overcome the obstacles to the domestic adjustment measures. More precisely, to compensate for any appearance of weakness involved in acceptance of IMF procedures, it will be essential to be able to show that the system is designed—and has the strength needed—to protect the U.S. economy from the periodic strains inevitable for the issuer of the principal reserve currency. It must also be totally evident that the sole condition for this protection is the achievement of sustainable overall payments balance.

As the main suppliers of resources, Japan and Germany would need assurance that the framework was secure in its eventual achievement of U.S. financial adjustment. "Eventual" would be the key concept, as they would have to be ready to accept a process designed to maintain pressure for further adjustment if initial efforts proved inadequate. They would be fully aware that in a simple confrontation they would have little choice but to provide the finance. Their greatest protection arises from the inevitable focus on successful adjustment that is ensured by maturing medium-term repayments in an IMF framework.

How would the process be initiated? The immediate step to show seriousness of intent would be an agreement on major new quota increases, giving Japan second place in the IMF and greatly increasing the relative role of other surplus countries. This would be important as much for its signal of renewed industrial country reliance on the IMF as for the resources provided. These resources would certainly need to be supplemented to meet the immense scale of present U.S. dollar liabilities. This would require an increase of the existing General Arrangements to Borrow (GAB)[3] at least to the level of $200 billion mentioned by Gyohten in his proposal last year for a new agency to underwrite stabilizing intervention.[4] For countries other than the United States, the necessary commitments to the GAB are not difficult, as they involve only the composition of central foreign assets. To underscore the comprehensiveness of the financing proposals, there should be a matching major increase in the swap lines between central banks of the main industrial countries. This would ensure that immediate resources could be made available while the adjustment measures are being developed to meet the IMF conditionality requirements.

Those developing an IMF role would have to focus early on their power to guide the formulation of these conditions. The most basic issue would relate to staff and management appointments. Renewed efforts would be imperative to ensure that all major parties felt secure about the integrity with which their plans would be executed. And a fresh look at their effective mechanisms for control over IMF decisions might lead to some upgrading of the status of their IMF Executive Directors, although their existing veto rights under the GAB may be considered to give adequate direct control.

As was the case for the United Kingdom, the mechanics of conditionality would have to evolve to meet the unique U.S. conditions. Although procedural decisions cannot be determined very far in advance, one innovation might involve the inclusion of a request for policy assurances from the U.S. Congress. The U.S. administration might well feel that continuing implementation of a fiscal program would be facilitated if it were endorsed by the U.S. Congress. In effect, Gramm-Rudman-Hollings would be adapted to a new mechanism of public commitment to the IMF.

In all probability, actual implementing decisions on the mechanics of conditionality might not be needed for some years. Agreement on an IMF framework by itself would most likely be used by the U.S. administration to press adjustment actions adequate to keep U.S. capital requirements down to sustainable levels. Many industrial countries have found the threat to involve the IMF helpful to preemptive action. Nevertheless, the acceptance of an IMF framework for the United States—even if in practice largely symbolic—would reinvigorate international cooperation. It would clearly maintain the usability of IMF conditional finance for other industrial countries. This may not be needed by most European countries now in the European Community, but even some of these countries—for example, Italy and the United Kingdom—might still welcome an IMF role to avoid appearing to act at the dictation of Germany, the strongest European Community country. The reassertion of an IMF role with industrial countries would, moreover, strengthen the prospects for a new IMF initiative to oversee an early definitive passage of individual Latin American countries from the devastating insecurity of perpetual debt negotiations.

The collective responsibility shown by an agreement on IMF financing would also greatly facilitate attempts to return to more stability of exchange rates between the major powers. The public political commitment to exchange rate stability necessary to deliver supporting fiscal and monetary actions will be much more easily given when the United States has accepted a system identifying its financing responsibilities and when all feel backed by assured resource availability. Such developments in the IMF field obviously work in favor of strengthening similar improvements for the GATT in the trade field.

There are many reasons for doubt. The loss of U.S. hegemony means that much more widespread support will be necessary for effective international operations. Much will depend upon the actual developments and whether they demonstrate early the dangers of regionalism in a dramatically changing world. But it is evident that the outcome will above all depend on the strength and effectiveness of the intellectual support developed for an international financing mechanism. It is to be emphasized that in no sense should support for the IMF be interpreted as a replacement of the G-7 or similar great-power arrangements. They will continue to be essential for the political cohesion without which the IMF will be irrelevant. Any IMF role is purely supplementary—designed primarily to provide centralized conditional financing. However, with memories of an IMF role with industrial countries fast fading, the time available for the IMF to recover its credibility is relatively short. Perhaps it is best if the debate before the informed public can be focused on the absence of workable alternatives. Somewhat like Churchill's famous defense of democracy, attempting to maintain international monetary order through a universal institution may have its problems, but it is far better than all the alternatives.

Notes

[1] The massive official effort to provide last-resort financing for Mexico is well documented by Joseph Kraft, "The Mexican Rescue," Group of Thirty, 1984. Although the IMF was central to the plans, it is remarkable how much importance is given to the framework and how little attention to the IMF staff.

[2] The overcoming of the 1976 sterling crisis is recorded step-by-step by Stephen Fay and Hugo Young, *The Day the Pound Nearly Died,* a reprint from the *Sunday Times* (London: *Sunday Times,* 1978). Once again, the account features the framework with no interest in the mechanics of IMF procedures.

[3] This is in accord with the intent of the original arrangements, completed in 1962. They were made "when it seemed possible that the United States might wish to use the Fund's resources in substantial accounts." Joseph Gold, *Legal and Institutional Aspects of the International Monetary System: Selected Essays* (Washington, D.C.: International Monetary Fund, 1979), p. 448.

[4] Proposal made by Toyoo Gyohten in "Collaring Exchange Markets," *The International Economy,* May-June 1988, pp. 36–38.

IV. The IMF and the Developing Countries

Chapter 3

Strengthening IMF Programs in Highly Indebted Countries

Jeffrey D. Sachs

Introduction

The International Monetary Fund is a great institution that has not lived up to its potential in recent years. Its design, creation, and operation are among the most splendid achievements of the postwar era. The IMF represents the most important attempt in history to apply the scientific understanding of economic forces to improve the stability of the world economy, and it is the world's greatest repository of practical macroeconomic experience. Moreover, successful economic policymakers around the world received their on-the-job training as staff members of the Fund.

Yet today the IMF's stewardship is clearly in crisis. This is nowhere more evident than in its role among the highly indebted countries (HICs). One motivation for creating the IMF was to help the world economy overcome an occurrence such as the debt crisis.[1] Article I, Section (v), of the Articles of Agreement states that one goal of the Fund is to provide members "with the opportunity to correct maladjustments in their balance of payments without resorting to measures destructive of national or international prosperity."[2] This goal obviously has not been met. Latin America and other highly indebted regions have suffered profound setbacks to "national prosperity" in the past decade—even with the constant guidance and support of the IMF.

After almost seven years of crisis, the debtor countries are still far from regaining creditworthiness; many if not most IMF programs in the HICs are now honored in the breach; and the IMF is the object of intense dislike among large segments of the population in Latin America and Sub-Saharan Africa. Many governments have forgone economic and technical assistance from the IMF merely to keep the it at arm's length.

In this chapter, I speculate on some new directions for the IMF to help improve its record in the indebted developing countries.[3] The new Brady Plan offers a critical opportunity for the IMF to redirect its policies. By shifting the IMF's focus from debt servicing to debt reduction, the Brady Plan offers the hope that the IMF can formulate more realistic programs for the heavily indebted countries. There are, however, several disquieting problems already evident in the early stages of the Plan's impelementation.

This chapter is organized as follows. The next section discusses the increasing non-compliance with IMF programs and argues that the deterioration is closely related to the flawed management of the debt crisis. Attention is given to the proper role of the IMF in the newly formulated Brady Plan. The third section turns to the specifics of the IMF's "standard" program, and the question of exchange rate management is discussed at some length. I suggest that the Fund has become too aggressive in urging devaluations, partly as a result of its attempt (during the pre-Brady Plan phase of the debt crisis) to maximize a country's debt servicing capacity in the short term to the neglect of other goals. The next section addresses the distributional effects of IMF programs, stressing how remarkably little the IMF has focused on this most important problem and proposing some steps for increasing the attention devoted to this issue.

The IMF's Excessive Secrecy

Before proceeding, I must stress the limitations of this review of IMF policies, which is necessarily impressionistic and non-quantitative because of the secretive nature of IMF programs. This secrecy makes it extremely difficult for outside observers to prepare a serious quantitative appraisal of IMF policies.[4] In an earlier draft of this chapter, I sought to include a brief quantitative assessment of compliance with IMF programs prepared by the IMF itself, but was requested by the Fund to eliminate the material on the grounds that it was confidential.

For these reasons, I must limit myself to a selective view of IMF programs. My detailed knowledge and expertise regarding IMF programs rests mainly on the experiences of Latin American countries. My most intimate knowledge of Fund programs arises from the direct experience of working with several governments (Bolivia, Ecuador, and Venezuela) in IMF negotiations in recent years.

There is no legitimate reason for the IMF to operate in such secrecy. Aside from very special matters (e.g., the timing of exchange rate changes), there is little in country programs that could not usefully be made public. A good model for the Fund would be the Federal Open Market Committee of the U.S. Federal Reserve System, which meets privately to discuss highly sensitive matters, but then, with a lag of several weeks, issues the minutes of each meeting. When IMF country programs are approved, these programs and the supporting technical analysis could be made public with a similar time lapse. For historical purposes, all archival materials related to IMF programs and broader policy issues more than five years old could be made available for scholarly analysis.

The excessive secrecy of the IMF also hinders a proper oversight of the institution by the legislatures of the member countries, which are regularly asked to approve budgetary appropriations to support IMF activities. When the U.S. Congress is asked, probably in 1990, to approve a new quota increase for the IMF, it should be able to assess that quota increase in light of the record of the IMF. Under current arrangements, there will be no way for Congress to obtain an objective assessment of the Fund's activities based on the full documentary evidence now held by the IMF itself.

The Debt Crisis and the Failure of the IMF in the 1980s

The IMF's recent record in the debtor countries is one of failure. The failure was predictable, and the IMF could have done much better. The IMF is committed to restoring balance-of-payments viability in the medium term to countries with an external financing crisis. Viability here refers to the capacity of a country to meet its international financial obligations without undermining national prosperity and on a *routine* basis (i.e., without further reschedulings, new concerted loans, or further negotiated reductions in the debt). Viability by this standard has been restored for few if any of the thirty-nine or so countries that have been engaged in the past decade in the restructuring of their commercial bank debt.[5] On the even tougher standard of renewing creditworthiness (that is, the capacity to borrow from international capital markets on normal market terms), none of the thirty-nine countries has clearly succeeded. Most of the problem debtor countries are further away than ever from renewed creditworthiness.

There are several indicators that point to a prima facie case of failure. First, there has been a sharp decline in compliance with IMF conditionality in recent years, suggesting that IMF programs are unrealistic in their design. Second, the secondary market prices of commercial bank debts have plummeted over the past four years, indicating that countries are drifting further and further away from a restoration of creditworthiness. Third, so-called new money packages have virtually disappeared since 1984, with only a few of the largest countries able to attract any of the new money.[6] Even for these countries, the new money packages have become less and less routine and have required ever greater lengths to negotiate. Fourth, traditional indicators of debt-servicing burdens have hardly improved, or have even worsened since 1981, despite the repeatedly optimistic forecasts of the IMF. Fifth, and most damning, the overall macroeconomic situation in Latin America has steadily deteriorated, with outbreaks of virulent high inflations in Argentina, Brazil, and Peru, and growing social unrest and violence in almost all countries in the region.

These indicators of failure are particularly troubling for the IMF since the institution transferred billions of dollars of resources to the heavily indebted countries during the 1980s, ostensibly to help them restore viability to their balances of payments, as shown in Table 1.[7] It now seems clear that the lending had a different effect, if not a different purpose: It helped the debtor countries meet their interest payments to the commercial banks, without restoring the medium-term viability of their balances of payments. Throughout the 1980s, until 1987, official creditors put net money (i.e., net resource transfers) into the debtor countries, while the banks took the money out in interest payments—a pattern evident in Table 1. By 1989, it had become clear that the IMF and the World Bank had put their funds at significant risk, to the benefit of the commercial banks that held claims on the heavily indebted countries.

The IMF can defend itself against some of the disastrous record of macroeconomic collapse of the debtor countries in the 1980s. Clearly, the IMF did not create the debt crisis, and it was bound to lose popularity in countries facing a period of prolonged austerity in response to the cutback in private lending. The IMF also played a vital role in helping to avert a financial crisis in the early years of the debt crisis (particularly 1982–84). Moreover, there is no evidence that IMF programs have actually hurt the countries that have undertaken them—at least compared with countries that have had no program at all. Indeed, there is evidence that Fund programs, when followed, have actually helped countries to meet their economic objectives.

Some Reasons for Failure

The IMF's greatest shortcoming was to suppose, up until the announcement of the Brady Plan, that the only way to solve a country's debt crisis was through internal adjustment sufficient to fully finance the external

Table 1. Net Resource Transfers from Official and Private Creditors to the Heavily Indebted Countries, 1980–87 ($ millions)

Net Resource Transfers	1982	1983	1984	1985	1986	1987
Official Creditors						
IMF	2,320	6,518	3,325	1,671	− 275	− 1,383
World Bank, IDA	921	1,398	1,597	949	1,078	− 557
Other	1,866	1,288	4,354	− 316	− 223	− 404
Subtotal	5,107	9,204	9,276	2,304	580	− 2,344
Private Creditors						
Suppliers	522	1,009	− 432	− 254	− 301	− 60
Financial Markets	5,780	− 3,785	− 10,449	− 18,375	− 19,096	− 14,106
Subtotal	6,201	− 2,861	− 10,950	− 18,670	− 19,428	− 14,198
Total	11,308	6,343	− 1,674	− 16,366	− 18,848	− 16,542

Source: *World Bank Debt Tables, 1988–89*, Volume 1, Analysis and Summary Tables, "Highly Indebted Countries," pp. 30–31. Note that net resource transfer is defined as net flows minus total interest payments for all creditors except the IMF. For the IMF, net resource transfer is defined as IMF purchases minus repurchases.

debt. This is of course is a radically historical proposition. In almost every historical episode of a widespread debt crisis, significant debt reduction has been a part of the resolution.[8] The bias against debt reduction in the 1980s of course can be explained by the focus on saving the major commercial banks that had overlent in the 1970s. The official community was successful in that goal, and by 1986 the acute financial crisis for the creditor institutions had passed. But even as late as the Fund's 1988 review of conditionality, the Fund showed its continuing neglect of a central role for debt reduction.

Clearly there is the question of how much responsibility should be attributed to the IMF versus the U.S. government for the neglect of debt reduction until U.S. Treasury Secretary Nicholas Brady's speech of March 10, 1989. Reliable press reports have indicated for the past three years that the IMF Managing Director, Michel Camdessus, was prepared to lead the Fund in the more constructive direction of debt reduction, but that he encountered enormous resistance from the U.S. Treasury.[9] Nonetheless, the IMF management has the role of clearly advising the world community as to what is needed to restore financial and economic stability, even in the face of U.S. Treasury resistance. Similarly, the IMF's professional staff has the responsibility of clearly advising the Executive Board as to what is needed. In both respects, the IMF fell short of meeting its responsibilities.

Because of its neglect of the debt reduction option, the IMF placed itself in a position of great vulnerability vis-à-vis the commercial banks. No matter how high a country's commercial bank debt, or how small the prospect for repayment, IMF programs were designed under the *presumption* that the interest on bank debt would be fully serviced. Indeed, under the doctrine of "assured financing" (which is now being modified by the Brady Plan), countries generally had to agree to continued debt servicing in their negotiations with the creditor banks as a precondition for getting an IMF program.[10] In this sense, the IMF found itself playing the role, wittingly or unwittingly, of bill collector for the banks. The IMF has vigorously rejected this characterization, but it is easy to see how it came to be viewed this way by the debtor countries.

The presumption of full-interest servicing has given enormous bargaining power to the commercial banks in recent years and also has led to a burgeoning of unrealistic programs. The banks understood, very simply, that if the debtor countries did not agree to a schedule for clearing arrears and did not agree to keep current on interest payments, they would not get an IMF program. Thus the banks were able to "hang tough" and wait for recalcitrant debtors to return to the fold.

In the beginning years of the crisis, this bargaining power was tempered by the Fund's insistence that the creditor banks agree to a "new money package" (i.e., a partial refinancing of interest due) as a prerequisite to an IMF agreement. Over time, however, the Fund's interest or ability to press for new money packages waned, to the point where the vast majority of countries have had little chance of getting a new money package, and where the packages that have been concluded generally provide for only a low level of financing. In 1987 and 1988, only two countries were able to arrange new money packages (Argentina in 1987 and Brazil in 1988), despite the fact that dozens of countries were actively involved in bank debt restructurings. The vast majority of countries were left without any refinancing of the interest payments falling due.

The result is that for several years, almost all IMF programs have been based on the unrealistic assumption that the country will remain current on all interest payments to the commercial banks. This, in turn, has led to two kinds of problems: the increasing rate of breakdown of Fund programs, as a result of their built-in unrealism about the extent of feasible debt servicing; and the pressure on the Fund to consent to programs that are clearly inadequate.

Weakness of IMF Conditionality with a Debt Overhang

Elsewhere, I have argued that an overhang of debt greatly weakens the prospects for Fund conditionality.[11] This is because the debt overhang acts like a tax on economic reforms: The country bears the cost of reforms (like an investment), while the foreign creditors appropriate much of the benefits. This overhang acts not only as a disincentive to a government to carry out a program of economic reform, but also as a political barrier to the election of reformist candidates, who seem to offer more years of austerity for the sake of continued debt servicing. One result, not surprisingly, is that a debtor government with an IMF program has had a very hard time making a reform effort stick: it simply has been too vulnerable to internal political attack to be able to follow through on the program.

The evidence on compliance with Fund programs would seem to bear out this worry. As detailed in Sachs, compliance with Fund programs has long been mediocre. Beveridge and Kelley, Doe, and Haggard all find a record of mediocre compliance at best, but one that seems to be getting worse over time. Edwards presents some evidence on the mediocre compliance with conditionality of programs negotiated in 1983, with his key results reproduced in Table 2.[12] The evidence presented in the IMF's 1988 review of conditionality also suggests that, since 1983, the rate of compliance has been decreasing sharply, down to less than one-third compliance with program performance criteria in the most recent years. Of course, given the secrecy surrounding IMF programs, it is impossible to evaluate the seriousness of the breaches or the reasons for them (e.g., internal policy failures versus external shocks).

David Finch, former Director of the Department of Exchange and Trade Relations of the IMF, has written eloquently about the flip side of these failures: the pressures on the Fund from "major shareholders" to adopt unrealistic programs, even when it is clear that the terms of an agreement will almost surely *not* be fulfilled. He writes of Argentina as a case in which there were "pressures to involve the IMF in an agreement where political solutions [in Argentina] won't allow a solution to the balance of payments problem . . . [T]he IMF has been forced to continue lending [to Argentina] to maintain the facade of the debt strategy."[13] In plain terms, the U.S. government was fearful that Argentina would default to the commercial banks in the absence of new IMF money, which was helping to fund the interest payments. The United States therefore pressured the Fund to maintain a program with Argentina despite the failure of the Argentine government to live up to earlier agreements.

Table 2. Compliance with Conditionality of Thirty-Four Programs Approved in 1983 (percentage of countries that comply)

Target	1983	1984	1985
Government deficit to GDP	30.3	18.8	43.5
Changes in domestic credit	54.8	46.4	40.9
Changes in net domestic credit to the government	72.0	52.8	52.4

Source: S. Edwards, "The Internatioal Monetary Fund and the Developing Countries: A Critical Evaluation," *NBER Working Paper Series*, No. 2909, March 1989, compiled from internal IMF data.

This charade finally collapsed in 1988, but not in a constructive way. When it became overwhelmingly clear that Argentina was unable to service its debts—and therefore to comply with any IMF program based on the assumption of substantial interest servicing—the IMF Managing Director tried privately to arrange a program of debt reduction for Argentina. According to press reports, this initiative was stymied by the U.S. Treasury. As a result of the failure of the attempt, and the consequent inability to piece together a program for Argentina with even a fig leaf of plausibility, the IMF finally pulled back from new lending in the fall of 1988. As the U.S. Treasury had long feared, Argentina did indeed fall into deep arrears to the commercial banks and eventually into hyperinflation in the spring of 1989.

Strengthening Conditionality through Debt Reduction: The Example of Bolivia

Bolivia represents an important exception to the overall debt strategy during 1986–89—one that demonstrates the merits of a program of deep debt reduction as well as the need for the IMF's tolerance of arrears during the period of negotiations over debt reduction.[14]

As is widely known, the Bolivian situation as of mid–1985 was unparalleled in the world. Inflation had reached 24,000 per cent in the twelve-month period prior to July 1985. Real per capita Gross Domestic

Product (GDP) had declined by about 30 per cent since 1980. Debt-service payments to the banks had been suspended in May 1984, almost sixteen months before the Paz Estenssoro government took office. The new Bolivian government came to office in August 1985 and immediately launched a stabilization and liberalization program of remarkable dimensions.[15] The program almost immediately stopped the hyperinflation and stabilized the exchange rate. However, serious external shocks (the collapse of tin and natural gas prices on world markets) soon shook the program and threatened to plunge the country back into hyperinflation.

In early 1986, the Bolivians and the IMF began negotiations for a stand-by program to help support a stabilization program that had been put in place the previous summer. In March 1986, the Fund mission in Bolivia was insisting upon another politically explosive devaluation of the peso (just two months after the peso had been stabilized!), with the stated purpose of making room for Bolivia to resume partial interest payments to the commercial banks. The Bolivian authorities vigorously resisted IMF demands for a new devaluation and a resumption of interest payments. In the end, the Fund staff backed down, and the IMF Board allowed the stand-by program to go forward with a continuing buildup of arrears to the commercial banks.[16]

With three years of hindsight, this decision seems emphatically correct, even fairly obvious.[17] The arrears served two purposes. First, they "financed" a realistic adjustment program, so that the IMF could set realistic targets. Second and equally important, they demonstrated to the commercial banks that the IMF was not simply going to defend their loans, and that the time had come to make a more realistic accommodation with the Bolivian government.

As a result of this realism, the Bolivian program has been among the most successful in the world, with continued low inflation and rising growth, based on a strategy of liberalization and budget austerity. Bolivian politics have become far more stable and supportive of stabilization, even as the political situation in Bolivia's neighbors has deteriorated sharply, and the role of the IMF is widely accepted.[18] The government's political opponents could not accuse the IMF and the government of squeezing Bolivia for the sake of the foreign banks. The IMF was recognized as a net provider of funds—and not as a bill collector for the banks.

In the face of continuing arrears, the commercial banks finally acceded to significant debt reduction for Bolivia with the debt "buyback" program of 1988 and 1989.[19] This program has led (as of May 1989) to a reduction of more than two-thirds of the bank debt at a price of 11 cents per dollar, but only after years of negotiation and stalling by the banks. Without the Fund's forbearance of Bolivia's arrears, and without the time granted Bolivia to negotiate the program, the buyback would not have taken place.

The IMF and the Brady Plan

The Brady Plan introduced in March 1989 represents an important new step in the debt strategy, with the focus shifting finally to debt reduction. Secretary Brady outlined three major roles for the IMF in this new phase of debt management. First, as before, the IMF is to oversee programs of economic reform in the debtor countries. Second, the IMF is to allow some of its lending to be used to support debt reduction operations, mainly by financing direct debt buybacks or enhancing bonds to be used in debt-for-bond swaps.[20] Third, the IMF is to have new freedom to commence lending to debtor countries under an IMF program even before negotiations with commercial banks have been completed.[21] The idea is to relax the policy of "assured financing" so that commercial banks cannot delay an IMF program by refusing to agree to the requisite amount of new loans or debt reduction.

The Brady Plan is clearly a vital step forward in restoring realism to IMF programs. There are, however, some reasons for worry about the formulation of the Brady Plan as of July 1989. The main and overriding problem is the Plan's focus on so-called voluntary, market-based mechanisms for debt reduction. "Voluntary" debt reduction is almost surely going to prove inadequate to meeting the financial needs of the debtor countries.[22]

The basic idea of "voluntary" mechanisms is that individual banks should have the option of choosing to participate in a debt reduction operation, or instead, to hold on to the original bank claim. In a typical debt reduction operation, for example, a debtor country might offer to exchange existing debt for a collateralized bond with a sub-market interest rate. The bond would offer a lower present value of repayments but would have the enhancement of collateralization, perhaps made possible by loans from the IMF. Each bank would then have the option to accept the new bond or to stick with the original claim, which would lack the enhancement.

The fundamental problem with such a voluntary approach, of course, is the "free rider" problem. Even if each bank fully understands that the debtor country can service only half of the debt (and therefore needs an overall reduction of the debt by half), each bank will resist participating in the debt reduction so that the other banks will grant the necessary reduction. Suppose that enough banks in fact do grant the reduction so that the country becomes fully creditworthy. Then, any bank that holds out (that is, rejects the bond swap) with its own small claim on the country will find that it is fully repaid. The paradox is clear: If debt reduction is to be adequate to restore creditworthiness, then each bank will have the incentive to avoid participation!

There are other related reasons why voluntarism is harmful to the process of achieving deep debt reduction. First, bank managers are particularly afraid of granting a debtor country concessions that are greater than those offered by their competitors. Morgan Guaranty, for example, might be willing to grant a 50-per-cent cut in the debt burden to Mexico, but only if Citicorp does so as well.[23] Second, bank managers want debt reduction to appear unavoidable—"forced" upon the bank by bank regulators and official creditor institutions. By being forced to take action, the management cannot be second-guessed by disgruntled shareholders. For these reasons, many if not all leading banks privately reject the workability of "voluntarism" on the grounds that it actually undermines the flexibility of bank managers to agree to debt reduction.

The key to achieving adequate debt reduction, therefore, is to avoid the voluntarism of the Brady approach and to insist on an across-the-board participation of the banks, with no free riders. The IMF would be well-placed to lead the effort in achieving across-the-board participation, just as it led the effort to achieve concerted participation in the "new money packages" of the earlier phase of the debt management strategy. In the case of the new money packages, the need for the IMF to press the banks for across-the-board participation was obvious. The same role for the IMF is needed in the case of debt reduction.[24]

The IMF can go beyond moral suasion. Recent legal analysis, both within the IMF and among independent commentators, suggests that the IMF Articles of Agreement provide a mechanism for enforcing across-the-board bank participation in debt reduction. Article VIII, Section 2(b), allows the Fund to approve exchange restrictions of member countries, thereby protecting the countries from any legal challenge that might arise from those restrictions. It appears that the IMF could use this mechanism to allow debtor governments to restrict interest payments to recalcitrant banks that refuse to participate in concerted debt-reduction programs. By doing so, the IMF would immunize the debtor country from lawsuits by the hold-out banks and thereby eliminate any incentive that they might have to resist participation in the debt reduction scheme.

In light of this analysis, it is particularly disappointing that the IMF's initial staff assessments of the Fund's role in debt reduction following the announcement of the Brady Plan virtually neglected any analysis of the strategic difficulties with the Plan's voluntary approach. As usual, the U.S. Treasury called the shots, and the IMF staff has followed in step with the U.S. framework.

In order for the IMF to adopt a bolder role in guiding a process of concerted debt reduction—a role that will soon prove necessary after the limitations to "voluntarism" are more widely appreciated—the Fund must become better equipped to judge how much debt reduction is actually necessary. In principle, such a judgment already lies within the purview of the IMF, since the technical staff is already supposed to assess the medium-term viability of a country's balance of payments. In practice, however, the IMF still focuses far too much attention on short-term cash flow needs rather than on medium-term viability. Under current IMF methodology, for example, the IMF makes little distinction between a scenario in which half the interest due is permanently cancelled via debt reduction and a scenario in which half the interest due is refinanced through a new long-term loan. These two cases differ, of course, in their effects on the country's medium-term prospects, but from a short-term cash flow perspective, they might look identical. Thus the IMF continues to be vague about how much of a given financing gap should be filled by "new money" (i.e., interest refinancing) rather than debt reduction.

Recent theoretical analyses of the "debt overhang"[25] distinguish between even the *short-term* consequences of new money versus debt reduction by arguing that a debt overhang has deleterious effects on the economy even when the cash-flow burden of an overhang is relieved in the short term by new lending. Even when a country "solves" its cash-flow problem by new loans rather than sustained debt reduction, the public is still aware of the long-term burden of the debt on the national budget. This can result, even in the short term, in higher interest rates on domestic public sector debt; in anticipations of future tax increases that depress current investment rates; in concern about stalemates over future debt negotiations; in expectations of future inflationary financing, etc. The IMF should be far more conscious of the differences between new money and debt reduction (and the relative advantages of debt reduction in the case of a large overhang) than it has been to date.

Another source of concern about the efficacy of the Brady Plan is the Fund's wavering approach to the question of debtor-country arrears to commercial banks. As of July 1989, the IMF stand on arrears in the context of the Brady Plan has been cautious and ambiguous. The Executive Board has recognized that arrears might be unavoidable during the process of negotiating a debt reduction program, but it has at the same time continued to insist that arrears should be avoided as much as possible.[26]

The problem with this approach is that the Fund has so far failed to acknowledge (at least in public) that arrears play a strategic role in bringing about debt reduction—and not just a role in filling a financial gap during a negotiating period. The banks will be willing to make concessions on debt reduction only if they believe that the alternative for them would be a still smaller cash flow because of arrears. Official forbearance of arrears (e.g., continued IMF lending in the face of a country's growing arrears to the commercial banks—or better yet, the invocation of Article VIII approval for non-payments) would send a strong signal to the banks that they will not gain by holding out in negotiations. Thus if the IMF wants to speed the process of debt reduction, it should be less coy in its attitude to arrears.

The Content of IMF Conditionality

Most of the focus of this chapter has been on the debt crisis as a barrier to effective IMF programs, in the belief that the debt overhang has represented by far the greatest source of failure for IMF programs in the 1980s. This section and the next turn to the substance of IMF conditionality, focusing mainly on the questions of exchange rate management and the income distributional effects of IMF conditionality.

On the whole, the Fund's basic economic framework, which links most countries' external problems either to fiscal mismanagement or to clearly identifiable external shocks merits *strong* endorsement. The Fund's emphasis on fiscal policy mismanagement as the key source of balance-of-payments problems is its main strength and is indeed the core "truth" of its strategy. The Fund's great contribution, in my opinion, is to act as an outside "auditor" of governments that have been prone to fiscal abuses. This helps not only foreign creditors but also the debtor country's citizens, who are the main victims of fiscal abuses.

Exchange Rate Management and Conditionality

The greatest need for conceptual rethinking comes not in the emphasis on fiscal balance but in exchange rate management. For its twenty-five years, the Fund championed exchange rate stability. Exchange rates were to be changed only rarely, and the fixed rates were to serve as a discipline on fiscal policy and inflation. IMF loans were often made to help countries preserve a given exchange rate. More recently, the Fund has abandoned this policy and now almost invariably *demands* devaluations to spur the growth of the tradeables sector, even in circumstances where a given pegged exchange rate can be defended.[27] In this shift of emphasis, the Fund has downplayed the old argument that the fixed rate could be a fulcrum for fiscal discipline and a nominal anchor against inflation.

The change in focus probably has more to do with the debt strategy of recent years than with the error of the earlier Fund policies. The goal has been to depreciate the real exchange rate sharply in order to foster the maximal outward transfer of resources. This policy can be self-defeating, however: Nominal devaluations may not stick as real devaluations, and excessive inflation resulting from an aggressive attempt to achieve a real depreciation can undermine a government's legitimacy and thus its capacity to enforce fiscal discipline. In the end, I would suggest that the intense pressure for trade surpluses via devaluation has undermined many governments in Latin America and thereby may have reduced rather than enhanced the long-term capacity of many countries to transfer resources abroad.

It is beyond the scope of this chapter to give a detailed account of appropriate exchange rate policies, but at least a few basic points can be stressed. There are enormous efficiency gains associated with a *unified* exchange rate on the current account, so the Fund is almost always correct in stressing devaluations in circumstances in which governments otherwise would be *rationing* foreign exchange on the current account.

Similarly, when budget deficits are large and the government must rely on inflationary financing, there is little gained from a temporary fixing of the exchange rate. The result will almost surely be to run down the foreign exchange reserves, leading to a collapse of the pegged rate. The exchange rate should be pegged in the face of a large budget deficit only (1) if there are good prospects for closing the budget deficit during the period in which the exchange rate peg remains viable, or (2) if nonmonetary sources of financing are available. The Fund should remember, however, that fixing the exchange rate can be an important practical *prerequisite* for subsequent budgetary reforms. A pegged rate can lead to a slowdown in inflation, with automatic positive effects on real tax collections (the so-called Tanzi effect stressed by Vito Tanzi of the IMF) and perhaps with positive political effects that may strengthen a government's ability to bring about further fiscal reforms.

A more difficult case arises in which a country's exchange rate is fully unified *and* the budget is under control, so that the nominal exchange rate is sustainable. Even in these circumstances (e.g., Bolivia in 1987–88), the Fund staff often urges a devaluation in order to raise the profitability of tradeables production. It is in this case that one can have profound doubts about the advisability of such a move. *At best,* a devaluation in these circumstances is a conscious governmental policy to raise the price of tradeables and to reduce the real urban wage; this is deliberate inflation and deliberate redistribution—both of which can gravely undermine political support for the government. At worst, the devaluation simply leads to compensating for increases in wages and non-tradeables prices, so that little is achieved in the relative price of tradeables and non-tradeables.

The possibility of carrying out a successful devaluation depends heavily on the government already having the reputation as a credible, low-inflation government (so that the devaluation does not set off a spiral of further wage and price increases), and on its having either enough rural support, or enough support among powerful export interests to provide a political base for the exchange rate change.[28] If these conditions do not hold, the government will tend to lack the capacity to bring about a real devaluation by a nominal devaluation. This is especially true in Latin America, where there is a legacy of high inflation, little money illusion, and constant attention to the risk of renewed inflation. In these circumstances, workers are highly protective of their real incomes and are ready to strike or protest in the face of a significant move in the real exchange rate. Politicians in search of votes are also quick to support the protests.

Recent theoretical studies[29] have stressed that a government that too freely resorts to devaluation sacrifices its long-term reputation as an inflation fighter. The private sector repeatedly anticipates *future* devaluations by marking up their own prices in advance of an exchange rate change. The monetary authorities then respond by undertaking the devaluation that was widely expected. Since this sequence is then repeated, the result is ongoing inflation with no benefit to the underlying real exchange rate. It is much better, in these models, for the government to find ways to *forswear* future devaluations in order to convince the private sector not to mark up prices in anticipation of a future exchange rate change.

To summarize, once a country has succeeded in stabilizing inflation and the exchange rate, constant pressure toward devaluation—to promote tradeable goods production—can easily undo the earlier accomplishments. Devaluations should not, of course, be forsworn entirely in these circumstances, but should be left to cases where: (1) a clear external shock requires a depreciation of the real exchange rate; (2) the government has achieved a reputation as an inflation fighter, or the country has a long history of low inflation; and (3) the government has sufficient political support among exporters and other producers of tradeables to maintain political control in the face of a devaluation.[30]

Implementing Conditionality

Further important problems with conditionality revolve around its implementation rather than its broad economic content. Many justifiable complaints about conditionality involve the specification of quantitative performance criteria that determine whether a government can continue to draw on a stand-by line of credit. In many cases, the numerical targets that measure compliance with an IMF program are based upon a series of dubious empirical assumptions.

Most important, the IMF relies heavily on domestic credit targets that are calculated using a very rudimentary model of monetary control (e.g., a fixed velocity of money demand underpinning the allowable rates

of growth of domestic money). The IMF must improve its waiver procedure to make sure that such rudimentary targeting does not stand in
the way of *smooth* disbursements of IMF credits if technical violations of
performance criteria are due more to faulty technical assumptions than
to shortcomings in the government's implementation of policies.

The problems with the IMF's rudimentary methodology for setting
precise quantitative targets are likely to become more severe with the
implementation of the new debt strategy. It is not only in the area of
monetary control that overly simple formulas are currently used to prepare projections. In the preparation of medium-term scenarios for the
balance of payments, for example, the IMF typically makes an
extremely crude and imprecise linkage between economic growth rates,
investment requirements, and import needs. The analogy to the
assumption of fixed monetary velocity are the assumptions of a fixed
incremental capital output ratio (ICOR), linking aggregate growth and
investment demand, and the assumption of a fixed elasticity, linking
import demand and GDP growth. Thus the IMF calculates the financing gap and hence the need for debt relief (whether through new lending
or debt reduction) using extremely rudimentary empirical indicators.

In this regard, it will be crucial for the Fund to coordinate the
quantitative analysis of medium-term growth prospects with the World
Bank and to explore the use of more sophisticated models that allow for:
multiple sectors, changing internal relative prices, lags between the
installation of fixed capital and the economically effective expansion of
capacity,[31] and the presence of debt-overhang effects on key behavioral
relations (e.g., the effects of the debt overhang on domestic interest rates
and private investment).

The IMF and Income Distribution

IMF programs are frequently attacked by outside critics as fostering a
deterioration of income distribution. This view is not generally correct,
but it is easy to understand why the charge is made. First, it is true that
the stringent austerity measures associated with IMF programs often
reduce the real income levels of the poor, even if they do not worsen the
income distribution per se. Second, the IMF has traditionally paid very
little attention to the income distributional consequences of its recommendations. And third, as the IMF itself stresses, the Fund typically
leaves distributional concerns to the national authorities. If the authorities choose to adjust in a manner that makes the national income distribution more unequal, the IMF will not interfere. (Equally important, if
the government chooses to pursue greater income equality consistent
with budgetary constraints, the IMF would surely not stand in the way.)

In truth, it is fairer to say that the Fund simply *does not know* the distributional implications of the policies that it recommends. The Fund has paid remarkably little empirical attention to distributional issues in the design and monitoring of IMF programs. Only very recently, under the leadership of Managing Director Michel Camdessus, has the issue of income distribution been put high on the agenda. Yet there is still much to do.

To an important extent, the IMF surely must leave income distributional concerns to the national authorities, as the Fund itself argues. Many critics of the Fund who attack its effects on income distribution also object to the Fund's meddling in countries' internal affairs, putting the Fund in a no-win situation. Nonetheless, I would suggest that the prevailing neglect of income distribution is overdone for at least four reasons.

First, if an IMF program truly immiserizes the poorest parts of the population, or penalizes an unpopular social or ethnic group within the population, the program cannot really be said to be achieving the Fund's goal of promoting national prosperity. It has been well documented by UNICEF and others that the infant mortality rate, child morbidity, and malnutrition have all increased as a result of the debt crisis.[32] It is also known that public expenditures on health, food subsidies, and education have suffered among the *largest* proportionate declines in budgetary allocations in highly indebted countries.

Second, the long-term viability of an adjustment strategy may well depend on an adequate distribution of income. There is evidence in Berg and Sachs, for example, that extreme income inequalities and the resulting political pressures have played an important role in generating the fiscal mismanagement that drives many governments to the Fund.[33] Moreover, I argue elsewhere that income distributional pressures have contributed importantly to the highly destructive populist episodes in Latin America.[34] Thus the IMF has a pragmatic interest in income distribution in order to raise the prospects for the long-term success of IMF programs.[35]

Third, IMF programs often deviate from neutrality to the extent that they reflect the prevailing ideological beliefs of the U.S. administration in power. In practice, during the 1980s, IMF recommendations have not always been neutral between tax increases and spending cuts as ways to balance the budget. In line with the Baker and Brady proposals, the IMF staff has tended to emphasize a reduced size of government as an independent goal of economic adjustment. The irony of the emphasis on spending cuts is that it neglects tax collections in Latin America, the region of the world with the most inequitable and corrupt tax systems, where the upper classes pay almost nothing in taxes. Personal income taxes in Latin America yield little, and almost all revenues that are collected come from salaried workers (whose incomes can be with-held) rather than the self-employed. The elites do not pay their way. This may be the main economic and political "illness" of the region— yet the IMF has not spoken publicly and vigorously about this disas-trous situation.

Fourth, the IMF's neglect of income distribution is overdone, in that many governments want to pursue adjustment programs that minimize the hardships on the poor, but the IMF does not really know how to design programs to meet such an objective. Income distributional effects of adjustment programs are indeed complicated, and they have been little analyzed within the Fund.

For these reasons, the Fund should take three urgent steps with regard to income distribution—without abandoning the basic principle that the major responsibility for the issue must lie with the sovereign governments. The first is to work closely with the World Bank, UNICEF, and others to make sure that the basic needs of the most indi-gent are protected as much as possible during stabilization. The IMF should prepare studies detailing various tactics for adjustment pro-grams to achieve this aim. The second step should be to make the collec-tion of information on income distribution an integral part of every IMF program. Specifically, each program should allocate some IMF funds to study the distributional effects of the specific program on a prospective basis in advance. The details of the monitoring can be worked out with the national authorities and should certainly be carried out in conjunc-tion with World Bank efforts in the country. But at this late date, the Fund should at least be in a position to know, beyond hopelessly outworn platitudes,[36] the distributional effects of its policies.

The third step, especially in Latin America, should be to restore progressive taxation as a *fundamental* policy prescription for the region's budgetary problems, and to give progressive taxation at least equal weight with privatization and "smaller government" in the litany of measures advocated by the IMF. There is enough evidence to suggest that without a fairer tax system in Latin America, the region's chronic fiscal crisis will not be resolved.

Review of Major Conclusions

The broad policy framework of the IMF, with its focus on fiscal prudence as the ultimate source of macroeconomic stability, is an appropriate starting point for IMF programs. Nonetheless, there are many ways in which this basic insight can be more effectively implemented by the IMF in the heavily indebted countries.

The first and most important is to combine the pressure for fiscal adjustment with a realistic dose of debt reduction. As described at length in this chapter, a major cause of the shortcomings of IMF programs in the 1980s has been the neglect of the debt reduction alternative. The new Brady Plan represents a major cause for hope in this regard, but there are several unsettling features about the early implementation of the new strategy. Most important, the reliance on "voluntary, market-based" debt reduction mechanisms makes little economic or institutional sense. Meaningful debt reduction will only be achieved once the official creditor institutions decide to lead a process of concerted debt reduction. Such concertation is necessary to overcome various manifestations of the "free rider" problem that currently cripples "voluntary" debt reduction operations.

Once debt reduction is achieved, there will be a prospect for more realistic programs. The basic emphasis on fiscal discipline should be continued, but the emphasis on devaluation in recent IMF programs should be toned down. Repeated devaluations can undermine a government's reputation as an inflation fighter and weaken the resolve to maintain budgetary discipline. The Fund is typically overoptimistic in its assessment of the extent to which nominal exchange rate changes can lead to sustained real exchange rate changes.

Another area for the reform of IMF practices is in the specification of numerical targets for Fund conditionality. Even in well designed programs, the Fund lacks the capacity to specify meaningful and precise numerical guidelines for money growth and other intermediate targets. The IMF needs to develop more procedures for waiving specific performance tests in circumstances in which the government has effectively undertaken the policy actions demanded but has not satisfied the technical assumptions underlying the IMF's targets. Also, in implementing numerical targets for debt reduction, the IMF must urgently move beyond the "back-of-the-envelope" calculations (e.g., assuming fixed ICORs and a one-sector economy) that now underlie the medium-term balance-of-payments scenarios.

Finally, the IMF must pay far more attention than it has to date to the income distributional consequences of adjustment programs. There is growing evidence, provided by UNICEF and others, that the poor have suffered heavily in the adjustment process of the 1980s. Far more care must be taken to protect the most vulnerable parts of the population, for both moral and pragmatic reasons. In Latin America, in particular, distributional goals could be linked to the adjustment process by a more explicit focus on an increase in progressive taxation.

Notes

[1] Some IMF reviewers of an earlier draft of this paper doubted that the Fund was created to help the world economy overcome an occurrence of the magnitude of the debt crisis, claiming that "an occurrence of these dimensions was probably not contemplated by the founding fathers." But the Fund was precisely created in the shadow of the Great Depression, with the idea that it could help to moderate, or prevent altogether, a new disaster of that magnitude.

[2] IMF Articles of Agreement.

[3] For a recent essay on the same themes, which reaches many of the same conclusions, see S. Edwards, "The International Monetary Fund and the Developing Countries: A Critical Evaluation," *National Bureau of Economic Research (NBER) Working Paper Series*, No. 2909, March 1989.

[4] As is well known, appraisals of the Fund based on "before-after" or "control-group" studies have deep methodological limitations. There is no substitute for a detailed knowledge of the IMF's policies in individual countries.

[5] The thirty-nine countries that have rescheduled their commercial bank debts in the 1980s are: Argentina, Bolivia, Brazil, Chile, the Congo, Costa Rica, the Dominican Republic, Ecuador, Gabon, Gambia, Guinea, Guyana, Honduras, the Ivory Coast, Jamaica, Madagascar, Malawi, Mexico, Morocco, Mozambique, Nicaragua, Niger, Nigeria, Panama, Peru, the Philippines, Poland, Romania, Senegal, Sierra Leone, South Africa, Sudan, Togo, Trinidad and Tobago, Uruguay, Venezuela, Yugoslavia, Zaire, and Zambia. This group has informally been designated by the U.S. Treasury as eligible for participation in the Brady Plan. Some IMF reviewers of an earlier draft of this chapter suggested that several countries "are making substantial progress." They cited three countries on the list of thirty-nine as examples: Chile, Morocco, and the Philippines. While these countires have indeed undertaken important reforms, there is little to suggest that they are close to achieving viability in the balance of payments, much less renewed creditworthiness. All three rely heavily on new official lending and continued bank debt restructurings to achieve balance-of-payments equilibrium. All are actively seeking to pursue new mechanisms of debt reduction. As of May 1989, the secondary market process for the three countries, respectively, were 59, 42, and 46 per cent of face value. See Salomon Brothers, "Indicative Prices for Less Developed Country Bank Loans," May 25, 1989, bid prices.

[6] In 1988, only Brazil among the forty or so countries suffering from an overhang of bank debt was able to negotiate a new money package, and that package soon proved to be wholly inadequate to Brazil's financial needs.

[7] The chapter in this volume by Louis Goreux also makes clear that in the 1980s an increasing share of Fund resources was devoted to the heavily indebted countries; see Table 1 and Charts 1-A and 1-B.

[8] For documentation of this point, see the essays on the history of past debt crises in Jeffrey D. Sachs, ed., *Developing Country Debt and Economic Performances*, Vol. 1, *International Financial System* (Chicago, Ill.: University of Chicago Press, 1989). See also Erika Jorgenson and Jeffrey Sachs, "Default and Renegotiation of Latin American Foreign Bonds in the Interwar Period," *NBER Working Paper Series*, No. 2636, June 1988.

[9] Since the announcement of the Brady Plan, Managing Director Michel Camdessus has been a vigorous, creative, and outspoken backer of significant debt reduction.

[10] The programs were also designed under the assumption that past interest arrears would be cleared, and once again, a program for clearing arrears, agreed to by the country and the commercial bank creditors, has generally been a precondition for the IMF program. As I mention in the next sub-section, there have been exceptions, of which the most widely known are Bolivia and Costa Rica. These countries have been able to get stand-by programs despite the absence of an agreement with the creditor banks. More recently, after the announcement of the Brady Plan, Mexico, the Philippines, and Venezuela also negotiated programs with the IMF before completion of negotations with the commercial banks.

[11] Jeffrey D. Sachs, "Conditionality, Debt Relief, and the Developing Country Debt Crisis," in Jeffrey D. Sachs, ed., *Developing Country Debt and Economic Performances*, op. cit.

[12] Ibid.; W. A. Beveridge and M. R. Kelley, "Fiscal Content of Financial Programs Supported by Standby Arrangements in Upper-Credit Tranches, 1969–78," *IMF Staff Papers*, Vol. 27, No. 2, pp. 205–49; L. K. Doe, "Fiscal Policy and Adjustment in the 1980 Fund Financial Programs," Departmental Memorandum 83/52 (Washington, D.C.: International Monetary Fund, 1983; S. Haggard, "The Politics of Adjustment," *International*

Organization, Vol. 39, No. 3 pp. 505–34; and Edwards, "The International Monetary Fund and the Developing Countries: A Critical Evaluation," op. cit.

[13] C. David Finch, "Let the IMF be the IMF," *International Economy,* January/February 1988, pp. 127.

[14] I have written a more detailed description of this case in "Comprehensive Debt Conversion: The Case of Bolivia," *Brookings Papers on Economic Activity,* No. 2, 1988.

[15] For details, see Jeffrey D. Sachs and Juan Antonio Morales, "Bolivia: 1952–1986," *Country Studies No. 6,* International Center for Economic Growth, San Francisco, California, 1988.

[16] There were, however, last-minute threats from U.S. officials who that it would be "very hard" to get the program approved unless Bolivia resumed interest payments.

[17] Some writers have even claimed that Bolivia was an "obvious" test case for debt relief in 1986. But at that time, nobody was looking for test cases; the program barely slipped through.

[18] In the Bolivian presidential elections of May 1989, all three of the major candidates, from the left to the right, explicitly called for a continuation of IMF programs in the next administration. The two parties that had backed the stabilization program, the MNR and the ADN, received a majority of the votes between them, with the rest of the votes distributed among several other parties.

[19] The program required about 18 months to negotiate and implement. Bolivia could afford this long period of delay because it paid no interest during the period.

[20] Specifically, the following terms for financial support of debt reduction were approved by the Executive Board on May 23, 1989, as reported by the *IMF Survey,* May 29, 1989. p. 161: "Around 25 per cent of a country's access to Fund resources—under an extended or stand-by arrangement—can be set aside to support operations involving reduction of debt principal. The Fund may approve additional funding—up to 40 per cent of the member's quota—for interest support in connection with debt or debt-service reduction operations where such support would be decisive in facilitating further cost-effective operations and in catalyzing other resources, including, where feasible, the debtor country's own efforts to contribute resources in support of the operations."

[21] As reported by the *IMF Survey,* op. cit.: "On a case-by-case basis the Fund may approve an arrangement outright, before the conclusion of a financing package between the member and its commercial bank creditors. It will give such approval in cases where Fund support is essential for program implementation, where negotiations with banks have begun, and where it is expected that an appropriate financing package will be concluded in a reasonable period of time."

[22] Jeffrey Sachs, "Efficient Debt Reduction," World Bank Symposium on Developing Country Debt, January 1989 (forthcoming in a conference volume); and Jeffrey Sachs, "Making the Brady Plan Work," *Foreign Affairs,* Summer 1989.

[23] There are two reasons for this interdependence of actions. If one bank makes greater concessions than another, it might weaken its competitive position relative to the other bank. Also, the shareholders of the first bank might question the management's decision if it appears that it has given up something that the other bank did not.

[24] It is interesting that concertation was applied to new loans, while it has been avoided so far in the strategy of debt reduction. In both phases of the debt strategy, it appears that the designers have responded to the desires of the most heavily exposed money-center banks. With new lending, it was the smaller regional banks that tried to avoid participation, so that the concertation ws used to draw in the smaller banks. With debt reduction, it is the hope of the money-center banks that they can get away with little debt reduction (i.e. that they can free ride), by having the regional banks accept the largest reductions in exposure. The regionals are much better placed to accept debt reduction because of their stronger balance sheets, and the money-center banks are therefore aware that these smaller banks are likely to accept the new debt reduction options even if the larger banks refuse to participate.

[25] See Sachs, "Conditionality, Debt Relief, and the Developing Country Crisis," op. cit., and references therein.

[26] "In promoting orderly financial relations, every effort will be made to avoid arrears, which could not be condoned or anticipated by the Fund in the design of programs. Nevertheless, an accumulation of arrears to banks may have to be tolerated where negotiations continue and the country's financing situation does not allow them to be avoided." *IMF Survey,* May 29, 1989, p. 173.

[27] As mentioned by Edwards, only 30 per cent of upper-credit tranche programs between 1963 and 1972 included a devaluation. That proporation rose to 50 per cent between 1977 and 1980. Edwards, op. cit., found that fully 79 per cent of programs ap-

proved in 1983 included a devaluation, and that those programs that did not correspond to countries with institutional constraints on the exchange rate, such as membership in a monetary union or the use of another nation's currency. Edwards, op. cit., pp. 10, 27–28 (Table 2). I would venture a guess that the proportion of programs with devaluations has generally been above 75 per cent of programs since 1980.

[28] Clear examples where a tradeables-promoting devaluation was called for and worked successfully are Indonesia in 1978 and 1983, and Thailand in the early 1980s.

[29] H. Horn and T. Persson, "Exchange Rate Policy, Wage Formation, and Credibility," *European Economic Review*, Vol. 32, October 1988, pp. 1621–36.

[30] The IMF reviewers of an earlier draft of this paper properly stressed a number of examples of effective devaluation, including Bangladesh, Chile, Ghana, Indonesia, and Morocco. The case of Ghana was a case where exchange rate rationing was rampant before the devaluation, so that by my own criteria, the choice to devalue was clear. In the other cases, the governments were not struggling precisely with inflation stabilization at the time of devaluation, but rather with the adjustment to adverse terms of trade shocks. It is harder to remember distinct "successful" devaluations in most Latin American countries in recent years since in most cases the depreciation of the real exchange rate has proved to be short lived.

[31] In some industries, years of lead time are required to turn physical investments into new production (e.g. in the planting of tree crops, or in industries where learning curves are important).

[32] UNICEF (United Nations Children's Fund), *The State of the World's Children, 1989* (Oxford, England: Oxford University Press, 1989).

[33] Andrew Berg and Jeffrey Sachs, "The Debt Crisis: Structural Explanations of Country Performance," *NBER Working Paper Series*, No. 2607, June 1988; my co-author and I have shown that high income inequality in the 1970s is an important predictor of which developing countries fell into crisis in the 1980s.

[34] Jeffrey Sachs, "Social Conflict and Populist Policies in Latin America," *NBER Working Paper Series*, No. 2897, March 1989.

[35] This point of view is well expressed in an IMF publication, "Fund-Supported Programs, Fiscal Policy, and Income Distribution," *Occasional Paper No. 46*, September 1986, p. 1: "If Fund-supported adjustment programs imply that specific income classes (and in particular the poor) inevitably bear the brunt of the economic costs involved [with adjustment programs], then those programs would be both less acceptable, and in the long run, less effective than the available alternatives."

[36] The IMF's constant refrain, for example, is that devaluation is good for decreasing income inequality because it raises the incomes of the rural (and presumably poorer) sector relative to the urban sector. This conclusion must surely be qualified, however, depending upon the pattern of land tenure and the nature of agricultural crops. In Latin America, with highly unequal land holdings and a huge number of landless peasants, the effects of devaluation are almost surely less beneficial to income distribution than in parts of Africa and Asia characterized by a large proportion of landowning farmers.

Chapter 4

The IMF and the Debt Strategy

Guillermo Ortiz

Introduction

The role of the International Monetary Fund in the debt strategy has taken a major turn since the unveiling of the Brady Plan last March. While the full extent of Fund participation in the "new" debt strategy is an evolving process, the important steps that have already been taken mark a sharp departure from previous policies and point to the direction in which the Fund may be moving in the future.

The most important recent steps taken in connection with the changing role of the Fund include: the use of the Fund's own resources for debt and debt-service reduction operations; the enhancement of the Extended Fund Facility (EFF), which can now be extended to a fourth year with the possibility of greater access; a parallel financing agreement with Japan that enhances the Fund's catalytic role; the modification of the policy of financing assurances, which now enables the Fund to release its own resources prior to the completion of a financing package with other creditors; a cautious but explicit tolerance of arrears to commercial banks in certain circumstances; and the new Compensatory and Contingency Financing Facility (CCFF), which, in addition to providing compensatory financing, is aimed at protecting adjustment pro-

---

Note: The opinions expressed in this chapter are those of the author and do not necessarily reflect official views.

grams from adverse external shocks such as a fall in the terms of trade or a rise in interest rates.

The new approach constitutes a positive response to long-standing demands made by indebted countries both at IMF Board sessions and in other fora regarding the role of the Fund in the debt strategy. It stems from recognition that the debt strategy has failed to achieve its basic objective of restoring economic growth and stabilization in indebted countries, and that the financing arrangements for these indebted countries envisaged under the Baker Initiative have all but broken apart. It became increasingly clear that a new course was needed. Persistence in the "muddling through" approach under the old debt strategy would have implied not only a continued deterioration of the situation of indebted countries, but also a clear danger to the financial position of the Fund.

For quite some time, the Fund's major shareholders resisted (and some still do) the notion of facilitating debt reduction operations by utilizing resources from multilateral organizations on the grounds of "protecting taxpayers' money" and avoiding "bailing out the banks." These catch-all phrases were later replaced by another, coined during the 1988 IMF/World Bank meetings in Berlin: "avoiding the transfer of risks to the public sector." It is clear, however, that these phrases are equally misleading: The risk already has been transferred to public sectors (and to taxpayers) of creditor countries, and banks have been bailed out. This transfer has not been "transparent," however, since it took place "through the back door"—by the substitution of commercial bank finance for resources from multilateral organizations.

Perhaps it was the realization that this transfer was indeed taking place—and that commercial banks, instead of increasing financing to indebted countries as envisaged under the Baker Initiative, were sharply reducing their exposure—that led to the shift in emphasis in the debt strategy toward debt reduction. Apart from the unsustainability of the strategy from the viewpoint of debtor countries, the combination of reduced lending from commercial banks and rising (but insufficient) financing from multilateral organizations (while the economic situation of indebted countries continued to deteriorate) was bound to affect the financial position of the Fund.[1]

Clearly the problem of arrears to the Fund is closely associated with the general debt problem and with the risk transfer from commercial banks. The Fund began registering arrears in 1983, and there is currently some SDR 2.7 billion in overdue credit outstanding. While the amount of these arrears is not such as could seriously affect Fund operations or undermine its basic solvency in the near future (especially if IMF gold holdings at market value are taken into account), it has already awakened considerable concern on the part of creditors as to the quality of the assets committed to the Fund.[2]

From the viewpoint of debtors, arrears present several difficulties. First, there is the immediate problem of the higher cost of Fund finance. Although under current arrangements the costs implied by lost income are shared between creditors and debtors, in 1988 the burden of arrears to the users of Fund resources was reflected in a rate of charge 1 per cent higher than would have been the case in the absence of arrears. This is no negligible amount. A second and more significant aspect of this problem is that the increase of arrears has created pressure for a tightening of conditionality and reduced access to Fund resources. This problem is likely to affect the extent of commitment of the Fund in the new phase of the debt strategy, potentially undermining its effectiveness. Some of the major shareholders have expressed concern that the arrears situation will weigh heavily in their decision to vote for a substantial quota increase later this year. This in turn could seriously limit the scale of Fund financing of adjustment programs and debt reduction operations in indebted countries.

Recent developments in the debt strategy brought about by the Brady Plan, as well as the stronger than expected endorsement of the Plan by the G-7 during the last summit in Paris, indicate that the role of the Fund in the international financial system over the next several years will be inexorably linked to the resolution of the debt crisis. The restoration of growth in problem debtor countries is increasingly perceived as essential for the economic and political health of the world economy. In turn, the role that the Fund can play in this major task will largely shape the future scope of the institution.

The Debt Situation: Current Perspectives

There is ample consensus that the three basic objectives of the debt strategy have been:

- Maintenance of an open and viable financial system;
- Restoration of economic growth in problem debtors; and
- Reestablishment of normal debtor/creditor relations.

The debt strategy has evidently been successful in preventing a collapse of the international financial system. It has also provided the time and space necessary to strengthen the financial position of creditor banks. In turn, the preservation of an open financial system has facilitated the longest continued expansion of the industrial economies in the postwar era. Since it is clear that neither creditors nor debtors would have benefitted from a breakdown of the system, and the stronger position of banks has all but eliminated the possibility of a systemic collapse on account of the debt problem, it should be recognized that this is an important achievement.

It is widely accepted, however, that the costs of maintaining an open financial system have been disproportionately borne by the debtors. The contraction of real wages and consumption levels, the decrease in investment, and the general deterioration of living standards in practically all indebted countries over the past six years has been amply documented.[3] On the other hand, commercial banks reported a steady *rise* in net income during the period 1982–86. It was only in 1987 that banks began reporting losses, although these losses were reported mostly because of a steep increase in provisioning, with the purpose of further strengthening their financial positions.

Perhaps the most disturbing fact, however, is that despite the costs incurred in terms of both economic stagnation and political fatigue, the majority of indebted countries are no closer to achieving the conditions necessary for the restoration of economic growth or to regaining access to voluntary finance than at the outset of the debt crisis.

The adjustment efforts undertaken by indebted countries have produced a major shift in their current account positions (equivalent to more than 35 per cent of their exports since 1981) in the face of a cumulative deterioration of the terms of trade of about one-quarter over the period 1985–86. The counterpart of this shift in the external positions—the transfer of resources abroad—has been a contraction in consumption levels and a sharp fall in investment. According to the latest information compiled by the U.N. Economic Commission for Latin America (ECLA), the investment/GDP ratio in Latin America in 1987 was 17.7 per cent, compared to 22.8 per cent in 1981. During this period, per capita GDP fell by approximately 3 per cent.

The long period of depressed investment has probably reduced potential output growth in the indebted countries over the medium term. In addition, the sharp curtailment of public investment has probably reduced the overall efficiency of investment.[4] This outlook is further complicated by the current status of financial arrangements, which suggest that negative resource transfers will remain an obstacle to the resumption of growth. The main debt indicators for this group of countries are considerably worse than at the outset of the debt crisis, yet—as recent events in Venezuela and Argentina sadly demonstrate—the room for maneuver at the political level has been sharply curtailed.

From 1982 to 1987, the debt/exports and debt/GDP ratios of the fifteen heavily indebted countries rose from 268.3 to 338.7 and from 41.6 to 45.7, respectively. Considering the overall deterioration of both living standards and debt indicators, it is evident that the creditworthiness of these countries has eroded even further. The marginal improvement observed in some countries in 1988 and 1989 has not been significant enough to encourage any hopes that access to the international financial markets is within reach in the near future. In this fundamental sense, it is evident that the debt strategy has failed. The new emphasis on debt reduction of the Brady Plan is a clear—and long overdue—recognition of this fact.

The Debt Overhang: Impact on Indebted Countries

The *direct* impact of the debt overhang on economic growth caused by the reduction in investment implied by the resource transfer is a well-documented effect.[5] However, the *indirect* effects of the debt overhang on the ability of governments to implement stabilization policies and structural reforms have not been sufficiently emphasized in debt discussions.

Creditor governments, banks, and multilateral financial institutions have consistently maintained that an element essential to the alleviation of debt problems is the implementation of strong adjustment programs; it has been repeatedly stressed that the main responsibility lies with the debtor countries themselves. From this perspective, regaining growth and creditworthiness depends on the restoration of confidence on the part of foreign and domestic investors. As a recent publication states:

> The evidence is very clear that restoration of the debtor's market access cannot be accomplished without the return of confidence in these countries on the part of their own residents. Consistent programs by the debtors in stabilization and reform would lure back flight capital, not merely for temporary and foot-loose financial investment but for permanent investment in productive domestic enterprise. After all, as Secretary Baker observed when propounding his 1985 initiative, if a country's own citizens have no confidence in its own economic system, how can others?[6]

Yet the implications of excessive debt for the probability of success of adjustment efforts have not generally been taken into account. This is true at the level of official discourse; but worse still, these effects have not been taken into account—until recently, as described in the next section—in the design and implementation of Fund-supported adjustment programs.

It is a fact that most stabilization programs attempted during the past six years in heavily indebted countries have failed. It may be argued that, in most cases, the main culprits behind the failure of adjustment programs were insufficiently strong action on the part of domestic authorities, problems of coordination, or the lack of political will in the implementation and follow-through of the adjustment effort. But it is also true that unfavorable external shocks—such as adverse shifts in the terms of trade—and the difficulties associated with the debt overhang have made adjustment extremely difficult, even in cases where the authorities are fully committed to the implementation of the programs.

Two of the most recurrent examples of the types of difficulties posed by the existence of excessive debt are the impact on *economic stabilization* and the effect on *income distribution* derived from the resource transfer. These, in turn, are closely associated with the fiscal dimension of the debt problem.

An important feature of the current situation is that external debt obligations represent a fiscal commitment of public sectors in debtor countries. Thus governments of debtor countries face the additional problem of extracting resources from the public to effect the transfer abroad demanded by debt service. Clearly, the different sectors of society tend to resist the government's attempts to levy additional taxes or to gather resources by increasing the real price of goods and services produced by public enterprises. This has produced two kinds of effects: First, as noted above, public investment expenditures have declined to the point where, in a number of indebted countries, the capital stock has depreciated. The World Bank estimates a *cumulative fall* of real investment of 27 per cent in highly indebted countries during the period 1982–87.[7] Second, governments have had to resort to the inflation "tax" as a means of overcoming the resistance of society to the internal resource transfer to the public sector.

In several cases, inflation has played a catalytic role in this transfer—realized through reductions in real wages. These reductions, in turn, often have been brought about by abrupt exchange rate depreciations. To the extent that formal or informal indexation mechanisms are present, inflationary impulses tend to replicate themselves. These effects may help to explain why it has proven so difficult to implement successful stabilization programs in indebted countries—even though these countries in many cases have attained larger external surpluses than originally envisaged. Lowering inflation has proven much more difficult than reducing external disequilibria.

In turn, the constraints imposed by the fiscal situation have important implications for income distribution that have not been generally recognized in debt discussions: First, the debt overhang implies a perennially precarious situation for public finances. Even if the government of an indebted country is following "correct" macroeconomic policies, and investors perceive that the public sector is in a position to maintain debt service for a given set of terms of trade and real interest rates, the uncertainties associated with debt payments and prospective financial flows are such that they will demand a very high real rate of return in order to hold domestic assets.

An alternative manner of stating the above argument is that the market's assessment of a country's payment capacity (including the perceived ability to enforce real resource transfers across sectors of society and the outlook for financial flows) determines the discounts at which debt sells. This calculation in turn sets the real return at which these assets are voluntarily held. Furthermore, since domestic financial assets can easily be taxed through inflation or through a discrete depreciation of the exchange rate, any external or supply-side shock that modifies the public's perception of the ability of the government to service its internal or external debt will immediately induce capital flight. It is thus entirely possible that capital flight may be observed even when consistent policies are being implemented.[8]

Second, it is clear that, at least in the short run, substantially higher real returns on investment—in physical or financial assets—can be realized only at the expense of lower real wages (efficiency and productivity gains being achieved only through time). In addition, as explained before, external shocks produce uncertainties regarding the debt-servicing capacity of the government and stimulate capital flight, which contracts the tax base of the economy. The ensuing adjustment therefore requires an additional fall of real wages. Although exchange controls may, in theory, be used to prevent capital flight, experience shows that these seldom work in practice and usually have the undesirable effect of introducing additional distortions. Since investors able to transfer their resources abroad are normally among the most prosperous sectors of society, it is evident that capital flight is highly regressive. Adjustment falls on the "captive" tax base: wage earners and others who do not have the means to transfer their assets abroad.

One conclusion that may be drawn from the above considerations is that a set of "correct" macroeconomic policies sufficient to stabilize an economy and generate growth in the absence of a debt overhang may not attain the desired objectives—and could conceivably have perverse effects—in highly indebted countries through their impact on income distribution. That is, the income distribution scheme resulting from the application of "sufficiently strong policies" needed to restore investor confidence and to stabilize the economy may be inherently unstable in the most indebted countries.

IMF Stabilization Programs: The Next Phase

The Fund-supported programs that were put in place during the early stages of the debt crisis were largely successful in bringing about a domestic correction of the balance of payments but were much less effective in bringing about a reduction of inflation and fiscal deficits. This asymmetry has led to frequent statements (by key participants from creditor countries and heads of multilateral financial institutions) that while efforts to reduce external imbalances on the part of creditor countries have been commendable, those directed at eliminating internal imbalances have been insufficient.

It is true that inflation and fiscal deficits have tended to rise rather than diminish in the course of the adjustment process undertaken over the past six years in a number of heavily indebted countries. But this largely has been the domestic reflection of the external resource transfer effected; the point is that the dynamics of the internal adjustment often result in higher inflation. In addition, the perceived "asymmetry" between the strong correction observed in the external account and persistent—and sometimes rising—public sector deficits is often prompted by focusing on the conventional definition of the deficit, the Public Sector Borrowing Requirements (PSBR). In times of high inflation, the PSBR conveys a distorted image of the fiscal stance of the government if the level of internal debt is substantial. From a national accounting perspective, no such asymmetry exists between internal and external adjustment: The counterpart to a reduction of the trade balance must be a rise in net savings on the part of private and public sectors; thus a reduction of the external imbalance of a certain magnitude implies an internal adjustment of a similar magnitude.

Consider, for example, the Mexican case. The 1983–84 program agreed with the Fund produced a very large overshooting of the balance-of-payments targets; during that period, a $9.6 billion current account surplus was obtained compared to the $5.2 billion deficit contemplated in the program. Compliance with the nominal performance criteria under the 1983–84 arrangements implied a much harsher real adjustment than originally envisaged. The counterpart to the balance-of-payments overshooting was, of course, a very steep recession: GDP fell by about 5 per cent in 1983, in contrast to a program target of zero growth. The impact of the initial exchange rate depreciation on inflation was grossly underestimated, while the setting of performance criteria of financial and fiscal variables in nominal terms under conditions of higher than expected inflation produced a very sharp contraction of aggregate demand. Programs implemented in a number of other debtor countries encountered similar difficulties: Either performance criteria were not observed or the contractionary effects were almost systematically larger than expected.

A second episode of the Mexican experience was also quite revealing. During 1986–87, the rate of inflation jumped from 65 per cent to 160 per cent at a time when the public sector deficit—measured by the PSBR—nearly doubled. This suggests that during this period there was a strong link between inflation and the large increase in the fiscal deficit. In the case of Mexico's recent experience, however, the order of causality was reversed—that is, the rise in the fiscal deficit was due to the rise in inflation and not vice versa. In fact, it was the effect of inflation on the fiscal deficit—through its impact on the nominal interest rates paid on domestic debt—that explained the coexistence of the large borrowing requirements of the public sector and a surplus in the external account during that period. A more accurate measurement of the fiscal stance of the government, the operational balance, in fact showed an improvement of 3.3 per cent of GDP. The doubling of inflation, in turn, was caused by the policy actions taken to protect the balance of payments in the face of the 1986 fall in oil prices and the lack of foreign finance.

These examples serve to illustrate a more general point: Fund programs have generally been designed and implemented with insufficient regard for the effects of the debt overhang on the adjustment process. Traditional Fund programs are designed to deal with "flow-type" imbalances, while the existence of debt overhang implies—by definition—a situation of stock disequilibrium that is extremely difficult to correct by means of a traditional adjustment program. This probably explains the failure of a number of stabilization attempts in highly indebted countries over the past several years. On the other hand, it is easy to bring about a turnaround in the balance-of-payments imbalance: All that is needed is a contraction of aggregate demand of sufficient magnitude.

For the Fund, a first step would be to recognize the effects of the debt overhang on growth and adjustment. Fortunately, the Fund has explicitly—if belatedly—acknowledged these effects at both the conceptual and the practical levels.[9] Again, this point is well illustrated by the latest Mexican program—an Extended Fund Facility approved by the Executive Board in May 1989—which, in our view, constitutes a significant landmark in program design for the following reasons:

1. *It is a "true" growth-oriented program.* The traditional approach to program design begins by assessing the amounts of external finance available on a "voluntary" basis from different creditors and by estimating the potential flows of domestic savings. Then the necessary adjustment of domestic expenditures needed to restore external balance is derived through a financial programming exercise. In this type of program, growth is clearly a mere residual. In contrast, in the recent Mexican program, the growth objective is up front; the financial programming exercise was carried out in the opposite sequence of traditional programs. First, a realistic growth objective was postulated in light of Mexico's pre-debt growth record and the urgent need to absorb a growing labor force. Then, given this growth objective, and after assessing the availability of internal sources of finance, the external financing gap was obtained as a residual.[10]

2. The program explicitly recognizes the existence of a debt overhang and the problems posed by excessive debt—both for economic policy implementation and for the resumption of economic growth. As mentioned above, this recognition has been the subject of numerous discussions by the Executive Board and between Mexican representatives and the IMF. It represents a major step at a conceptual level and constitutes the basis for Mexico's negotiations with commercial banks, providing the rationale and support for the country's demands for debt and debt-service reduction. In contrast to previous practice, and for the first time in the case of a major debtor, the Fund supports the position of the Mexican authorities on the need for a drastic reduction of the net resource transfer abroad—of which a substantial portion must be effected by debt reduction. This is acknowledged to be essential for the resumption of durable economic growth with price stability.

3. Again for the first time in the case of a major debtor, the program was unanimously approved by the Executive Board without financing assurances from commercial bank creditors. Although official creditors grouped in the Paris Club were expected to conclude a multi-year arrangement with Mexico shortly after Board approval of the program, no such expectation existed regarding the conclusion of a rapid negotiation with commercial banks. In fact, although Mexico had not incurred payment arrears with commercial banks, the decision approved by the Board did not imply that if negotiations were prolonged and Mexico had to generate arrears at some point to protect its reserve position, this would constitute a cause for program suspension. In other words, there was an understanding that arrears would be tolerated if Mexico conducted its negotiations in good faith.

4. The program was framed in a medium-term context, stipulating that financing should be provided on a multi-year basis in order to reduce the uncertainty associated with yearly negotiations. In addition, it was agreed that 30 per cent of each purchase made by Mexico under the extended arrangement would be set aside for debt reduction operations. The Executive Board decision also noted Mexico's intention to request an augmentation up to the equivalent of 40 per cent of its quota in support of debt-service reduction.

In sum, Mexico's recent program incorporates the new features or "innovations" that form the core of the Fund's new approach to the debt strategy. In fact, to some extent, the policy guidelines that set out the modalities of Fund participation in this stage of the debt strategy were shaped by the negotiations of the Mexican program itself. These guidelines were approved by the Executive Board only a few days prior to the presentation of the program; negotiations had concluded about four weeks prior to the formal Board meeting. This is not the first time that negotiations between Mexico and the Fund have had a direct and significant impact on the shaping of Fund policy. On this point, it is illustrative to quote a recent article by Joseph Gold, a former General Counsel and Director of the Legal Department of the IMF:

> Mexico has had a striking influence on the IMF's Articles and on the development of some of its most important policies both before and after the present version of the Articles took effect. In more recent years, the problem of Mexico's external debt has produced changes in the IMF's relations with commercial banks, its practice of surveillance, and on the use of its resources under stand-by arrangements. In addition, impending changes in the IMF's response to external contingencies can be attributed to experience with Mexico. One of the generalizations drawn from this experience is that the IMF's practice is not determined solely by the major industrialized countries.[11]

The Role of the Fund in the New Debt Strategy

The significance of the role of the Fund during the first stages of the debt crisis is widely recognized. The success of the early developments in the debt strategy in preventing a collapse of the international financial system was in no small measure due to the initiative and leadership shown by the Fund. This clearly was a major achievement. But then, as the financial position of banks became stronger—since the indebted countries, despite their difficulties, largely maintained debt-service payments—the debt problem evolved from a systemic threat to a chronic disease.

The situation of indebted countries (with some ups and downs) continued to deteriorate, while industrialized countries and the international financial institutions (IFIs) insisted that adherence to the basic premises of the debt strategy was essential, since better times were just around the corner. But of course the favorable conditions that were repeatedly predicted failed to materialize.[12]

Muddling through on the debt front became standard policy until the recent action taken in the context of the Brady Plan. But despite the important steps taken by the Fund in this connection, the modalities of its participation in the debt strategy remain the subject of considerable debate. For quite some time, members have been confronted with a dilemma between the preservation of the monetary character of the Fund—implying revolving resources and short-term assistance—and the realities of the debt situation, which have imposed demands seemingly at odds with this monetary character. Meanwhile, some of the Fund's original functions and purposes have been considerably diluted.[13]

Some voices, concerned with maintaining the "purity" of the institution, repeatedly have stressed that the Fund should disengage itself from the debt problem and let borrowers and lenders solve their problems without official interference. While this view may be justified on the grounds of reaffirming the monetary character of the Fund, the force of circumstances has determined that the Fund will continue to play a key role in the resolution of the debt problem. Nevertheless, the remaining skepticism on the part of some industrial countries as to the need for more active official intervention has already set limits on the scope of Fund action and may hamper its future effectiveness.

It is now a fact that, despite remaining doubts, a central role for the Fund in the new debt strategy has been established; the question now is, how can the Fund contribute more effectively to the lasting improvement of the situation of indebted countries? First, it should again be stressed that the steps already taken constitute a significant and positive response to changing circumstances and to the needs of indebted countries. The focus on the recovery of economic growth on a sustained basis is most welcome and, at least in the Mexican case, certainly has gone beyond rhetoric. The emphasis on reduced resource transfers in a medium-term context, implemented through substantial debt alleviation, is an essential element for the *reduction of the level of macroeconomic uncertainty* caused by the debt overhang. This is a necessary condition for the recovery of economic growth.

"Stop-go" policies in indebted countries have largely resulted from discouragement with the results of short-term, demand-oriented adjustment, and from the lack of a financial perspective that facilitates the persistence of macroeconomic and structural policies within a medium-term horizon. This is why a departure from the "short-leash" approach is so important; adequate finance should be assured for a period of three to four years. Debtors need to be freed from the debt negotiation/renegotiation loop and to focus on the task of macroeconomic management and structural reform—as the Fund has recognized by emphasizing the utilization of an enhanced EFF.

In the context of medium-term macroeconomic projections, the Fund needs to be explicit regarding the amount of debt reduction needed for the restoration of economic growth. This will of course remain a controversial issue, and the Fund will be challenged by commercial banks—as the balance-of-payments projections of the Mexican program have been challenged during the recent negotiations with commercial banks.

The Fund must take a clear and firm stance with respect to the banks. Just as it was influential in overcoming the resistance of banks to participation in concerted financing packages in the earlier stage of the debt strategy, it can now use its considerable leverage in facilitating debt reduction operations. Again, in this respect, both the recent policy changes and direct Fund action clearly have been supportive of the Mexican negotiations with commercial banks. The modification of the policy on financing assurances is a major movement in this regard. Instead of waiting for firm financing commitments on the part of banks, the Board has recently approved programs without these assurances not only for Mexico but also for the Philippines, Venezuela, and Costa Rica. The rationale for the traditional policy on financing assurances was to "safeguard" Fund resources. But this policy implied placing pressure on indebted countries to maintain debt-service payments, since negotiations had to be concluded with commercial banks before the program could be submitted for Board approval. This of course was the main reason for the contention that the Fund was acting as a debt collector for commercial banks.

A second major policy modification has been a cautious, if explicit, tolerance of arrears to commercial banks. Some of the programs recently approved by the Executive Board contemplate both the existence and the further accumulation of arrears. This is also an important development in Fund policies that—in my view—tends to balance its participation in the debt strategy with respect to previous practice.

Turning now to the amounts currently available for debt and debt-service reduction from the international financial institutions, three points are worth mentioning:

First, these funds seem insufficient for a scale of operations that would produce a significant impact on indebted countries. This has been a difficult issue in the Mexican negotiations with commercial banks.[14] Thus it will be important to strengthen the catalytic role of the Fund, perhaps along the lines agreed with Japan for the provision of parallel financing for debt reduction.

A *second* point has to do with the timing of the delivery of these funds, which are the "enhancements" for debt and debt-service reduction operations. Creditor banks have insisted that the benefits of debt relief be passed on to countries only to the extent that these enhancements (which cover the purchase of guarantees for principal and interest on new bonds) are delivered to the banks. This raises some important difficulties, since current arrangements with the international financial institutions envisage that these enhancements will be made available only gradually, to the extent that countries are in compliance with adjustment programs. Although this is a sensible policy from the point of view of the financial institutions, the benefits of debt alleviation for indebted countries will be considerably diminished if debt reduction is not "front-loaded," since the effect on expectations—an essential element in the restoration of confidence—will be considerably diluted. The Fund should then front load the enhancements as much as possible, requiring early repurchases in cases of failure to comply with program targets.

The *third* point has to do with the unnecessary rigidities introduced in the utilization of the "set-aside" and "interest-support fund" portions of the resources available for debt reduction. These funds should be fungible and utilized for any type of debt reduction operation.

A final comment on two issues that have surfaced insistently in recent debt discussions and in the Mexican negotiations with commercial banks: debt-equity swaps and capital repatriation. The substantial debate on the relative merits and difficulties of debt-equity swaps is not reproduced here.[15] Suffice it to mention that, by and large, the economics profession has come out strongly against these types of operations. However, this view has not permeated official circles. The official discourse of creditor governments and multilateral institutions is that public sectors should contract and that private investment should be the engine of growth. But it is evident that the debt strategy has conspired directly against this objective. On the one hand, the contraction of public investment—especially in infrastructure—reduces the productivity of private investment, which is also discouraged by the contraction of domestic markets caused by recessionary policies. On the other hand, short-term financial arrangements (at a macro level) do not facilitate private investment decisions. And then, to counter these negative incentives, the magic solution is: Subsidize investment through debt-equity swaps. It is paradoxical that some of those who call more insistently for price stabilization and the reduction of subsidies are the very ones who push hardest for debt-equity swaps—seemingly oblivious to the inflationary and distorting effects of these operations. The Fund should be more candid regarding these effects and the limited cases in which they could be avoided.[16]

The Brady Plan has placed a good deal of emphasis on the return of flight capital. The potential source of finance represented by the deposits held abroad by residents of highly indebted countries has been rediscovered once again. The repatriation of flight capital is certainly desirable and should remain a central objective of indebted countries. But this requires two conditions: (1) persistence in following sound macroeconomic and structural policies and (2) the perception that these policies are indeed viable and will result in the restoration of economic stability and growth. Again, the establishment of adequate conditions will take time and should result from the reduction in macroeconomic uncertainty associated with the debt overhang. Capital repatriation will take place as part of the virtuous circle resulting from strong, credible, and viable programs that are adequately financed and implemented in a context where the debt overhang has been (or is in the process of being) eliminated. It would be unrealistic to assume that capital repatriation will take place before substantial progress has been made toward a lasting solution for the debt problem.

Concluding Remarks

Mexico has recently concluded a difficult and prolonged negotiation with its commercial bank creditors (an agreement in principle with their Steering Committee). This has been the first "test" case under the new approach to debt strategy—the Brady Plan—in which the basis has been laid for substantial debt and debt-service reduction as well as for multi-year financing.[17] The agreement with the IMF on a three-year EFF program was of course an essential element for the conclusion of this negotiation. The Mexican program is significant in the context of the new debt strategy for several reasons:

- It is a program that promises growth in the medium term, since the financing of the term requirements of the program were determined as a function of the growth target and not the other way around—as is normally the case in "traditional" programs;
- It recognizes the existence of a debt overhang and the problems this entails for stabilization and growth, and calls for a substantial reduction of net transfers and debt alleviation;
- It was framed in a medium-term context;
- The program was approved without financing assurances from creditor banks;
- The Fund committed its own resources for debt reduction.

In sum, the program incorporates the modalities of the Fund's participation in the new debt strategy, some of which were given shape by the program itself.

The Fund has moved in a rapid and effective way in this new stage of the debt strategy. This has not been an easy process, and there are still considerable doubts on the part of a number of industrialized countries as to the nature and depth of involvement of the Fund in the resolution of the debt problem. Several difficulties arise in this connection, such as the magnitude, structure, and timing of the delivery of resources available for debt reduction, and other important considerations regarding program design. Given the attitude of commercial banks, it is not clear to what extent the Mexican experience can be replicated by other countries. It should be kept in mind that Mexico has had a long—and largely sustained—record of adjustment and has undertaken deep structural reforms. Not all indebted countries are in the same position or can count on the same degree of political support from some of the major industrialized countries. Despite the long-standing opposition to the creation of a debt facility along the lines proposed by Sachs and others,[18] such a facility may have to be established to deal in a systematic manner with other more difficult cases. It seems difficult to envisage general application of the Mexican experience.

A final word on quotas. A substantial quota increase is clearly needed for several reasons. First, there is the need to increase the amounts of resources devoted to finance both adjustment and debt reduction. It also will be important to maintain adequate levels of liquidity. Other developing countries that are not heavily indebted have expressed concern that the resources of international financial institutions are being used to finance debt reduction operations. The argument is that "bad behavior" (as evidenced by the accumulation of excessive debt) is now being "rewarded" by the extension of additional finance with respect to countries that followed prudent policies and avoided excessive debt. While this argument is debatable, it must be assured that these countries will not be "crowded out" of the use of Fund resources by indebted countries.

Notes

[1] During the period 1983–88, total bank lending to the fifteen heavily indebted countries was practically nil: Banks lent $16.6 billion during 1983–84, and then, from 1985 to 1988, reduced their exposure by $15.5 billion. The Fund's net credit during this period was approximately $7.5 billion. See the IMF's *World Economic Outlook*, 1989.

[2] This point is stressed by Jacques Polak in his chapter in this volume.

[3] See, for example, the reports of the Economic Commission for Latin America and the Caribbean (ECLAC). See also Jeffrey D. Sachs, "The Debt Overhang Problem of Developing Countries," Paper presented at the conference in memory of Carlos Díaz-Alejandro Helsinki, Finland 1986.

[4] There is some evidence of complementarity between public and private investment in developing countries; see Mario Blejer and Mohsin S. Khan, "Government Policy and Private Investment in Developing Countries," *IMF Staff Papers*, June 1984; and Guillermo Ortiz, "Public Finance, Trade, and Economic Growth: The Mexican Case," Paper presented at the 1988 Congress of the International Institute of Public Finance, Istanbul, Turkey, August 1988.

[5] See Sachs, op. cit., and Guillermo Ortiz, "Adjustment, Indebtedness, and Economic Growth: Recent Experience," in A. Martirena-Mantel, ed., *External Debt, Savings, and Growth in Latin America* (Washington, D.C.: IMF, 1987).

[6] Morgan Guaranty Trust, *World Financial Markets*, December 1988.

[7] World Bank, *World Debt Tables 1988–89*, p. xvii.

[8] See Alain Ize and Guillermo Ortiz, "Fiscal Rigidities, Public Debt, and Capital Flight." *IMF Staff Papers*, June 1987.

[9] In recent statements, the Managing Director of the Fund has alluded to this point. See Michel Camdessus, "La Contribución del FMI al Problema de la Deuda," *Excelsior*, Mexico City, July 7, 1989. See also Chapter IV of the IMF's *World Economic Outlook*, 1989.

[10] The program contemplates a recovery of economic growth, with a rate of 6 per cent toward the end of the current administration. A financing gap of about 2.5 per cent of GDP is envisaged for the duration of the program.

[11] Joseph Gold, "Mexico and the Development of the Practice of the International Monetary Fund," *World Development*, September 1988, p. 1127.

[12] The IMF's 1989 issue of the *World Economic Outlook* includes a revealing estimation of the source of projection errors incurred by the Fund in its assessment of the outlook

for indebted countries. The 1988 debt/export ratios turned out to be 50 per cent higher than predicted in the 1985 *WEO*. The projection errors were due to valuation effects on the stock of debt (as the U.S. dollar weakened from early 1985, the dollar value of debt denominated in other currencies rose sharply) and lower export volumes and prices, i.e., terms of trade deterioration.

[13] See the chapters in this volume by Jacques Polak and Peter Kenen.

[14] In Mexico's case, the total amount of enhancements available from the IMF and the World Bank is $3.4 billion. Funds available from a parallel arrangement with Japan reach approximately $2 billion. This sum is insufficient to cover the purchase of thirty-year zero-coupon bonds and to guarantee two years of interest payments for a base of $53 billion, assuming a 35-per-cent discount of the principal or an equivalent reduction in interest payments.

[15] See, for example, Rudiger Dornbusch, "Mexico: Stabilization, Debt, and Growth," Photocopy, Massachusetts Institute of Technology, May 1988.

[16] In addition to the well-known inflationary and distorting effects of swaps, it is worth noting that swaps may have the effect of discouraging investment rather than the other way around. Since a swap program has to be limited in any case (due to the effects on inflation and/or public finances), there is usually a long list of projects waiting for swaps. Investment decisions are postponed many times in the hope of obtaining a subsidy, the magnitude of which usually makes this wait worthwhile. The Mexican government agreed to a swap program limited exclusively to the privatization of public enterprises. Since this involves the direct swap of government debt for government assets, it avoids undesirable effects on inflation and public finances.

[17] Mexico and the banks have agreed on a basic package consisting of a three-time "menu": a debt exchange for thirty-year bonds with a 35-per-cent discount on a basis of $54 billion of outstanding medium-term public sector debt; an exchange for bonds of the same maturity bearing a reduced interest rate (a fixed 6.25 per cent); and "new money" in amounts that imply an increase in exposure of 25 per cent on the outstanding debt over a period of three-and-a-half years. About $7 billion will be available for enhancements for debt or debt-service reduction operations.

[18] See John Williamson, *Voluntary Approaches to Debt Relief,* IIE Policy Analysis, first edition (Washington, D.C.: Institute for International Economics, 1988).

Chapter 5

The Fund and the Low-Income Countries

Louis M. Goreux

During the last thirty years, the number of International Monetary Fund members has more than doubled, and the type of countries making use of IMF resources has changed. Industrial countries accounted for about half of outstanding Fund credit until the mid–1970s, but no industrial country had a program with the Fund during the last twelve years. In contrast, among the forty-seven countries that had an arrangement with the Fund at end–June 1989, twenty-eight were African countries and another eight were non-African low-income countries eligible for International Development Association (IDA) assistance.[1] How successful has the Fund been in adjusting to the change in the composition of its clientele? Should it remain so deeply involved with low-income countries encountering structural problems that can be solved only in the long term? And if so, how can the effectiveness of the Fund's assistance be enhanced?

This chapter addresses these questions in four sections. The first reviews the Fund approach in theory and practice. It argues that the Fund is best equipped to design a macroeconomic framework, and that this framework is necessary but not sufficient to secure the needed supply response. It stresses that the Fund has to rely largely on the World Bank for the supply side, and that closer interactions between demand and supply considerations are needed. The second section deals with the financial aspects of Fund assistance. It shows that the use of Fund credit, which was intended to be temporary, has become quasi-permanent in the case of most low-income countries. It argues for the establishment of a soft-loan window for these countries and reviews possible ways of financing it. The third section deals with the catalytic role of the Fund in mobilizing external financial assistance for low-income countries, with particular attention to the refinancing or reduction of external debt and to program lending by the World Bank. It notes that the expansion of program lending by the Bank and structural adjustment credit by the Fund has resulted in a sizable overlap between the respective functions of the two institutions. The last section deals with possible ways of solving the overlap problem. It concludes that the Fund should remain involved with low-income countries, that the Bank-Fund overlap is unavoidable, and that closer cooperation between the Fund and the Bank is the only solution.

The Fund Approach in Theory and Practice

It should be stressed from the start that any arrangement supported by the Fund is tailor-made to the particular conditions of the economy concerned. For that reason, the Fund approach has evolved as the Fund has faced new problems and new clients. Fund missions in low-income countries were concerned with structural adjustment long before the Fund established structural adjustment facilities. Nevertheless, changes in terminology are not without significance, because they reflect changes in emphasis.

Fund programs have been frequently referred to in the past as "stabilization models." This terminology reflected the belief that when a country was facing temporary balance-of-payments difficulties, a cooling-off period often was the price to pay for reestablishing a sound basis for economic recovery. This belief has not disappeared, and the rationale underlying the design of Fund programs remains influenced by a short-term monetary model sometimes referred to in the economic literature as the "Polak model" or the "monetary approach" to the balance of payments. When it was found that recovery did not occur as rapidly as anticipated, and that, in many low-income countries, the first Fund program had to be followed by a second and a third, Fund programs began to be referred to as "adjustment programs," the duration of arrangements was lengthened, and more emphasis was placed on the supply side.

In brief, Fund programs aim to limit the balance-of-payments deficit to the amount that can be financed by placing ceilings on money creation and on the government budget deficit.[2] The Fund believes that countries (like individuals) should not spend more than they have, and that attempting to avoid this constraint by printing more money would only lead to more inflation. The Fund also believes that resources can be allocated more efficiently through the price mechanism than through quantitative restrictions. Consequently, when the Fund analysts consider that the overvaluation of a member country's currency is such that balance-of-payments objectives cannot be reached without having to impose excessive quantitative restrictions, the Fund asks the country to depreciate its currency. Similarly, the Fund asks the national authorities to raise the nominal interest rate when it is lower than the rate of inflation.

In designing a macroeconomic framework, the Fund might appear to be concerned essentially with a few prices (exchange rate, interest rate, and inflation rate, in particular) and with a small number of economic aggregates. But Fund missions often have to go into considerable detail when they negotiate a program.

Suppose that the government deficit, as it appears from a country's initial budget proposal, has to be cut by half. The Fund mission has to discuss with the authorities how to implement this cut by analyzing the budget line by line. One solution is to increase revenues—and tax reforms are often a major feature of the fiscal program recommended by the Fund—but the posssibilities for raising revenues are usually limited in the short term. Raising tax rates could be counterproductive if this had the effect of inducing more fraud and transferring activities from the formal sector (which pays taxes) to the informal sector (which does not). Therefore, in the short term, most of the reduction in the budget deficit often has to come from an expenditure cut. The least painful cut is a reduction in capital expenditures. If the cut would have the effect of eliminating "prestige" projects that would have generated sizable recurrent expenditures without significant output, the cut would stimulate future growth. However, the opposite effect would be produced if prestige projects were preserved at the expense of productive ones.

Turning now to current expenditures, reducing the public wage bill and/or the subsidies to urban consumers is politically very sensitive. These reductions could be avoided by cutting the consumption of goods and services instead; but if the cuts were excessive, civil servants might become unable to perform their duties. One way to avoid such an outcome is to underbudget expenditures on goods and services without reducing actual consumption, which leads to arrears. Enforcing a tight ceiling on domestic credit to governments without being concerned with the accumulation of government payment arrears would make no sense. Consequently, the Fund has to measure the budget deficit not only on a cash basis but also on a commitment basis—the difference between the two being the change in arrears. In spite of the difficulties of measuring variations in domestic government arrears, reduction in domestic arrears is used as a performance criterion in a number of Fund programs.

Finally, the budget of the central government provides only part of the public finance picture. In a number of countries, there are a multitude of special treasury accounts that need to be consolidated to obtain the overall picture. There is also the problem of public enterprises kept afloat with commercial bank credit instead of government subsidies. Ideally, the accounts of the entire public sector should be consolidated, but this is a difficult and lengthy undertaking. It is clear from these examples that Fund missions are not and cannot be concerned only with broad economic aggregates.

The monetary survey is the second set of data that Fund missions analyze in great detail. Given the increase in the demand for money-compatible price expectations, the survey provides the link between the balance-of-payments objectives of the program (which defines the net foreign liabilities target for the banking system) and the permissible expansion of domestic credit. The latter is divided into: (1) net credit to government, which to a large extent defines the permissible budget deficit, and; (2) credit to the private sector, which affects the level of economic activity.

The first task of the mission is to check consistency among the various components of the monetary survey, as well as between the statistics of the central bank and those of the ministry of finance. When the banking system is well organized and the data are presented in a transparent manner, this task is easy. If this is not the case, the Fund may need to send banking experts for extended periods of time in order to establish a reliable monetary survey. The second task is to assist the authorities in defining the monetary and credit policies most appropriate to achieve the objectives of the program.

The balance of payments is the third set of data on which Fund missions concentrate their attention. Frequently, the balance of payments of the previous year has to be extensively revised—starting with numbers that are reasonably well known (such as the overall deficit, official transfers, and official capital flows) before going to those that are known less precisely (such as exports and imports) and ending with those about which little is known (such as private transfers). In the case of exports and imports, recorded transactions often have to be adjusted by estimating unrecorded transactions. The Fund attaches special importance to the determination of the external account deficit because it represents the amount that has to be financed by drawing on the member's reserves, borrowing, refinancing the external debt, or accumulating external arrears. With the frequency of debt rescheduling, Fund missions have had to spend an increasing amount of time in simulating various debt refinancing schemes and in assisting members in negotiations with their creditors.

The balance of payments, the monetary survey, and the table summarizing the financial operations of a government are the three pillars on which Fund programs are built. These pillars are progressively strengthened by regular Fund missions; by technical missions organized by the fiscal, central banking, and statistics departments of the Fund; and by technical experts sent to countries for periods ranging from a few months to several years. Because of the thoroughness of this technical work, because Fund discipline requires perfect consistency between these three basic sets of data, and because of the probing nature of Fund missions, the IMF data is considered by virtually everybody (including bilateral and multilateral aid agencies) to be the most authoritative and timely source of information for countries that have a Fund-supported program. These programs therefore have the considerable merit of providing an improved information base for assessing changes in the economic and financial situation and, consequently, for making rational policy decisions. The importance of this contribution of Fund programs cannot be overemphasized.[3]

Fund missions have gained a reputation for competence, integrity, and power. But they have also acquired, on occasion, the image of inquisitors who have to check everything. Although this perception cannot always be avoided without a lowering of Fund standards, it should be stressed that fruitful cooperation cannot develop without establishing relations of reciprocal confidence and even friendliness between the mission and national authorities. To assist the country's authorities in designing measures that are feasible and sustainable, Fund missions have to understand the nature of the various political constraints; good judgment therefore may be as important as sound economics.

Devaluation is probably the most controversial aspect of Fund programs, but it is unavoidable when a currency is grossly overvalued. In some countries where devaluation was the centerpiece of the Fund program, the disparity between parallel and official rates exceeded ten to one; the parallel market was widespread, and the same good was sold at prices ranging from one to ten depending on how the item was obtained, which was a major source of corruption and inefficiency. Dual exchange rate systems sometimes have been used as temporary devices to facilitate the reentry into regular channels of transactions previously conducted through parallel channels. The Fund has acquired considerable experience in designing fiscal, monetary, and credit measures to avoid a surge in inflation, but the results have been mixed. Among the devaluations made in Africa, there have been failures (such as Sierra Leone and Zambia), semi-successes (such as Zaire and Nigeria), and successes (such as Guinea, Ghana, the Gambia, and Mauritius).

Looking back at the adjustment programs that have been conducted in various African countries and in other countries with similar levels of development during the past ten years, it has to be recognized that the results have been less favorable than anticipated. This has sometimes been due to policy slippages or unforeseen external events such as a sharper-than-assumed deterioration in the terms of trade, but the main reason is generally that the supply response has been weaker and has taken more time to materialize than expected. It was known that Fund prescriptions (such as limiting the expansion of credit and raising the interest rate) could have an immediate recessionary effect. But the recovery did not happen as rapidly as expected, and the Fund was not able to come quickly, do the job, and go. Once the Fund became involved with a country, it generally had to remain involved year after year.

It became clear that the Fund had to take a longer-term perspective and to devote more attention to the supply side and to the various impediments to growth. However, Fund missions, which had been used to discussing policies and adjustment measures with officials of the central banks and the ministries of finance, could not be expected to cover all aspects of the real economy; they could not be expected to find the engine for growth, start it, and maintain it in running order. They therefore had to rely increasingly on the staffs of other institutions—of the World Bank in particular—to deal with the supply side of the economy.

Plugging a number of supply measures advocated by the Bank into the Fund model is not the appropriate solution, however. Supply and demand considerations need to be integrated into the formulation of the model to determine the speed of adjustment that is both technically feasible and politically sustainable. The speed of adjustment often has been overestimated, partly because the length of the grace period attached to Fund purchases was too short. If the Fund is to provide financial assistance to low-income countries, the terms of this assistance should be fitted to the repayment capacity of the borrowing country.

Fund Financial Assistance

Prior to 1977, outstanding Fund credit was shared about equally between industrial and non-industrial countries, but after 1980, outstanding credit to industrial countries became insignificant (Table 1). The turning point occurred in the mid–1970s. In the three years that followed the first oil shock, three industrial countries made credit-tranche purchases and six made purchases under the oil facility; three industrial countries drew resources under the Compensatory Financing Facility in 1976, and another did so in 1978. Since then, no industrial country has requested the use of Fund resources.

The rapid expansion of Fund credit to developing countries started in 1974 with the first oil shock and the ensuing worldwide economic recession. In Africa, outstanding Fund credit rose from SDR 100 million

Table 1. Outstanding Fund Credit[a]: Total, Industrial Countries, and Non-Industrial Countries by Regional Groupings (billions of SDRs at end of period)

	All Countries	Industrial Countries[b]	Non-Industrial Countries in:				
			Africa	Asia	Europe	Middle East	Western Hemisphere
1950	0.2	0.1	—	0.1	—	—	—
1955	0.1	—	—	—	0.1	—	0.1
1960	0.4	—	—	0.1	—	0.1	0.2
1961	1.4	0.7	0.1	0.2	0.1	—	0.4
1965	3.0	1.9	0.1	0.4	0.1	0.1	0.4
1970	3.2	2.4	0.1	0.4	0.1	0.1	0.1
1973	1.0	—	0.1	0.4	0.1	0.1	0.3
1974	3.7	1.5	0.3	1.2	0.2	0.1	0.4
1975	7.4	3.3	0.6	1.8	0.6	0.3	0.8
1976	12.6	5.7	1.2	2.1	1.4	0.5	1.7
1977	13.1	6.5	1.4	1.8	0.8	0.6	1.6
1978	10.3	4.1	1.5	1.7	1.3	0.6	1.1
1979	8.8	1.7	1.5	1.7	1.4	0.5	1.2
1980	8.5	1.0	1.8	2.4	1.9	0.3	1.0
1981	13.4	0.6	3.3	5.2	2.8	0.2	1.3
1982	19.3	0.1	5.2	7.3	3.9	0.1	2.7
1983	29.9	—	6.5	9.6	5.3	0.1	8.4
1984	34.9	—	7.1	10.0	5.9	0.1	11.8
1985	35.2	—	7.3	9.2	5.4	0.1	13.2
1986	33.4	—	6.6	8.7	4.6	0.1	13.4
1987	28.8	—	5.6	7.0	3.2	0.2	12.8
1988	25.5	—	5.8	5.7	1.7	0.2	12.1

[a] Excludes SAF purchases and Trust Fund loans. At end-June 1988, SAF disbursements amounted to SDR 0.6 billion and Trust Fund loans outstanding to SDR 0.5 billion, of which SDR 1.1 billion were to India and China. Includes principal in arrears.
[b] Twenty countries classified by the Fund as industrial.

Source: Derived from Tables on "Use of Fund Credit," *International Financial Statistics* (Washington, D.C.: IMF), various years.

in 1973 to a peak of SDR 7.3 billion at the end of 1985 before declining to SDR 5.8 billion by the end of 1988. In Western Hemisphere (mainly Latin American) countries, due to Fund involvement in the debt crisis, the use of Fund credit increased from SDR 1.3 billion at end–1971 to a peak of SDR 13.4 billion at end–1986.

Until recently, the Fund extended financial assistance to all of its members essentially in the form of purchases that had to be repurchased within three to five years. By that time, it was reasoned, the member's balance-of-payments problems should have been resolved. If not, the repurchase would have a destabilizing effect unless it was offset by a second purchase, which in turn might have to be followed by a third. In order to prevent a temporary credit from becoming permanent, the Fund was supposed to grant a request for a stand-by arrangement only if it was satisfied that the member's balance of payments would become viable within three to five years. Viability was understood to mean that the member would not need exceptional financing such as Fund purchases or debt rescheduling.

These expectations have been generally satisfied in the case of industrial countries and the largest developing countries. Of the twenty-one countries now classified as industrial, eleven have made use of Fund resources and, among them, only two (Iceland and New Zealand, which have been classified by the Fund as industrial only since 1979) have had Fund credit outstanding for more than eight consecutive years. Of the eight developing countries with Fund quotas exceeding SDR 1 billion, Saudi Arabia has never made use of Fund credit; Venezuela used Fund credit for the first time in 1989; four (Argentina, Brazil, China, and Mexico) never used Fund credit for more than ten consecutive years, and only two (Indonesia and India before 1975) have had Fund credit outstanding for more than ten consecutive years (Table 2). For many other developing countries, however, outstanding Fund credit has not been temporary. Six of them have had Fund credit outstanding for 20 to 29 consecutive years, and fifteen others for 14 to 19 consecutive years.

As the Fund became more involved with low-income countries, it established new facilities with financing terms better fitted to the needs of these countries. Through the establishment of the Extended Fund Facility (EFF) in 1974, the Fund was enabled to support three-year programs with credits repayable within four to eight years and following the 1979 review, within four to ten years. This facility was used mainly in the early 1980s, but very few members have been able to meet the performance criteria throughout the program period. The EFF, which had been used infrequently from 1984 to 1987, was revived in 1988; as of end–June 1989, five countries had an EFF arrangement with the Fund.

Table 2. Fund Credit to Developing Countries, Number of Consecutive Years Outstanding[a]

Countries with a Quota Exceeding SDR 1 Billion[b]:			Countries with a Quota Exceeding SDR 1 Billion[b]:		
	Period	*No. consec. yrs. outstanding*		*Period*	*No. consec. yrs. outstanding*
Argentina	1958–66	8	Egypt	1959–88	29
	1972–77	5	Chile	1961–88	27
	1983–88	5	Sri Lanka	1962–88	26
Brazil	1957–67	10	Mali	1964–88	24
	1982–88	6	Sudan	1964–88	24
China	1981–82[c]	2	Philippines	1968–88	20
	1986–88[c]	2	Chad	1970–88	18
India	1957–70	13	Uganda	1971–88	17
	1974–77	3	Zambia	1971–88	17
	1980–88	8	Yugoslavia	1961–69	8
Indonesia	1958–74	16		1971–88	17
	1983–88	5	Turkey	1955–71	16
Mexico	1976–80	4		1975–88	13
	1983–88	5	Zaire	1972–88	16
			Romania	1973–88	15
			Jamaica	1973–88	15
			Central Africa	1974–88	14
			Kenya	1974–88	14
			Korea	1974–88	14
			Madagascar	1974–88	14
			Panama	1974–88	14
			Sierra Leone	1974–88	14
			Tanzania	1974–88	14
			Ghana	1962–64	3
				1966–72	7
				1975–88	13

[a] Outstanding Fund credit of no less than SDR 1 million at the end of the calendar year. A country may have outstanding Fund credit throughout a series of consecutive years without purchasing from the Fund each year. For example, a country making its first purchase in year one, repurchasing in years three to five, making a second purchase before the end of year five, repurchasing it before the end of year ten and not making a third purchase before year eleven would have had outstanding Fund credit for nine consecutive years.
[b] Venezuela used Fund credit for the first time in 1989.
[c] First credit tranche.
   Source: International Monetary Fund, *International Financial Statistics* (Washington, D.C.), various years.

As long as Fund exposure increased, it was relatively easy for countries to remain current with the Fund. However, once Fund exposure stabilized or declined—while the financial situation of borrowing countries remained difficult—paying interest charges at market-related rates became a problem. Moreover, it did not appear consistent for the Fund to tell a country that it should not borrow at commercial terms and simultaneously to extend credit to that country at market-related rates. For these reasons, when new facilities were established to assist low-income countries in implementing structural adjustments, interest charges became highly concessional.

While stand-by and EFF purchases carry interest charges slightly below market rates and have to be repurchased within three to five years, credits extended under the new facilities carry an interest rate of half of one per cent a year and are repayable over five to ten years. The Structural Adjustment Facility (SAF) established in March 1986 was financed from reflows of the Trust Fund loans made between 1977 and 1981, which had themselves been financed from one-sixth of the proceeds of the Fund's gold sales from 1976 to 1980. The SAF was restricted to IDA-eligible countries, as the Trust Fund had been. Because China and India—which together account for some 52 per cent of the sum of the quotas of IDA-eligible countries—expressed their intent not to make use of the SAF, the other IDA countries were able to draw the equivalent of 70 per cent of their respective Fund quotas in support of three-year adjustment programs.

SAF resources amounted to only SDR 2.7 billion. An additional SDR 6 billion was sought through voluntary contributions for the Enhanced Structural Adjustment Facility (ESAF), which was established by the IMF Executive Board in December 1987 and became operational in April 1988.

The two concessional facilities (SAF and ESAF) provide assistance to support three-year adjustment programs on the same financial terms, but differ in several respects. The amount of assistance a member can obtain under the ESAF is more than twice that available under the SAF. But the conditionality attached to ESAF arrangements is stronger than that tied to SAF arrangements. The main differences between stand-by, ESAF, and SAF arrangements may be summarized as follows. With stand-by arrangements, purchases are subject to the observance of quarterly quantitative performance criteria, such as ceilings on net bank credit to the government or net domestic assets of the banking system. With ESAF arrangements, disbursements are made every six months, and performance is assessed on the basis of several considerations: observance of quantitative and structural performance criteria; discrepancies from quantitative or qualitative benchmarks; and completion of mid-year reviews, including understandings on key policy issues. With SAF arrangements, disbursements are made upon approval of yearly programs, and performance is assessed in relation to benchmarks.

The first SAF and ESAF arrangements were approved by the Executive Board in August 1986 and July 1988, respectively. By end–June 1989, twenty-one SAF and eleven ESAF arrangements were in effect; but only two SAF-eligible countries had a stand-by arrangement, and none had an EFF arrangement.[4] In contrast, eighteen SAF-eligible countries had either a stand-by or an EFF arrangement with the Fund at the end of 1986. It is therefore clear that SAF and ESAF resources have been used to replace the Fund's ordinary resources. Substituting Fund resources with SAF and ESAF resources relieves low-income countries of the burden of market-related Fund charges and enables these countries to repay the Fund while avoiding negative transfers. But the SAF and ESAF resources will have to be replenished.

SAF reflows could be used to replenish the ESAF during the second half of the 1990s. Assuming that the GDP of SAF countries increases by 7 per cent a year in terms of current SDRs—which, after accounting for inflation, may correspond to only a limited improvement in real GDP per capita—SAF reflows in relation to the current GDP of SAF countries would represent only half of the original SAF in relation to the GDP of the same countries ten years earlier. Moreover, SAF reflows would become available several years after the expected exhaustion of ESAF resources. If the original SAF resources were recycled once more, the reflow would become insignificant in terms of current gross domestic product. ESAF reflows could not be recycled because, under present arrangements, they must be used to repay the original lenders.

In accordance with the Board decision establishing the ESAF, all ESAF funds had to be committed by November 1989, with the last disbursement to take place before June 30, 1992. By end–June 1989, only SDR 1.15 billion had been disbursed and SDR 2.8 billion committed under the SAF and ESAF facilities, out of a total of SDR 8.7 billion. The deadlines for commitments and disbursements were extended by one year in March 1989, and they may be further extended. In any case, the problem of replenishing the ESAF facility or of funding an interest subsidy account will arise soon.

One solution would be to rely on voluntary contributions, as was done when the ESAF was established. A second solution would be to institutionalize a periodic ESAF replenishment by the aid agencies of industrial countries. In either case, however, the ESAF replenishment would, to some extent, compete with the IDA replenishment. A third solution would be for the Fund to take advantage of its monetary power and make an SDR allocation to its members, with the understanding that industrial countries would transfer the whole or part of their allo-

cations to the subsidy account. Creating money instead of asking industrial countries to make adequate aid appropriations in their budgets
could, however, be considered a misuse of the SDR, which should remain
a liquid and safe reserve asset. A fourth solution would be for the Fund
to sell part of its gold, either through public auctions (as it did in the late
1970s) or to central banks with surplus liquidity.

The Fund holds about 103 million ounces of gold, valued at SDR 35
per ounce on its balance sheet. At prices prevailing in mid–1989, this
gold constitutes a hidden reserve of about SDR 27 billion. If the Fund
sold one-fourth of its gold and invested the proceeds at the prevailing
SDR interest rate, it would receive enough income to subsidize down to
zero the interest on an amount in excess of SDR 6 billion, which is the
maximum credit that can be extended under current ESAF arrangements.[5] If the Fund wanted to preserve the real value of the invested
proceeds, it would have to sell a larger share of its gold. Selling part of
the gold owned by the Fund raises very sensitive issues, and the conditions under which the Fund is authorized to make gold transactions is
tightly restricted by its Articles of Agreement—but it represents an
option well worth serious consideration.

By selling part of its gold, the Fund could finance ESAF credits
from its quota resources and subsidize charges from its own revenues.
The Fund and the Bank would use different sources of financing for
their soft windows, which would eliminate the problem of competition.
The Fund could simplify the complex structure of its facilities (stand-by,
EFF, SAF, and ESAF), which partly reflects the historical context in
which they were established. As in the Bank, low- and medium-income
countries could use the same facilities but receive financing at different
levels of concessionality.[6]

The Catalytic Role of the Fund

The leverage of Fund programs results not only from the money lent by
the Fund but also more broadly from the doors opened to countries
implementing such programs. Fund programs have become increasingly important in the last ten years because of their impact on debt
refinancing by official and private creditors and on adjustment lending
by the World Bank.

Refinancing External Debt

The close linkage between Fund-supported programs and debt rescheduling has given a prominent role to the Fund, but it has also on occasion
placed the Fund in an uncomfortable position. In some cases, strong
pressures have been exerted on the Fund to conclude a program in the

absence of adequate finance either because the terms of debt rescheduling were not appropriate or because the country's adjustment efforts were not sufficient. In other cases, the Fund has played the role of debt collector because the accumulation of arrears owed to an external creditor was treated as a breach of performance criteria—even when it appeared that no viable long-term solution could be found without some form of debt reduction. Some debt issues relating to debt financing are reviewed below for the three main categories of creditors: bilateral, private, and multilateral.

The debt of low-income countries to *bilateral creditors* is by far the largest of the three categories. It has been rescheduled in the context of the Paris Club, which relies heavily on the assessment presented in Fund-supported programs. But the successive reschedulings have resulted in an accumulation of claims that cannot be repaid. From 1980 to 1987, the claims of bilateral creditors on SAF-eligible countries in Africa almost tripled in relation to the export earnings of the debtor countries. The need for debt reduction is clear. A first step was made at the Toronto summit, but more needs to be done.

Although the alternative to debt refinancing is often the accumulation of unpaid bills, bilateral creditors have tied assistance in the form of debt refinancing much more tightly to Fund programs than they have assistance in the form of new credits and grants. This anomaly has now been partly corrected by several donor countries that have established adjustment lending facilities that are generally linked to the adjustment programs supported by the Fund and the Bank; the European Community, for example, is planning to set up an adjustment facility within the context of Lomé IV.

Because attention is focused on the commercial debt of the middle-income countries, the problem of the low-income countries is often overlooked. But even if *private creditors* account for a small share of the debt of low-income countries, they may receive a substantial part of the debt service paid. In 1987, the public and publicly guaranteed long-term debt owed by low-income African countries to private creditors was only 15 per cent of that owed to official creditors, but the debt service paid to private creditors was 46 per cent of that paid to official creditors.[7] The discrepancy was even greater for countries with Fund programs. A sizable part of the assistance provided by the Fund and the Bank has therefore been used to pay interest to commercial banks on the face value of claims that are highly discounted on the secondary market and that have been abundantly provisioned by the banks.

It may appear paradoxical that banks could gain in lending to Madagascar and lose in lending to Mexico and Brazil, which have per capita incomes eight times higher than Madagascar. But in the first case, the banks knew that they would be bailed out by the Fund and the

Bank; and in the other, they knew that they would not because the debts of Mexico and Brazil were too large.

Consider a low-income country receiving official assistance in excess of the debt service due to the banks; suppose that this assistance is tied to the observance of the Fund performance criteria and that one of these criteria is to be current with the banks. As long as the country has a program with the Fund, the country will be better off paying the banks than not paying them. On the other hand, the banks will not be interested in negotiating a debt reduction scheme as long as they believe the Fund will act as their de facto debt collector. Serious negotiations can start only if the Fund makes it known that arrears to the banks will not be treated as a breach of performance criteria.

The Fund rarely took this position prior to 1989; it did so in 1987 with Bolivia, which, for this reason, was able to conduct a successful debt buyback. What was exceptional before the Brady Plan could become normal practice. Accumulation of arrears to banks may now be tolerated when the country is engaged in bona fide negotiations with its creditors. A creditor would not, however, be interested in participating in a debt reduction scheme if this creditor knew that, if it did not participate, the non-servicing of its original claim would be treated as a breach of Fund performance criteria. Every creditor would want to become the free rider, and no scheme could be agreed upon.

The free ride would disappear if creditors knew in advance that, if the Fund considers that the debtor country has offered a fair package of options to its creditors, the debtor will be granted a waiver on arrears to those creditors having chosen not to participate. In this case, however, the Fund could not remain neutral; it would have to decide whether the deal is fair or not. Rather than place itself in this delicate position, the Fund may follow a case-by-case approach and rely essentially on the leverage that governments of creditor countries are willing to exert on their banks.

Assuming the appropriate leverage could be exerted and the bank claims could be bought for 10 cents to the dollar, the simplest solution would be a buyback, as in the case of Bolivia. If the claims could be bought in the range of 15 to 40 cents to the dollar, a direct buyback could present two drawbacks: First, a large disbursement would have to be made at the beginning of the program period, and the resources might not be available at the time; second, the financial leverage of the Fund and the Bank would be sharply reduced after the buyback. These two drawbacks would disappear with a lease-purchase agreement.[8] Assuming rollover of the principal, the debtor would have to reach an agreement with its London Club creditors on a payment schedule corresponding to the interest due on the face value of its debt and on the price at which the debt would be purchased if all interest payments were made on schedule. If the debtor interrupted its payments, the contract would not be fulfilled, and creditors would keep their full claims—previous payments being treated as interest charges on the face value of the claims. With a purchase price of 30 cents to the dollar and an interest rate of 10 (or 12) per cent a year, the debt could be paid back in 44 (or 37) months.[9] The debtor country would be induced to make regular payments because it would see the light at the end of the tunnel. The motivation would become stronger as time went on, since interrupting payments would mean forgoing benefits of increasing magnitude. The scheme would complement an adjustment program supported by the Fund and the Bank. The size of the financial gap would remain unchanged during the repayment period but would be reduced afterward, which would strengthen the member's capability of repaying the Fund and the Bank.

The possibility of linking debt service to changes in export earnings is one of the avenues that could be explored for countries heavily dependent on primary commodity exports (for example, linking the repayment of the Congo to earnings from oil). In managing the Compensatory Financing Facility, the Fund has acquired considerable experience in assessing changes in the value of export earnings, and much discussion has been devoted to the pros and cons of using nominal or deflated export earnings. For the sake of simplicity, one might also consider the possibility of linking debt payments to the price of a key commodity, as quoted in a professional journal or the *International Financial Statistics (IFS)* published by the Fund. When earnings (or the price) fell sharply, creditors would receive very little—but without the scheme, they would not have received much either. When earnings (or the price) shot up, creditors would receive more, and debtors might eventually be prevented from using their windfall earnings for launching prestige projects.

The last category of creditors consists of the *multilateral agencies* (the Fund, the World Bank, and the regional development banks), which have not yet rescheduled their claims. Arrears to the Fund became a problem after the use of Fund credit started to decline. To encourage its members to remain current, the Fund decided that a member with protracted arrears would be declared ineligible to use Fund resources. This procedure induced countries to make special efforts to repay the Fund to avoid the declaration of ineligibility; but, once declared ineligible, countries generally ceased to make any payments at all. As a result, the problem of arrears has been limited to a small number of countries with large arrears. Four countries (Sudan, Zambia, Peru, and Liberia) have accumulated arrears of SDR 2,230 million, which represents 80 per cent of the total arrears due to the Fund.[10]

The Fund so far has held the view that a request for an arrangement with the Fund cannot be submitted to the Board before the country has become current. This should not mean, however, that once a country has accumulated large arrears it should remain isolated from the international financial community forever. When such a country becomes genuinely committed to better policies, the Fund can intervene in two ways.

The first procedure has already been applied when it has been possible to mobilize enough outside resources to repay the arrears to the Fund and other multinational agencies and, at the same time, to support a credible adjustment program. In such cases, the Fund has been able, when needed, to provide larger-than-usual access to its resources and to arrange a bridge loan allowing the member to become current before presenting the arrangement to the Board.[11] When it is not possible to reduce the Fund arrears immediately, but a plan can be worked out for reducing arrears progressively and eliminating them within the program period, the Fund can monitor a program supported by resources other than its own—as was done for the first time in the case of Guyana in April 1989. When arrears are very large, as in the case of Sudan, it may not be possible to apply this second procedure, but the Fund should be prepared to monitor a credible adjustment program supported by resources other than its own even if arrears to the Fund could not be reduced over the program period. If the program proves to be successful, it may become possible to apply one of the two above-mentioned procedures. If the program fails, it will not have the effect of increasing Fund arrears.

Structural Adjustment Lending by the World Bank

Structural Adjustment Loans and Credits (SALs and SACs) and Sector Adjustment Loans (SECALs) were introduced by the World Bank in 1980 "to assist countries prepared to undertake an adjustment program to meet an existing balance-of-payments crisis or to avoid an impending one." Unlike project lending, adjustment lending is fast-disbursing and can be used to finance imports not linked to any specific investment program. It can therefore be used to fill up the ex ante balance-of-payments gap in much the same way as Fund credit; 95 per cent of the countries that have received SALs or SECALs also had Fund programs.

The share of adjustment in total Bank lending increased from 3 per cent in 1980 to about 25 per cent in 1988; for low-income African countries, it reached 37 per cent in FY'88.[12] For SAF-eligible countries, the decline in Fund outstanding credit since 1984 has been almost offset by Bank adjustment lending. As a result, total outstanding credits extended by the two institutions for balance-of-payments support has remained almost stable over the last four years (middle line of Figure 1-A). Total Fund and Bank outstanding credit (inclusive of Bank project lending) doubled from 1980 to 1984, but it has increased only marginally since 1984 (upper line of Figure 1-A). The share of Fund and Bank credit to SAF countries in Sub-Saharan Africa (SSA) rose from 57 per cent in 1980 to 62 per cent in 1987. For this subset of countries, the small decline in outstanding Fund credit has been more than offset by the increase in Bank credit (Figure 1-B); lending by the Bank was equivalent to almost one-third of outstanding Fund credit by end–1987.

For the fifteen highly indebted medium-income countries covered by the Baker Initiative, adjustment lending by the Bank increased sharply after 1982; by the end of 1987, it was equivalent to almost one-third of outstanding Fund credit (Figure 1-C). For the three major debtors—Argentina, Brazil, and Mexico—outstanding credit by the Fund and the Bank increased almost threefold from 1982 to 1985 (Figure 1-D).

The rapid increase in Bank adjustment lending provided an effective way of filling the financing gap of many countries, but it also created problems. Through its adjustment lending the Bank was able to do virtually the same thing that the Fund was trying to do through its structural adjustment facilities. It soon became clear that the two institutions had to harmonize their strategies so that they would not provide conflicting advice to the same countries. The instrument for enforcing this harmonization has been the Policy Framework Paper (PFP) that was introduced in 1986 with the establishment of the Structural Adjustment Facility.[13] The PFP has greater operational significance in the Fund than in the Bank, since its approval by the Fund Board is a prerequisite for the establishment of an SAF or an ESAF arrangement. In the Bank, PFPs have only provided the background for possible future negotiations of SALs or SECALs.[14]

The Future of Fund Financial Assistance to Low-Income Countries

When the Bank was dealing essentially with investment projects and the Fund with short-term balance-of-payments problems, the borderline between the respective functions of the two institutions was clear. When the two institutions moved into structural adjustment and extended program loans to the same countries for similar purposes, the boundary became blurred. This overlap could be eliminated in two ways: Either the Bank could return exclusively to project lending or the Fund could leave the problems of low-income countries to the Bank. Alternatively, one could recognize that an overlap is unavoidable and even beneficial, provided that the two institutions are complementary and do not compete in the overlapping zone.

Figure 1. Fund and World Bank Outstanding Credit, 1980-87

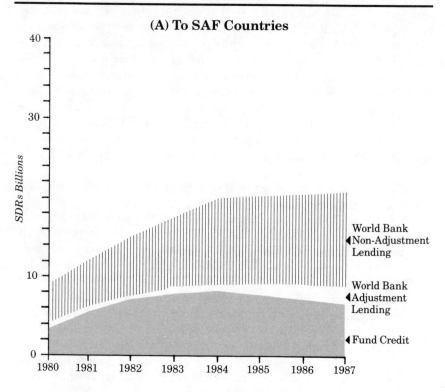

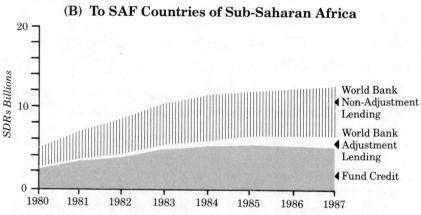

Source: Outstanding Fund credit calculated from International Monetary Fund, *International Financial Survey* (Washington, D.C., IMF), various issues. World Bank outstanding credit derived from World Bank, *World Bank Debt Tables 1988* (Washington, D.C., World Bank). World Bank adjustment lending calculated from structural adjustment loans and credits country by country.

(C) To Fifteen[a] Highly Indebted Countries

(D) To Argentina, Brazil, and Mexico

[a]Bolivia and Jamaica excluded.

The key issues for the Fund are (1) whether or not the institution has an essential role to play in the economic policies of low-income countries, and (2) whether or not the financial assistance required to play this role effectively is compatible with the "monetary character" of the Fund. If the answers are positive, the nature of financial assistance that the Fund extends to low-income countries would differ from that envisaged when the Fund was established. The need for a soft window was recognized when the SAF and ESAF were initiated, but these facilities were established on a temporary basis only. Since it is now clear that ESAF resources will be fully committed long before the financial problems of the low-income countries are solved, Fund shareholders will have to decide soon how to finance the soft window.

If Fund shareholders decide against a soft window, two developments are possible. Under one, the Fund would progressively withdraw from low-income countries needing structural adjustment and leave the problems of these countries to the Bank. Under the other, the Fund would remain very much involved—but without using its resources. Should the Fund maintain a soft window, the remaining problem will be to define more clearly the respective responsibilities of the Fund and the Bank.

Scenario 1: No Soft Window

Without a soft window, the Fund could follow two different roads:

1. *Reduced number of programs.* Since the repayment capabilities of most low-income countries are not expected to improve substantially in the near future, the number of programs supported by the Fund would have to decline under this scenario. The Fund would pursue policy dialogue with low-income countries in the context of Article IV consultations, but its impact on the policies of these countries would be reduced. The staff and the Executive Board would have more time to concentrate on issues affecting the world financial system. But if key actors continued to prefer discussing the most sensitive issues within restricted circles (the Groups of Three, Five, or Seven), rather than within the Fund, the Fund would lose some of its financial clout and would become more research-oriented and less action-oriented.

2. *Programs without financial commitments.* It could be argued, however, that the above scenario need not occur because the power of the Fund depends largely on the doors it opens—not merely on its financial resources. A country's participation in a program approved and monitored by the Fund could be a prerequisite for debt rescheduling or aid by official creditors—as well as for commitments and disbursements of structural adjustment credits by other multilateral institutions. The

Fund would thereby retain its leverage without having to be concerned with the risk of building up future arrears.

This might be considered an ideal position for the Fund, but one unlikely to last, as it would become more difficult for the Fund to resist political pressures in the absence of a financial commitment. The agencies committing their own resources would resent their dependence on the Fund giving a green light before they could act. More basically, decisionmaking power without financial responsibility is not a sound management principle.

Scenario 2: A Soft Window

The basic reason for funding a soft window is that over the years the Fund has acquired unique experience in the macroeconomic aspects of adjustment programs—and this existing capital should be efficiently utilized. As stressed earlier, the Fund provides the most accurate and up-to-date picture of the overall financial situation of a country, and it is best equipped to assist national authorities in assessing the consistency of their proposed fiscal and monetary policies with their balance-of-payments objectives. Moreover, the Fund's procedures have been designed to allow it to act expeditiously when temporary balance-of-payments disequilibria need to be corrected.

The Fund's expertise is necessary but by itself insufficient to solve the economic and financial problems of the low-income countries. The Bank is better equipped than the Fund to deal with the supply side of the economy and with long-term problems—in particular the formation and maintenance of physical and human capital. Taking into account the comparative advantages of each institution, it would appear logical for the Fund to deal with the macroeconomic sphere, with emphasis on short-term problems, and for the Bank to focus on sectoral microeconomic issues, with emphasis on long-term problems.

While it is relatively easy to identify broad areas in which each institution has a comparative advantage, it is difficult to draw a firm borderline between their respective responsibilities. For the least-developed countries, especially when they are small, a distinction cannot be drawn easily between the macro, micro, or sectoral issues, and it is difficult to isolate short-term from long-term movements. These difficulties can be illustrated in the case of an exchange rate adjustment, which typically falls within the Fund's domain. It is critical to the success of adjustment to pass on the cost of the devaluation to consumers and the benefits to producers. For these reasons, the levels of producer prices for a country's main export crop (e.g., coffee or cocoa) and of retail prices for the main consumer goods (e.g., rice and petroleum products) often have been key issues in the negotiation of Fund programs.

Moreover, the distinction between the short and long term has become of little operational value for defining the borderlines between the respective responsibilities of the Fund and the Bank. Between the short term and the long term, there is a grey area called the medium term, and the Fund has become increasingly involved in this middle zone. The Fund had to become involved not only because of the debt crisis, but also because it had to assess the repayment capabilities of the members to which it extended credit.

If an overlap between the respective responsibilities of the Fund and the Bank is unavoidable, one solution would be to merge the two institutions. This solution has been advocated at times, but it should be resisted because the Fund discharges an essential monetary function that is quite different from the functions assigned to the Bank. The Fund's most important shareholders already exhibit the tendency to discuss sensitive monetary issues within restricted circles rather than in the Fund in order to preserve confidentiality. This tendency would become greater if the size of the institution quadrupled through a merger.

Assuming that the Fund and the Bank continue to function as separate institutions, and that the Fund remains involved with the problems of low-income countries, how should the two organizations cooperate to assist these countries most efficiently? The joint preparation of the Policy Framework Paper (PFP) has certainly contributed to greater cooperation between the Fund and the Bank, but it has also raised difficulties. First, this procedure has resulted in the preparation of at least three separate documents for each debtor country (the PFP, the Fund document describing the SAF or the ESAF arrangement, and the Bank document), which in many respects repeat each other, but in others may differ in matters of substance. Second, three separate negotiations are required, which is time-consuming and may sometimes lead to confusion. Third, the Fund program may have a financing gap without the Bank's contribution, and the Bank may not wish to specify the timing and amount of its disbursement before starting to negotiate its own program.

These difficulties could be partially avoided if the PFP became the main document describing the most important policies that the government intended to follow in its three-year program. Unfortunately, the PFP so far has been primarily a subject of negotiation between the staffs of the Fund and the Bank, and it has been written in sufficiently general terms to leave enough margin of maneuver to each staff for negotiating its own arrangement. It is now recognized that the borrowing-country authorities should play a much more active role in the preparation of the PFP, which should be *their* document—not one written essentially in Washington. The purpose of the PFP could be better achieved if it were negotiated between the authorities and a joint Fund-Bank mission with a single head and a single brief. If the mission chief were from the Fund, its deputy should be from the Bank, and vice-versa, with each institution heading the same number of joint missions. It is encouraging to note that the desirability of such joint missions recently has been acknowledged by the management of both organizations. Such joint missions could prove particularly valuable in difficult cases where the assistance of both the Bank and the Fund is critical. The countries would lose the opportunity of playing one institution against the other, and they could concentrate their attention on a single key negotiation.

Such a procedure should not raise technical difficulties for the Fund's staff, since the PFP and the document describing the SAF (or ESAF) arrangement are generally prepared concomitantly and discussed simultaneously by the Executive Board. It would, however, essentially reverse the relative importances of the two documents. For the Bank staff, the adoption of the proposed procedure could have more important implications: The Bank's lending program should be tied to the PFP, and policies that the Bank might wish to recommend in its future adjustment lending should be integrated in the PFP if they are likely to affect the structure of the three-year program described in the paper. Because the PFP would commit the Bank on key features of its program lending, it would require advance preparation by the Bank staff. This should nevertheless be feasible; since PFPs are rolling programs covering the three-year period ahead, most PFPs produced in a given year are merely updated versions of previous PFPs. In view of the proposed upgrading of the PFP, the Bank heads of the joint missions should hold sufficiently senior positions, and the Bank's Executive Board should review the PFP document.

To conclude, the Fund has accumulated unique expertise in the formulation of macroeconomic adjustment programs. This expertise should be utilized, but it should be complemented by World Bank expertise on the supply side, and these two expertises should be integrated through closer cooperation between the staffs of the two institutions. The Fund's contribution to the design and monitoring of adjustment programs should be supported by financial assistance on terms compatible with the repayment capacity of the low-income countries, which means that a soft window should be established in the Fund when the ESAF resources are committed. Closer cooperation between the staffs of the Fund and the Bank could be enforced by upgrading the status of the PFP, which would specify the key features of the three-year adjustment program and of the Bank's lending program. The upgraded PFP should be negotiated by a joint Fund-Bank mission with a single head.

Notes

[1] In this chapter, the term "low-income countries" refers to the sixty countries eligible to draw resources under the Fund's Structural Adjustment Facility (SAF), other than India and China, which are eligible to draw but have expressed their intent not to do so. The SAF countries were originally those eligible to receive concessional resources from the IDA, the World Bank's soft-loan window. But the list of IDA countries varies from time to time, because it is based primarily on a per capita income threshold.

[2] Most Fund programs specify a ceiling on total domestic credit and a subceiling on net credit to the government, which are both performance criteria of the program. The subceiling on net credit to government is the most sensitive to negotiate and the one most frequently broken. Its purpose is to contain the budget deficit and to avoid crowding out the private sector. This subceiling is usually reinforced by a ceiling on external commercial borrowing and other external arrears, which provides an effective way of capping the government deficit measured on a cash basis.

[3] The information collected by the Fund on countries without a program is of more limited value; it is often outdated because the visits of Fund missions are much less frequent; it is also of lower quality, because the authorities are often unwilling to discuss sensitive information with the missions if they do not expect anything from the Fund.

[4] International Monetary Fund, *IMF Memorandum*, for release August 7, 1989.

[5] Such an operation has a precedent in the Fund's early history, when the low interest rate it charged on the limited amount of outstanding credit did not suffice to cover its administrative expenditures. To meet the deficit, and thereafter to build up a reserve, the Fund sold some of its gold for dollars, which it invested in U.S. Treasury bills. The investment, which at its peak reached 23 million ounces, lasted from 1968 to 1972.

[6] The author benefitted from lengthy discussions with Jacques J. Polak on the gold sale proposal.

[7] From 1982 to 1987, private creditors did not increase their exposure in these countries, while official creditors increased theirs by 130 per cent.

[8] *Dettes Africaines, les oubliés du plan Brady,* "L'abandon conditionnel de créances," *Repères,* N.S.E., No. 167, July 24, 1989, pp. 3–4.

[9] For a claim with a face value of 100, the first semiannual interest payment of 5 would be accounted in two parts: 1.5 as interest on the discounted value of 30 and 3.5 as repayment of the discounted principal, which would then be reduced to 26.5.

[10] Obligation overdue by six months or more as of April 30, 1989, as reported in International Monetary Fund, *Annual Report 1989,* Annex Table II.14.

[11] Several bridge loans have been arranged with commercial banks on the understanding that the bank would be repaid by the country from the proceeds of the initial Fund purchase. But this practice has proved to be expensive and somewhat risky.

[12] Fiscal years cover the period from July 1 to June 30.

[13] Because of its limited operational significance, the PFP has been considered by the Bank's Executive Directors meeting as a "Committee of the Whole" and not as the Executive Board.

[14] It may be noted that the problems that occurred recently between the Fund and the Bank related primarily to non-SAF countries for which no PFP is prepared.

Comment by Joan M. Nelson:
The IMF and the Impact of Adjustment on the Poor

The IMF has been sharply criticized for failing to assess the impact on the poor of the policies it recommends to member governments. The Fund's Managing Director and its Executive Board agree that much more vigorous action along these lines is not only feasible but merits high priority. The issue is not one of principle, but of precisely what the IMF can and should do to reduce the transitional effects of stabilization measures on the poor.

Only a handful of developing countries now have reliable data on basic questions: Where precisely are the poor located? Who, again precisely, are they? How do they make a living? What do they buy? What public services are reaching them? Gathering such data takes time and money. Immediate relief programs do *not* depend on such data. As UNICEF has cogently argued, less accurate but much quicker and cheaper techniques can be used to assess, for instance, the extent and trends in malnutrition among children in various districts of a country. But to gauge how particular policies will affect the poor and to design policy packages that are less damaging, it is essential to have better data than are now available. The World Bank has ambitious programs under way to establish data-gathering and monitoring institutions in many African and other low-income countries in the next several years. Clearly the IMF should not attempt to duplicate this effort. However, as data on the poor become available for individual countries, the IMF can integrate the new information into its analyses.

A serious assessment of stabilization's impact on the poor also requires better theories and knowledge about the complex ways that various policies (singly and in combination) can affect the incomes of different groups. Devaluation, for example, has both direct and indirect effects on prices of imported and domestically produced staples, on employment, and on wages (among other effects). Both the earnings and the expenditures of most groups will be affected. Many will gain in some ways and lose in others. The gains and losses change over time; the immediate impact is different from the effects several months later.

If devaluation is part of a larger package of policies—as is usually the case—the impact on any particular group is still more complicated. IMF research staff, working in consultation with related efforts in the World Bank, other development agencies, and universities, should considerably increase their efforts to understand how combinations of policies affect different groups, in varying circumstances.

What additional action should the IMF take beyond research on the distributive impact of adjustment measures and full use of data on individual countries as it becomes available? How actively should it press developing-country governments to pay more attention to income distribution and advancement of the poor?

In 1986 and again in 1987 the IMF made clear that it is willing, in the course of preparing stabilization programs and when requested by a member country, to discuss "the implications of alternative approaches to adjustment for distribution of income, with a view in particular to sheltering the poorest."[1] The invitation thus far has gotten little formal response—perhaps partly because the officials with whom IMF teams deal are not those mainly charged with worrying about welfare effects. Moreover, many governments are not strongly concerned with protecting the poor, although they may give high priority to easing pressures on middle-income groups that pose a political threat.[2]

Even without an initiative from a member government, when the Fund recommends measures highly likely to directly harm poor people, it has a clear responsibility to press the government to take compensatory measures. For instance, the Fund often urges that food subsidies be reduced because they are a heavy fiscal drain and mainly benefit middle- or even upper-income people. But if those subsidies also benefit some among the poor, the Fund should press for substitutes targeted more precisely to the poor and near-poor. It should stand prepared to adjust its timetable and perhaps even to approach other multilateral or bilateral agencies to assist in setting up targeted programs.

Beyond such damage-limitation measures, perhaps the most effective way for the IMF to contribute to pro-poor adjustment is to redouble efforts already under way to increase the compatibility of stabilization and growth. But the IMF's mandate and the nature of its operations are not suited to direct relief. Other international actors—including the World Bank and the regional banks, bilateral donors, and PVOs—are also generally better suited than the Fund to promote directly the longer-run interests of the poor in the course of adjustment. The Fund focuses on immediate macroeconomic policies. Most of the steps needed for durable improvements in the prospects of the poor require medium-run reform or reorientation of institutions and programs. However, as Jeffrey D. Sachs emphasizes, in many countries (particularly in Latin America), the wealthy and near-wealthy largely escape taxation. Tax policy falls squarely within the traditional mandate of the Fund. Perhaps most appropriately through Article IV consultations rather than stand-by arrangements, the Fund could and should systematically press for revisions in tax structure and administration, to ease the acute fiscal crisis that is strangling crucial public investment, maintenance, and services.

In the 1990s, adjustment programs in Latin America and Africa are likely to face increasing threats from popular political pressures—perhaps particularly in those countries turning or returning to democracy. Many, including IMF Managing Director Camdessus and a number of Executive Board members, have suggested that adjustment programs that better protect the poor would be more politically sustainable. Sachs argues both in this volume and in greater detail elsewhere that badly skewed income distribution and resulting resentments fuel the periodic populist political pressures that have so often triggered severely damaging economic policies in Latin America.[3]

This proposition needs to be more carefully stated. Emergency relief for the poorest and most vulnerable groups may well improve a government's domestic and international image. But the very poor are rarely a major political threat. The poorest thirty or forty per cent of the population are heavily rural and seldom politically organized. The groups most likely to threaten governments, and therefore adjustment efforts, are the more vocal and organized urban near-poor and middle strata and elite vested interests. These middle groups have also been extremely hard-hit by the crisis of the 1980s. They are not the poorest nor the most at risk, but they are often the most aggrieved and politically volatile. Tightly targeted pro-poor measures are irrelevant to the fears and grievances of these groups. Indeed, some reforms—such as reallocation of public expenditures to better serve the poor—are directly opposed to the interests of the so-called middle classes (who in fact are usually among the top ten or twenty per cent in the national income distribution ladder), and sometimes conflict with the interests of the urban lower-middle and near-poor classes as well. In short, the *equity* issue that Sachs rightly underscores is not the same as the *poverty* issue that has captured international attention and concern.

How then can the triple goals of economic adjustment, political sustainability, and pro-poor action be reconciled? In large part, different measures must be designed to address the different goals, which will often be promoted by different external agencies. Immediate and longer-term programs to shelter and promote the truly poor should be pursued (a) because it is right to do so, and (b) because they are a sensible long-term investment. Both short- and medium-run adjustment tactics and strategies must also be designed to be *politically sustainable*, which may require concessions to middle-sector groups. Better information and knowledge about the distributive effects of alternative policy packages would facilitate both poverty alleviation and political sustainability, consistent with the requirements of adjustment.

Notes

[1] Statement of Managing Director Michel Camdessus to ECOSOC, Geneva, June 26, 1987—reaffirming a statement to the same group a year earlier by then Managing Director de la Rosière.

[2] See Chapter 4, "The Politics of Pro-Poor Adjustment," in Joan M. Nelson and contributors, *Fragile Coalitions: The Politics of Economic Adjustment* (New Brunswick, N.J.: Transaction Books in cooperation with the Overseas Development Council, 1989).

[3] See Jeffrey Sachs, "Social Conflict and Populist Policies in Latin America," Working Paper No. 2897 (Cambridge, Mass.: National Bureau of Economic Research, March 1989).

About the Overseas Development Council

The Overseas Development Council is a private, non-profit organization established in 1969 for the purpose of increasing American understanding of the economic and social problems confronting the developing countries and of how their development progress is related to U.S. interests. Toward this end, the Council functions as a center for policy research and analysis, a forum for the exchange of ideas, and a resource for public education. The Council's current program of work encompasses four major issue areas: trade and industrial policy, international finance and investment, development strategies and development cooperation, and U.S. foreign policy and the developing countries. ODC's work is used by policy makers in the Executive Branch and the Congress, journalists, and those concerned about U.S.-Third World relations in corporate and bank management, international and non-governmental organizations, universities, and educational and action groups focusing on specific development issues. ODC's program is funded by foundations, corporations, and private individuals; its policies are determined by a governing Board and Council. In selecting issues and shaping its work program, ODC is also assisted by a standing Program Advisory Committee.

Victor H. Palmieri is Chairman of the ODC, and Wayne Fredericks is Vice Chairman. The Council's President is John W. Sewell.

Overseas Development Council
1717 Massachusetts Ave., N.W.
Washington, D.C. 20036
Tel. (202) 234-8701

The Editors

Pulling Together: The International Monetary Fund in a Multipolar World is the thirteenth volume in the Overseas Development Council's series of policy books, U.S.-Third World Policy Perspectives. The co-editors of this series—often collaborating with guest editors contributing to the series—are Richard E. Feinberg and Valeriana Kallab.

Catherine Gwin, guest editor of this volume, is currently the Special Program Advisor at The Rockefeller Foundation. In recent years, she has worked as a consultant on international economic and political affairs for The Ford Foundation, The Rockefeller Foundation, The Asia Society, and the United Nations. In the late 1970s and early 1980s, she was a Senior Fellow at the Council on Foreign Relations and at the Carnegie Endowment for International Peace, where she directed the Study Group on international financial cooperation and developing-country debt. During the Carter administration, she served on the staff of the International Development Cooperation Agency (IDCA). Dr. Gwin had taught at the School of International Affairs at Columbia University and has written frequently on international development cooperation, the World Bank, and the International Monetary Fund.

Richard E. Feinberg is Executive Vice President and Director of Studies at the Overseas Development Council and co-editor of the Policy Perspectives series. Before joining ODC in 1981, he served as the Latin American specialist on the Policy Planning Staff of the Department of State (1977–1979), prior to which he worked as an international economist in the Treasury Department and with the House Banking Committee. He also has been Adjunct Professor of International Finance at the Georgetown University School of Foreign Service. Dr. Feinberg has held fellowships from The Brookings Institution, the Council on Foreign Relations, and the Woodrow Wilson International Center for Scholars of the Smithsonian Institution. In the ODC Policy Perspectives series, for which he is a frequent contributing author as well as co-editor, he has moat recently directed and edited the policy study, *Between Two Worlds: The World Bank's Next Decade* (1986). He has published numerous articles and books on U.S. foreign policy, Latin American politics, and international economics, including *The Intemperate Zone: The Third World Challenge to U.S. Foreign Policy* (1983); (with Ricardo Ffrench-Davis) *Development and External Debt in Latin America: Bases for a New Consensus* (1988); (as editor) *Central America: International Dimensions of the Crisis* (1982); and *Subsidizing Success: The Export-Import Bank in the U.S. Economy* (1982).

Valeriana Kallab is Vice President and Director of Publications of the Overseas Development Council and co-editor of the ODC's policy book series, U.S.-Third World Policy Perspectives. She has been responsible for ODC's published output since 1972. Before joining ODC, she was a Research Editor and a writer on international economic issues at the Carnegie Endowment for International Peace in New York. She was co-editor (with John P. Lewis) of *Development Strategies Reconsidered; U.S. Foreign Policy and the Third World: Agenda 1983;* and (with Guy Erb) of *Beyond Dependency: The Third World Speaks Out.*

Contributing Authors

Jacques J. Polak has been a senior advisor to the Development Centre of the OECD and a consultant to the World Bank since leaving the International Monetary Fund after a distinguished career at that institution. He was Director of the Research Department from 1958 to 1980, and Economic Counselor from 1966 to 1980. From 1981 until 1986, he served as a member of the Fund's Executive Board. Prior to joining the Fund in 1947, he worked as an economist in the League of Nations from 1937 to 1943, in the Netherlands Embassy in Washington in 1943–44, and in UNRRA from 1944 to 1946. His major published works include: (with Jan Tinbergen) *The Dynamics of Business Cycles* (1950); *An International Economic System* (1952); (co-edited with Robert A. Mundell) *The New International Monetary System* (1977); and *Financial Policies and Development* (OECD Development Centre, 1989). Dr. Polak is a national of the Netherlands.

Peter B. Kenen is Walker Professor of Economics and International Finance and Director of the International Finance Section at Princeton University. From 1957 to 1971, he taught at Columbia University, where he was chairman of the Economics Department and Provost of the University. He has been a Fellow of the Center for Advanced Study in the Behavioral Sciences and of the Royal Institute of International Affairs; has been awarded fellowships by the Guggenheim Foundation and The German Marshall Fund; and has held visiting appointments at the Hebrew University, the Stockholm School of Economics, the Australian National University, and the University of California at Berkeley. His recent publications include: *Essays in International Economics, Asset Markets, Exchange Rates, and Economic Integration* (with Polly R. Allen); *Managing Exchange Rates; The International Economy;* and *Exchange Rates and Policy Coordination;* and he was co-editor (with Ronald W. Jones) of the *Handbook of International Economics*. Dr. Kenen has been a consultant to the U.S. Treasury, the Board of Governors of the Federal Reserve Board, the International Monetary Fund, and the World Bank. He is a member of the Group of Thirty.

C. David Finch is currently a Senior Fellow at the Institute for International Economics. From 1950 to 1987, he was on the staff of the International Monetary Fund in the Research, Western Hemisphere, and Exchange and Trade Relations Departments, most recently as Counselor and Director of the Exchange and Trade Relations Department.

Jeffrey D. Sachs is the Galen L. Stone Professor of International Trade at Harvard University and a Research Associate of the National Bureau of Economic Research (NBER). Dr. Sachs serves as an economic advisor to several governments in Latin America (notably Bolivia), Europe, and Asia, as well as to Solidarity in Poland. He also has been a consultant to the IMF, the World Bank, the OECD, and the United Nations Development Programme. His current research interests include the international debt crisis, international macroeconomic policy coordination, and macroeconomic policies in developing and developed countries. At NBER, Sachs has directed and edited the major NBER series, *Developing Country Debt and the World Economy* (1989). He is a frequent contributor to the *New Republic,* the *Nihon Keizei Shimbun (Japan Economic Journal),* and several magazines and newspapers in Latin America, Europe, and Japan, and co-author (with Michael Bruno) of *Economics of Worldwide Stagflation* (1985). Sachs is a member of the Brookings Panel of Economists, the Board of Advisors of the Congressional Budget Office, the Overseas Development Council's Program Advisory Committee, and several other organizations.

Guillermo Ortiz is the Undersecretary of the Ministry of Finance in Mexico. Prior to serving in his current position, Dr. Ortiz was the Executive Director representing Mexico, Spain, Venezuela, and Central America at the International Monetary Fund. He also served as an official in the economic research division of Mexico's Central Bank. He has published widely on matters of macroeconomic policy and international finance. Among his U.S. publications are "The Burden of the Mexican Foreign Debt" (with J. Sorra) in the *Journal of Development Economics,* Vol. 21, 1986; and "Currency Substitution in Mexico: The Dollarization Problem," in the *Journal of Money Credit and Banking,* May 1983.

Louis M. Goreux, now a private consultant, was until 1987 Deputy Director in the Africa Department of the International Monetary Fund. Prior to assuming that role in 1980, he was Assistant Director in the Fund's Research Department. In the late 1960s, Dr. Goreux served as Director of the Development Research Center and as Advisor in the Economics Department of the World Bank. In 1965–67, he was Deputy Director of the Food and Agricultural Organization's Indicative World Plan for Agricultural Development, prior to which he held numerous other posts in the FAO and, earlier, in CREDOC, a French research organization in Paris. Dr. Goreux is a national of France.

Joan M. Nelson is a Senior Associate at the Overseas Development Council. Before joining the Council as a Visiting Fellow in 1982, she taught at the Massachusetts Institute of Technology, the Johns Hopkins University School of Advanced International Studies, and Princeton University's Woodrow Wilson School of Public and International Affairs. Dr. Nelson has been a consultant for the World Bank, the Agency for International Development, and for the International Monetary Fund, as well as a staff member of USAID. She has published books and articles on development assistance and policy dialogue, political participation, migration, and urban politics in developing nations, and the politics of economic stabilization and reform.

BETWEEN TWO WORLDS:
THE WORLD BANK'S NEXT DECADE
Richard E. Feinberg and contributors

> **"essential reading for anybody interested in the Bank"**
> —*The Economist*

> **"well-researched analysis of some of the problems confronting the World Bank in the 1980s"**
> —*The Journal of Development Studies*

In the midst of the global debt and adjustment crises, the World Bank has been challenged to become the leading agency in North-South fiwhich must be comprehensively addressed by the Bank's new presinance and development. The many dimensions of this challenge are the subject of this important volume.

As mediator between international capital markets and developing countries, the World Bank will be searching for ways to renew the flow of private credit and investment to Latin America and Africa. And as the world's premier development agency, the Bank can help formulate growth strategies appropriate to the 1990s.

The Bank's ability to design and implement a comprehensive response to these global needs is threatened by competing objectives and uncertain priorities. Can the Bank design programs attractive to private investors that also serve the very poor? Can it emphasize efficiency while transferring technologies that maximize labor absorption? Can it more aggressively condition loans on policy reforms without attracting the criticism that has accompanied IMF programs?

The contributors to this volume assess the role that the World Bank can play in the period ahead. They argue for new financial and policy initiatives and for new conceptual approaches to development, as well as for a restructuring of the Bank, as it takes on new, systemic responsibilities in the next decade.

Contents:
Richard E. Feinberg—Overview: An Open Letter to the World Bank's Next President
Gerald K. Helleiner—Policy-Based Program Leading: A Look at the Bank's New Role
Joan M. Nelson—The Diplomacy of Policy-Based Lending
Sheldon Annis—The Shifting Grounds of Poverty Lending at The World Bank
Howard Pack—The Technological Impact of World Bank Operations
John F. H. Purcell and Michelle B. Miller—The World Bank and Private Capital
Charles R. Blitzer—Financing the World Bank

Richard E. Feinberg is vice president of the Overseas Development Council and co-editor of the U.S.-Third World Policy Perspectives series. From 1977 to 1979, Feinberg was Latin American specialist on the policy planning staff of the U.S. Department of State. He has also served as an international economist in the U.S. Treasury Department and with the House Banking Committee. He is currently also adjunct professor of international finance at the Georgetown University School of Foreign Service. Feinberg is the author of numerous books as well as journal and newspaper articles on U.S. foreign policy, Latin American politics, and international economics.

U.S.-Third World Policy Perspectives, No. 7   ISBN: 0-88738-123-5 (cloth) $19.95
June 1986, 208 pp.   ISBN: 0-88738-665-2 (paper) $12.95

FRAGILE COALITIONS:
THE POLITICS OF ECONOMIC ADJUSTMENT

Joan M. Nelson and contributors

The global economic crisis of the 1980s forced most developing nations into a simultaneous quest for short-run economic stabilization and longer-run structural reforms. Effective adjustment is at least as much a political as an economic challenge. But political dimensions of adjustment have been much less carefully analyzed than have the economic issues.

Governments in developing countries must balance pressures from external agencies seeking more rapid adjustment in return for financial support, and the demands of domestic political groups often opposing such reforms. How do internal pressures shape external bargaining? and conversely, how does external influence shape domestic political maneuvering? Growing emphasis on "adjustment with a human face" poses additional questions: Do increased equity and political acceptability go hand in hand? or do more pro-poor measures add to the political difficulties of adjustment? The capacity of the state itself to implement adjustment measures varies widely among nations. How can external agencies take such differences more fully into account? The hopeful trend toward democratic openings in many countries raises further, crucial issues: What special political risks and opportunities confront governments struggling simultaneously with adjustment and democratization?

The contributors to this volume explore these issues and their policy implications for the United States and for the international organizations that seek to promote adjustment efforts.

Contents:

Joan M. Nelson has been a visiting fellow at the Overseas Development Council since 1982; since mid-1986, she has directed a collegial research program on the politics of economic adjustment. She has been a consultant for the World Bank, the Agency for International Development, and for the International Monetary Fund, as well as a staff member of USAID. In the 1970s and early 1980s, she taught at the Massachusetts Institute of Technology, the Johns Hopkins University School of Advanced International Studies, and Princeton University's Woodrow Wilson School. She has published books and articles on development assistance and policy dialogue, political participation, migration and urban politics in developing nations, and the politics of economic stabilization and reform.

U.S.-Third World Policy Perspectives, No. 12 $24.95 (cloth)
Summer 1989, 192 pp. $15.95 (paper)

ENVIRONMENT AND THE POOR: DEVELOPMENT STRATEGIES FOR A COMMON AGENDA

H. Jeffrey Leonard and contributors

Few aspects of development are as complex and urgent as the need to reconcile anti-poverty and pro-environmental goals. Do both of these important goals—poverty alleviation and environmental sustainability—come in the same package? Or are there necessary trade-offs and must painful choices be made?

A basic premise of this volume is that environmental degradation and intractable poverty are often especially pronounced in particular ecological and social settings across the developing world. These twin crises of development and the environment can and must be addressed jointly. But they require differentiated strategies for the kinds of physical environments in which poor people live. This study explores these concerns in relation to irrigated areas, arid zones, moist tropical forests, hillside areas, urban centers, and unique ecological settings.

The overview chapter highlights recent efforts to advance land and natural resource management, and some of the real and perceived conflicts between alleviating poverty and protecting the environment in the design and implementation of development policy. The chapters that follow offer economic investment and natural resource management options for reducing poverty and maintaining ecological balance for six different areas of the developing world.

Contents:

H. Jeffrey Leonard, guest editor of this volume, is the vice president of the World Wildlife Fund and The Conservation Foundation and Director of the Fairfield Osborn Center for Economic Development. Dr. Leonard has been at The Foundation since 1976. He is the author of several recent books, including *Pollution and the Struggle for the World Product, Natural Resources and Economic Development in Central America*, and *Are Environmental Regulations Driving U.S. Industries Overseas?* He is also editor of *Divesting Nature's Capital: The Political Economy of Environmental Abuse in the Third World* and *Business and Environment: Toward a Common Ground.*

U.S.-Third World Policy Perspectives, No. 11
Summer 1989

$24.95 (cloth)
$15.95 (paper)

U.S. FOREIGN POLICY AND ECONOMIC REFORM IN THREE GIANTS: THE USSR, CHINA, AND INDIA

Richard E. Feinberg, John Echeverri-Gent, Friedemann Müller, and contributors

Three of the largest and strategically most important nations in the world—the Soviet Union, China, and India—are currently in the throes of historic change. The reforms in the giants are transforming global economic and geopolitical relations. The United States must reexamine central tenets of its foreign policy if it is to seize the opportunities presented by these changes.

This pathbreaking study analyzes economic reform in the giants and its implications for U.S. foreign policy. It assesses the impact of the reforms on the livelihood of the nearly half the world's population living in their societies. Each of the giants is opening up its economy to foreign trade and investment. What consequences will this new outward orientation have for international trade, and how should U.S. policy respond to these developments? Each giant is attempting to catch up to global technological frontiers by absorbing foreign technologies; in what areas might cooperation enhance American interests, and in what areas must the U.S. protect its competitive and strategic assets? What role can key international economic institutions like the GATT, the IMF, and the World Bank play to help integrate the giants into the international economy?

Economic reform in the giants has important consequences for their political systems. What measures can and should the United States take to encourage political liberalization? How will the reforms affect the foreign policies of the giants, and what impact will this have on U.S. geopolitical interests?

The contributors suggest how U.S. foreign policy should anticipate these new circumstances in ways that enhance international cooperation and security.

Richard E. Feinberg, John Echeverri-Gent, and Friedemann Müller—
Overview: Economic Reform in the Giants and U.S. Policy
Friedemann Müller—Economic Reform in the USSR
Rensselaer W. Lee III—Economic Reform in China
John Echeverri-Gent—Economic Reform in India
John Echeverri-Gent, Friedemann Müller, and Rensselaer W. Lee III—
The Politics of Economic Reform in the Giants
Thomas Naylor—Economic Reforms and International Trade
Richard P. Suttmeier—Technology Transfer to the Giants: Opportunities and Challenges
Elena Borisovna Arefieva—The Geopolitical Consequences of Reform in the Giants

---

Richard E. Feinberg is vice president of the Overseas Development Council and co-editor of the U.S.-Third World Policy Perspectives series. From 1977 to 1979, Feinberg was Latin American specialist on the policy planning staff of the U.S. Department of State.

John Echeverri-Gent is a visiting fellow at the Overseas Development Council and an assistant professor at the University of Virginia. His publications are in the fields of comparative public policy and the political economy of development in India.

Friedemann Müller is a visiting fellow at the Overseas Development Council and a senior research associate at Stiftung Wissenschaft und Politik, Ebenhausen, West Germany. His publications on the Soviet and Eastern European economies have focused on economic reform, energy policy, and East-West trade.

U.S.-Third World Policy Perspectives, No. 14
Winter 1989, 256 pp.

$24.95 (cloth)
$15.95 (paper)

STRENGTHENING THE POOR: WHAT HAVE WE LEARNED?

John P. Lewis and contributors

"bound to influence policymakers and make a major contribution to renewed efforts to reduce poverty"
—B. T. G. Chidzero, Minister of Finance, Economic Planning, and Development, Government of Zimbabwe

"deserves wide readership within the broader development community"
—Barber B. Conable, President, The World Bank

The issue of poverty alleviation—of strengthening the poor—is now being brought back toward the top of the development policy agenda.

The current refocusing on poverty is not just a matter of turning back the clock. Anti-poverty initiatives for the 1990s must respond to a developing world and a policy environment that in many ways differs dramatically from that of the 1970s and even the 1980s. Much has been accomplished during and since the last thrust of anti-poverty policy. The poor themselves have in some cases become more vocal, organized, and effective in pressing their own priorities. A great deal of policy experience has accrued. And national governments, donor agencies, and non-governmental organizations now employ a much wider range of tools for poverty alleviation.

Strengthening the Poor provides a timely assessment of these changes and experience. In an overview essay, John Lewis draws important policy lessons both from poverty alleviation's period of high salience in the 1970s and from its time of lowered attention in the adjustment-accentuating 1980s. An impressive cluster of U.S. and developing-country authors react to these propositions from diverse points of view.

Contents:

U.S.-Third World Policy Perspectives, No. 10
1988, 256 pp.

ISBN: 0-88738-267-3 (cloth) $19.95
ISBN: 0-88738-768-3 (paper) $12.95

GROWTH, EXPORTS, AND JOBS IN A CHANGING WORLD ECONOMY: AGENDA 1988

John W. Sewell, Stuart K. Tucker, and contributors

"particularly timely, as the Administration and Congress face critical decisions on the trade bill, the budget, and other issues affecting the economic future of the U.S. and countries around the globe"
—Frank C. Carlucci, Secretary of Defense

Agenda 1988, the eleventh of ODC's well-known assessments of U.S. policy toward the developing countries, contributes uniquely to the ongoing debate on U.S. jobs and trade competition with other nations.

The administration that takes office in 1989 faces a situation without precedent in the post-1945 period. Like many developing countries, the United States has to balance its trade accounts, service its foreign debts, and rebuild its industrial base. The challenge is twofold.

The immediate task is to restore the international economic position of the United States by taking the lead in devising measures to support renewed *global* growth, especially rapid growth in the developing countries.

Meanwhile, however, the world is on the threshold of a Third Industrial Revolution. Rapid technological advances are radically changing the familiar economic relationships between developed and developing countries. The kinds of policies needed to adjust to these technology-driven changes—policies on education, training, research and development—generally have longer lead times than the immediate measures needed to stimulate global growth. In the next four years, the United States must therefore proceed on *both* fronts at the same time.

John W. Sewell—Overview: The Dual Challenge: Managing the Economic Crisis and Technological Change
Manuel Castells and Laura D'Andrea Tyson—High-Technology Choices Ahead: Restructuring Interdependence
Jonathan D. Aronson—The Service Industries: Growth, Trade, and Development Prospects
Robert L. Paarlberg—U.S. Agriculture and the Developing World: Opportunities for Joint Gains
Raymond F. Mikesell—The Changing Demand for Industrial Raw Materials
Ray Marshall—Jobs: The Shifting Structure of Global Employment
Stuart K. Tucker—Statistical Annexes: U.S.-Third World Interdependence, 1988

John W. Sewell has been president of the Overseas Development Council since January, 1980. From 1977 to 1979, as the Council's executive vice president, he directed ODC's programs of research and public education. Prior to joining the Council in 1971, Mr. Sewell directed the communications program of the Brookings Institution. He also served in the Foreign Service of the United States. A contributor to past *Agenda* assessments, he is co-author of *Rich Country Interests and Third World Development* and *The Ties That Bind: U.S. Interests in Third World Development.* He is a frequent author and lecturer on U.S. relations with the developing countries.

Stuart K. Tucker is a fellow at the Overseas Development Council. Prior to joining ODC in 1984, he was a research consultant for the Inter-American Development Bank. He has written on U.S. international trade policy, including the linkage between the debt crisis and U.S. exports and jobs. He also prepared the Statistical Annexes in ODC's *Agenda 1985-86.*

U.S.-Third World Policy Perspectives, No. 9
1988, 286 pp.

ISBN: 088738-196-0 (cloth) $19.95
ISBN: 0-88738-718-7 (paper) $12.95